Copyright © November 2022
I, Andy Darby, hereby assert and
give notice of my rights under section 77 of the
Copyright, Design and Patents Act, 1988
to be identified as the author of this work.
All Rights Reserved. No part of this publication
may be reproduced, stored in a retrieval system
or transmitted at any time by any means
electronic, mechanical, photocopying, recording or
otherwise, without prior permission of the publisher.
All characters in this publication are fictitious and
any resemblance to real persons, living or dead,
is purely coincidental.
Cover art by Dave Howarth www.hmdesigners.com
ISBN: 978-1-8384577-6-1
published by www.badpress.ink

I feel a bit sick after licking that demon blood. Still, nothing that another Jack won't fix.

What? I know it's the third bottle but there are four of us! Anyway, the pizza delivery will be here in a minute, and we need something to wash it down with, ya fucking lightweight!

The Monkey

For Detective Minkowski

11 November

We met a German dude who is a professor of social anthropology and spends most of his free time off his tits on Amanita Muscaria – that's the red toadstool with the white dots to you and me – and he is also a bit of an expert in Norse legend and mythology. Seems that he discovered his taste for toadstools as a teenager after reading about their use in shamanic ritual and the berserker legends of the Northmen. They, apparently, changed his perception of reality on a permanent basis and cause him to have prophetic visions. Perhaps I should explain how we hooked up…

We had been to Amsterdam's Tropenmuseum because The Monkey had heard that there was a large collection of writings from the Far East and that there was possibly something that could shed light on the history of the Green and Red Society, their historical links with the Illuminati, plus, more importantly, legends about monkey deities. There was indeed a large collection – thousands of documents – and the curators were none too happy to let the likes of us go rummaging through them. As we were constructing a plan to break in and help ourselves a middle aged, very dapper German fella with an impressive beard, leant over one of the ornate gallery rails and excitedly started jabbering at us. We had no idea what he was saying but one phrase was repeated – '*Affengott*'. Kev's schoolboy German kicked in and fell straight over, so with the help of Google Translate he told us that our bearded friend was repeatedly saying 'Monkey God'. So, we took him for a drink…

*

And drink we did…

There's a rock bar in the Red Light District called Excalibur – loads of metal heads and bikers and people with attitude amongst the stoned sex tourists, vaguely scared 'cultural' visitors and other sheep that mill around the canal sides looking for shiny things and pretending to be bad asses – and that's where we went.

Herr Myer was completely at ease even dressed in his tweeds and waistcoat. He obviously dresses like that for effect, and he gets away with it well. He can't be more than about 38 but he has this sort of Sigmund Freud thing going on but with a much more epic beard (did I mention the beard – big fan). The massive biker by the door took one look at him and nodded in appreciation before making room for us to pass. We settled ourselves into an alcove and Kev got a round in while we began our chat. Herr Myer speaks enough English for us to cobble together sentences so we gradually worked out that he was at the museum looking for some ethnographic writings relating to the ritual use of mushrooms in shamanic cultures. We asked about the whole *Affengott* thing, and he told us about a series of psychotropic adventures he had about 15 years ago and how he had 'seen' The Monkey and knew him for who he was…

Me and The Monkey

*

One sunny day, in a dark forest in Northern Germany, the young Ruddi Myer and his best friend Max had decided that it was death or glory time in true Viking tradition. They had each swallowed a large quantity of the red and white spotted toadstool and come hell or high water vowed that they would either glimpse the gods in this life or meet again in Valhalla. After about twenty minutes they both had bad stomach cramps and then Max began to vomit, as Herr Myer put it, 'Like he would bring up his shin bones.' Ruddi felt as if he was burning up and ran off into the forest while tearing off his clothes. Some hours later a naked Ruddi found a puke-covered Max and they crawled into the tent they had set up that morning, and told each other their visions. Max had experienced a full-on Wagnerian opera worth of Teutonic nonsense in which he had gloriously battled giants and scaled mountains in search of dragon gold. Ruddi on the other hand, was rather perplexed by the mountain temples and terrifying Monkey deity that had picked him up in one massive paw and stripped the skin, flesh, organs, and finally bones from his body before shooting his consciousness into outer space. None of that fitted with what he had expected in his youthful heavy metal and Nordic mythology-influenced dreams – a different mythos from a different culture – and he had lost all his clothes…

It took Herr Myer the next 15 or so years to process what he had experienced. Through anthropological research and extensive travel, he had begun to piece together the whereabouts of the place he'd visited during his mushroom trip and after searching through the Tropenmuseum he homed in on a site in Tibet.

Through the aid of drunken shouty German, Google translate, and some sort of voguing arm movements he instructed us to go to a spot in the Himalayas where he said we would find the essence of who The Monkey was. He then reached into his leather satchel and gave The Monkey a cardboard tube which he said contained a facsimile of a map and some copies of ancient Tibetan texts, then he fell off his chair. This all sounded like the last conversation we had with our friendly Mao Shan sorcerer and the main reason for our museum-based excursion.

Kev muttered something about there being a club over the other side of the canal and we hoisted up Herr Myer and staggered off in the direction of the closest bridge. Across the canal we could see the lurid neon signs above the club announcing it as 'The Banana Bar' – it was going to prove to be very disappointing for The Monkey…

*

Ah, it was not good. We had been in The Banana Bar for about 20 minutes before the next live performance started. Herr Myer was slumped on a sofa giggling to himself as he watched topless waitresses manoeuvre between the tables of punters while trying to avoid getting groped. Kev got a round in, and The Monkey sat expectantly on the arm of the sofa waiting for his Jack and the apparent surfeit of bananas that he was sure would be delivered soon.

The lights dimmed, the music got louder, and a pretty much naked red-haired woman slithered onto the stage. When The Monkey saw what was actually happening to the bananas his mouth dropped open and then his eyes narrowed into little evil slits. You don't fuck with The Monkey's drink, and you literally don't fuck with his food.

Swinging through the lighting rigs he pelted all and sundry with bottles, glasses, furniture, and anything that wasn't nailed down. Bits of abused banana flew far and wide and we battled with the doormen who came crashing in to restore order but fortunately in the chaos they managed to hit just about everyone present except our party, and shouting to The Monkey to get the fuck out we legged it for the door dragging Herr Myer with us.

Into the night we fled with stupid grins on our very drunk faces – The Monkey still had a scowl but the carnage he had wreaked had cheered him up a bit. We carried Herr Myer back to his hotel and made sure he was safely in his room with promises to meet him the following lunchtime and then staggered off to find our own beds and maybe a nightcap – because we obviously needed one...

12 November

Hindsight is a motherfucker.

Maybe the clues were there. Maybe if we hadn't been so shit-faced we would have seen the express train. But we didn't and sitting here now with a Jack in one hand and no one trying to fuck us up it's easy to be all self-critical and *if only* – but we didn't see it...

We rolled out of bed at the crack of eleven and cleaned ourselves up a bit before heading out to Herr Myer's hotel. It was obvious, even to our hungover brains, that something was amiss. The flashing blue lights reflected back from the oily canal with a monotonous blinking like an insane child's fairground fantasy, and the cops outside the hotel entrance didn't give us much confidence in getting away without a thorough questioning. The Monkey gave me his day sack to hold and disappeared around the side of the building. Me and Kev tried to look nonchalant while staring into the window of an antique shop further along the towpath; the bay window provided us with a reflection to watch the goings on.

After about 20 minutes The Monkey appeared beside us and gestured us away. We walked for two streets and across the canal until we found a friendly looking café and sat inside by the window. Herr Myer was dead. The Monkey had climbed up the outside of the hotel and found our German friend's window ledge. Inside police forensics were hard at work bagging and tagging and Herr Myer was dangling naked, by his hotel dressing gown belt from the rail of his wardrobe. There were popper bottles scattered on the floor and it looked like a strangle wank gone wrong. But we knew Herr Myer was way beyond an erection when we left him...

Me and The Monkey

*

Kev sent a message to JudyZ, our resident not so artificial intelligence, and asked her to monitor radio, phone, and other electronic communications that the Amsterdam police were sending to each other regarding the death of Herr Myer. By early evening it was apparently a cut and dried case. The police had decided that it was death by misadventure – another salutary warning about the dangers of drunken wanking and an apparent fetish for capital punishment. Herr Myer was to join a long list of the famous and not so famous who had shuffled off this mortal coil, cock in hand and distended tongue hanging from mouth...

Utter shite of course. JudyZ has intercepted a short message sent from the investigating detective's mobile phone to a satellite phone somewhere on the other side of the world (signal was bounced through several transmitter stations so she couldn't get a lock) which said simply: JOB DONE 😊. Adding a smiley face to it – what a cunt!

Back at our apartment the old paranoia began to set in. The Monkey set about tearing the place apart 'just in case'. Well, 'just in case' was at home... After about two hours of violent searching, he slammed three small black lumps onto the kitchen table. They were about the same size as dice and had a tiny lens on one side. Kev photographed the James Bond kit with his phone and sent the pics off to JudyZ for a quick ID. I poured some drinks and The Monkey lit up a cigar. The minutes ticked and then there was a knock at the door. The Monkey chambered his favourite Glock and I peeked through the spy hole straight into the spoon warped face of a villain from a Chinese Kung fu movie...

*

The Green and Red Society's only remaining trustworthy member glided into the room as if he was attached to a skateboard, the long hem of his robe concealing the movements of his feet – and maybe a skateboard...

The Monkey kept the Glock pointed at the inscrutable oriental face as he hovered over to the window and turned to look at us. Long white eyebrows and moustache seemed to float about in their own air current or as if we were seeing him underwater. The Shaw Brothers kung fu movie bad guy look was still unnerving but then that's what happens when you spend long drunken hours watching bad Hong Kong martial art films. 'I am sorry for the loss of your friend,' he bowed his head slightly as he said this, and I saw the barrel of the Glock follow the movement.

'You have been in one place for too long and now they have found you again. There are many strange things happening in a world that they cannot control, things that you have set in motion, things that interfere with their plans.' This was directed at The Monkey. The Monkey lowered the gun slightly and squinted at the tall oriental.

'One – he wasn't really our friend; we had only just met him. And B – what fucking plans?'

We made ourselves comfortable as Hong Kong Phooey gave us the lowdown on what was happening in the world of people who hate us. Since the rebirth of Arno Whitaker, the Illuminati nut jobs in control had had a bit of a seizure. There had been major *reorganisation* within their ranks and over the pile of bodies Whitaker squatted like a big fat fucking spider. The Illuminati's aim – development of a super elite and use of ancient technology for the purpose of enslaving the masses and producing a utopian new world order. Same old shit.

And what did this have to do with us? The Monkey was seen as the one element of chaos of unpredictable, uncontrollable, spanner in the works lunacy who could derail their plans yet again. If he realised his full potential, he would be unstoppable and that made them very twitchy. The Monkey told him about the map and documents Herr Myer had given him and the sorcerer nodded but didn't ask to see them. I think that was wise…

'So, I must go to Tibet sooner than expected. I would ask you to go to South America and locate a second monkey temple, then you can join me, and hopefully we will have clues to the location of the ancient god and maybe then the map Herr Myer gave you will be of most use.' He stared hard at The Monkey from under long white eyebrows and said, 'You must be who you are destined to be.'

As he stood, he reached into one of his enormous sleeves and produced a yellow cloth covered in Chinese characters. He laid it on the table in front of me and opened it, and there, in all its gnarly glory was the monkey finger. I reached out and picked it up feeling that weird prickly sensation it emanates, and he scooped the cloth back up and returned it to his sleeve. 'That was in the possession of one of my former colleagues. It had been passed to the Green and Red Society so that they could use it to locate other artifacts of power for the Illuminati. When I broke free of the magic prison in which they had trapped me, it was there, as if it was waiting to be found and returned.' He raised his eyebrows as he looked at me, 'Try, not to lose it again. We may not be so lucky next time!'

*

The oriental has left and we are sitting around doing what we do best – drinking. Kev and me keep running through options and lurching from 'Fuck it,' to 'Fuck it let's do it.' The Monkey is sat on the bed and staring at a Dutch overdubbed *Bevis and Butthead* episode, his face expressionless.

Why can't they just leave us alone? The Monkey is okay if you don't stir him up. Like me and Kev, he just wants to forget all the crap, but no, they are going to poke him with a shitty stick, and you never poke The Monkey with anything he hasn't agreed to be poked with…

13 November

Eventually went to sleep – it was a fitful night. Dreamt of the girls. Squatting over me, all arms and legs like Kali, holding a severed leg and a string of skulls. The leg had bite marks. They were saying something to me, but I couldn't make it out, like it was being whispered from another room.

Woke suddenly and there was The Monkey, sitting in the chair by the bed, twisting the pendant back and forth between his long fingers. 'It's time to go,' was all he said…

*

Sitting in the back of our battered old Land Cruiser, Kev had pointed out an item on an internet news feed. Amongst all the refugee chaos and fucked-up stock exchange stories there was an odd little side bar about an increase in grave robbing in the north of England… The legacy of the Monster Highs lives on…

We are driving through the Arden on the way to a rendezvous with a man who knows a man who might be able to put us in touch with a man. This man is apparently going to get us, unnoticed, into Hungary so that we can get onboard a cargo plane at a dodgy airfield and then fly to some other dodgy airfield in South America. Very long winded but we are trying very hard to stay *under the radar* so to speak. JudyZ has been keeping us appraised of the chatter regarding us and it has become rather intense. There are several interested parties who would like our balls nailed to planks.

The Monkey is smoking a particularly foul-smelling cigar and reading a *Tintin* comic. He looks very serious – I don't think he trusts the Thompson Twins…

14 November

Finally met 'the man' in the early hours of this morning.

We rolled into a place called Kopstal, just northwest of Luxembourg, having followed the directions given us by a series of shady fuckers greased with handfuls of Euros. This grumpy looking twat whose name is Edward or something, has us holed up in a disused garage while he has gone to get stuff sorted out. The plan seems to be that we load the Cruiser and ourselves into the back of a lorry and then get driven across Germany and Austria to a meeting with some Triad goons in Hungary who are in the pay of our friendly Shaw Brothers Chinese sorcerer. The Monkey does not seem pleased and has taken to the upper gantry with a bottle of Jack and his favourite Glock.

15 November

Lots of hanging around – quite literally in The Monkey's case. He had us doing pull ups to keep active and reckons we need to start training more again. He is probably right... We have been lazy bastards for a while and now we are going to get back on it in proper full-on style.

Kev has been keeping us entertained this afternoon with downloaded TV shows on the laptop. Got massively confused by the second series of *True Detective* and to save violence we skipped it and went onto *Justified* which was a winner. I think Kev misses Tony who went back to the UK a couple of weeks ago, he doesn't really get the full-on nerd conversations that he is used to from me and The Monkey. But Tony is a bit broken mentally if not physically after the battles in Iceland and the warehouse, I think he has PTSD or something very much like it, which we are all getting bouts of. He is back at his place in Slough at the moment, laying low and hoping to do some research for us into our next little escapade. JudyZ talks to him several times a day and I think that helps, well, as much as a conversation with a ghost inhabiting an orbiting satellite can help...

*

The Edward dude has rocked up with an inconspicuous-looking lorry. The Cruiser loaded easy enough and there is plenty of room for us three, we even managed to drag a couple of sofas and three mattresses on to make it more homely – the porta potty though is leaving a lot to be desired!

The plan is to head off tomorrow afternoon so until then a game of drunken Jenga with The Monkey is in order. Need to try to lift the black mood that has settled over him these past months, if only so he doesn't kill someone out of hand...

16 November

What? We had only been going for an hour at most and came to a halt in a very noisy location. Sealed in the back of a lorry and weaving along various minor roads was not exactly the most fun we could have been having but at least we were moving. The Monkey gave me a look and slipped from the hammock he had constructed, gun in hand. Kev had his headphones on, and The Monkey tapped him lightly on the shoulder and motioned him to silence. Other vehicles came to a halt near the lorry, and I caught site of Kev's laptop screen and the message that popped up with JudZ's avatar at the top, I didn't have time to read it, but it was all in caps...

The doors of the lorry opened letting in a grey early evening light, still enough to dazzle us, and me and Kev dived for cover behind the Land Cruiser while The Monkey swung up between the opening doors and onto the roof of the lorry.

Me and The Monkey

There were no shots, just a couple of expletives and then a very British voice asking us to lower our guns and exit the lorry. The Monkey's face appeared at the top of the open doorway and grim faced, he nodded that we should do as we were asked. So, we put down our weapons, at least the firearms, and clambered out onto what I thought at first was a wide, deserted motorway. As my eyes adjusted to the light, I realised that there were the tail fins of commercial aircraft over to our right and Kev looked up from Google maps on his phone and said, 'Luxembourg Airport.'

*

It would be easy to look back over the last day with a degree of nonchalance on our unexpected airport arrival and the encircling ring of soldiers with their weapons firmly trained on us, but I would be lying if I said that thoughts of extraordinary rendition, summary execution, disappearing without a trace etc didn't take over in sphincter tightening fashion. But as The Monkey says – we always have the Monkey God nuclear option…

We were shepherded into the back of an armoured personnel carrier and driven across the apron to a row of hangars. As we exited through the rear doors I glanced back at the lorry and watched as it was driven towards the grey bulk of an Atlas military transport plane, then the hangar doors shut.

It was a very odd feeling. It had all been strangely civilised, if you don't mind having guns pointed at you that is. We were escorted up a short flight of metal stairs and into an office that had obviously been commandeered for the purpose as it didn't have that military look. The Monkey headed straight for the big swivel chair at the far side of the desk and me and Kev made ourselves at home in a couple of less grand chairs which we turned to face the door. The very polite officer had a bemused look on his face as he gestured to one of our escorts to remain by the door, then he left with the others, and we heard their boots on the metal steps. Kev started to speak but we heard voices outside, so he shut up and we waited for the ascending footsteps to reach the door.

In walked Captain Bartholomew Tempest-Stewart.

'What the fuck, Barty?' Well what else can you say at a moment like that?

Barty gave a toothy grin under his magnificent handlebar moustache and said, 'Sorry chaps.' Barty had helped us to get into the airbase near my house in Cornwall where we had found JudyZ trapped inside an old computer terminal into which her consciousness had escaped after she was tortured to death. He had seemed like a good bloke but maybe not…

Behind Barty came an Army officer and an alert looking civilian. 'This is Lieutenant Colonel McBride from British Army intelligence, and this charming young lady is Caroline Wright, I will allow her to fill you in on her role.' Ms Wright gave Barty a look of vague exasperation, possibly because of Barty's old school political incorrectness but more likely because he had forgotten what her role was. Barty perched on the corner of a two-drawer filing cabinet and absentmindedly began to flip through a comedy desk calendar, chuckling to himself every now and then. Lieutenant Colonel McBride rolled his eyes heavenward and then turned towards us and began his sell...

*

We listened and were quite well behaved as he told us how very naughty we had been and how Her Majesty's Government had a proposition for us that would let us off the hook rather than seeing us sent off to some black site from which we never returned. I felt The Monkey tense, even from the other side of the desk, and was waiting for shit to start flying but he just burst out laughing and jammed a cigar between his teeth. 'We are sort of busy at the moment,' was all he said.

'Perhaps Caroline can give a little background info?'

He turned to Caroline, and I was just about to launch into some witty, Oscar Wilde worthy comment about how they could go fuck themselves when she reached into the attaché case she was carrying and produced a green pendant carved in the shape of a monkey's face. Well, I simply said, 'Fuck.'

Over the next hour Caroline explained how the pendant had turned up during a drug raid on a major cocaine syndicate on the Peru/Bolivia border region around six months ago. It was just another piece of evidence gathered by the local police and may have stayed that way if not for an earthquake that flattened the town, including the police station. It was then, while an international rescue team began to dig through the wreckage to pull out survivors, including searching the police station, that a British aid advisor saw a glowing light. It was the eyes of the monkey pendant. This aid advisor was very much part of covert intelligence and smuggled the pendant back to the UK where it made its way to a classified unit whose job was to deal with stuff that no one else knew what to do with – Ms Wright's unit. Questions were asked and research done, and they became aware that other groups were very, very interested in the pendant, and a pissed-up South African mercenary had blabbed a bit too much about a monkey and his buddies to an arms dealer who was trading info with MI6. Obviously, the Monster Highs brain fog had kept us off their radar and though they had gotten close we had gotten lucky.

And then the eyes went dark again. Until last week...

*

'They aren't glowing now though,' I said, being a master at stating the obvious.

'No. They started and then, after a couple of hours they stopped again and have been dark since.' Caroline turned the pendant in her fingers as she spoke, and I was aware that we were all holding our breath.

So, we wanted to know exactly what it was that they expected from us, and McBride was only too happy to tell us. In exchange for not throwing us away with the key, we were to go to Peru and locate a jungle shaman who, rumour had it, knew the location of a hidden temple, which local legend said was linked to a monkey demon, blah, blah, blah. We didn't bother telling him that we were off to South America temple hunting anyway, but we got the picture – another jungle, another temple, and potentially another massive body count, and this time us returning with black hole tech to give to our 'friendly' government.

The Monkey hadn't taken his eyes off the pendant for the whole of the conversation and now they snapped round to the Lieutenant Colonel, and he growled out of the corner of his mouth, 'Okay.'

Kev looked at me, I looked at The Monkey, we all looked at McBride. 'But,' said The Monkey, 'you dickheads are going to have to give us something in return.'

He spelt out in no uncertain terms how extremely sensitive information regarding the British Government's failure to deal with secret societies operating within their borders would be released to the world press if they didn't agree to rebuild my house in Cornwall and then just fuck off and leave us alone. 'If you do this, we will find the shaman, and the temple.' McBride nodded and said that it could be arranged, and we all got the feeling that we could have asked for a hell of a lot more – bollocks…

*

Then, a very chiselled captain came in and he and Caroline filled us in on the plan. Get onboard the waiting Atlas; fly to Charles de Gaulle Airport in France; get on an Avianca Airlines flight to Lima in Peru (no official flights, no escort, HM Government deniability); then fly to Iquitos in the Amazon to meet with a shaman who claimed knowledge of the temple; and then? Well, that was down to us, apparently…

17 November

Barty flew us in the Atlas to Charles de Gaulle this morning, and he apologised profusely for being 'that' guy. He didn't have much choice but to help out the security services as he was conspicuous on the CCTV footage they pulled of us all drinking and laughing together, and he knew that they needed our help so we would at least get to put our side forward before they started getting heavy. We, of course, forgave him and promised to meet up for much gin on the other side of whatever this turned out to be.

As we sit in departures, drinks in hand, we have clocked the spooks sent to watch us and have given them little waves, much to their disgust. I sent a message through JudyZ to our Mao Shan man to let him know there has been a bit of a change of plan. Twenty minutes later his reply dinged on my phone. He had got wind of something happening but not in time to warn us, so, with his usual pragmatic composure he was going to let us be flown courtesy of the British Government to exactly the place he wanted us to be. Wasn't that great... wanker.

In the meantime, there is a bar, a surplus of baguettes, and some spooks to torment...

19 November

Ah well, we didn't fly business class but there was plenty of booze and a seemingly endless supply of movies and cartoons which kept us amused for the thirteen-hour flight, that and quite a bit of sleep. The Monkey had bought a Lonely Planet Guide to Peru in the airport booksellers and spent a while laughing at pictures of llamas with bits of coloured wool in their ears. We didn't talk much about our change of itinerary as we had bitched about it quite a bit while waiting for the delayed (yes, four fucking hours!) flight, and in the end, we decided that. *It is what it is* – very fucking Stoic of us!

I must say that I have never been on a flight where the passengers clap and cheer the take-off and landing. I asked a stewardess why and she said that it's always like that on these flights. I get the feeling that maybe the predominantly Catholic, very superstitious passengers, are just not convinced by the science of flight and are actually clapping God's good work in getting them from A to B safely.

The last couple of hours had been flying over jungle that was total blackness except for the occasional pinpoints of light made by the fires of tiny villages set in clearings. As we began our descent towards the airport all that changed, and we could see miles and miles of golden lights that marked roads and buildings as if someone had laid out the Christmas fairy lights over a giant Lego city play set.

It was nearly midnight when we landed at Jorge Chávez International Airport in Lima. We were the last flight in, and the airport seemed to have gone home! We were waved through passport control and customs without a second glance, carrying our bags which had been unloaded from the Land Cruiser back in Luxemburg. These had been searched before being returned to us on the Atlas and anything that could go bang had been removed but they had left us our stabby stuff which they had kindly put in zip-up knife cases. They had also given us some suitable clothes for pretending to be Dora the Explorer as opposed to the black/tactical gear we had been hauling around. They seemed to believe it would be less conspicuous as there are a few paramilitary groups in the country who we don't want to be mistaken for, and we would meet someone in the country who would give us some new tactical stuff anyway. The Monkey had insisted on retrieving the plastic Mousetrap game dude who had been taped to the strap of his tactical vest since our trip to Chernobyl. He is a little worse for wear, a bit melty in places and perhaps looks like he has 'seen too much man', but he is still the team mascot and doesn't get out of facing death that easily. The Monkey also grabbed the cardboard tube given to him by Herr Myer. I had made sure that I got the cigar tube from my bag, the cigar tube that contains the monkey finger bone wrapped in cotton wool – our lodestone for all things weird and wonderful. Kev had just clung to his laptop and growled a bit if anyone looked at it.

When we got to the exit, we could see that the locals on the flight had already been picked up by family and friends or had jumped on board the last of the nice official taxis. That left us with some decidedly dodgy looking transport. We have allowed ourselves to be shown to the first on the rank and jammed ourselves into the dirty yellow Daewoo Tico (believe me, the others are just as bad). I am sitting in the front and have given the driver the hotel address and we are now roaring off into the night in a cloud of blue/grey smoke...

*

An eventful taxi ride? I should fucking say so...

The road leading from the airport was quiet and so was the major road that we turned onto but when we joined with several other main roads it all got a bit special. There was obviously a pretty full-on riot happening at the top of the embankment that led up steeply from the road. Figures were silhouetted blackly against the orange fire and harsh spotlights. The driver muttered something under his breath, crossed himself and kissed his fingers before touching the religious icons Blu Tacked to his dashboard. Then he put his foot down – hard. The Tico put on an unexpected lurch of speed and suddenly we were level with the carnage above us. I watched a petrol bomb sail through the air and get blocked by a riot shield before rolling down the bank and exploding. The focus of attention was obviously the authorities, but you always get a few intent on ruining everyone's day. Figures ran onto the bridge above the road and lumps of concrete rained down, and then from off to our right, a burning tyre bounced down the embankment and the driver deftly touched the brakes, letting the tyre bounce past a few feet in front of us. Then he floored it again and we were past the rioters and rushing into the night, while he laughed and crossed himself again, shouting something in Spanish about Crazy kids! We laughed as well, cuz they were crazy kids, and I mean, what else could we do?

Ten minutes later we were navigating dimly lit streets in a built-up area. The driver asked me again for the address and I showed him on the screen of my phone. He shook his head and I guessed that he was saying he had taken a wrong turn. We stopped at a junction, and he appeared to be thinking, then he turned off his taxi sign and headlights and swung the car left down a dark side road. The Monkey leaned forward between the seats and colourfully threatened the driver with much violence if he was driving us into an ambush, but the driver kept reassuring us in broken English that everything would be fine. We got to the next junction and the driver visibly relaxed and switched back on his lights and with a big grin on his face headed to a brighter part of town and our hotel, even pointing out a couple of parks as we passed and a restaurant that I think was owned by his cousin – maybe?

When we checked into the hotel, I asked the manager what the riots were about, and he just shrugged and said that some people aren't happy with their lives, so they smash things. Okay... What about the taxi driver turning off his lights? Ah, well that would have been a dangerous part of town and there may have been criminals watching who would have stopped a taxi carrying foreigners. I laughed, Kev looked nervous, and The Monkey just said, 'I think I'm going to like it here.' The manager has kindly opened the bar for us and so we have bought him a drink or several...

20 November

Morning, and over a very late breakfast of strong coffee and pork tamales we looked at the map that Ms Wright had given us. Not a huge amount of help really, just a circle around a section of jungle next to the Amazon River northwest of Iquitos.

Something has been nagging at me over the last few days and I have suddenly found words for it. Why is The Monkey so calm about this enforced hijacking of our mission? He has been full on about the chance of finding the Monkey God site in Tibet, in fact he had been nearly unbearable hanging around in Luxembourg (to be honest, The Monkey can be a little bastard when he is impatient) and was determined to get the South America trip out of the way as quickly as possible, so why was he taking this all so well? He poured another coffee and said, 'Sometimes you don't get a choice, so why try to change what you can't? Anyway, we get the house back and they might just leave us the fuck alone for a bit. And... there is now a second monkey pendant and definitely another monkey temple somewhere in all that,' he jabbed his finger at the green area that covered most of the map. Curiosity... I might have guessed.

But why, if the second pendant's eyes had sparked up, hadn't ours? The Monkey shook his head and confessed, 'I thought I saw the eyes alight, but it was the middle of the night and I had just woken up, and we had drunk that bottle of tequila. I went for a piss and when I got back there was no light again, so I thought I had dreamt it. Don't look at me like that...' Oh the joys of tequila.

*

Our flight to Iquitos isn't until tomorrow so we are having a bit of a wander, and so far, surprisingly, we have stayed out of trouble. The many, many bike carts selling street food have done a good trade from us and I can recommend the anticuchos, although Kev and The Monkey seemed to prefer the less carnivore option of the awesome sugar-heavy rice pudding dishes. But we are all agreed that the yucca root donut thingies with honey are epic!

The Monkey is fascinated by the idea that a bunch of Spaniards could pitch up and basically take over a whole country just because they had steel, and not for the first time. He has borrowed Kev's laptop to do a bit of background reading. I hope it doesn't give him any long-term ideas...

In the meantime, we are drinking JD and playing poker with the hotel manager. We have promised ourselves an early night...

21 November

Yeah, right!

This morning, we woke extremely late, and laughing like idiots, frantically jumped in a taxi and headed back to the airport. More of a *Ben Hur* chariot race than our previous ride. Reminded me of taxi journeys in Paris but with an assortment of cars that looked like they had been stock car racing, or maybe had appeared in *Mad Max*, as well as some very expensive vehicles and lots of horn blowing. They either don't have working indicators, or they think that they are only for special occasions, either way, it did nothing for our bad heads. And why so many old VW Beetles?

A one-hour wait at the airport had us drinking Pisco brandy in the bar – I know, we never learn... Kev raised the question of what exactly The Monkey had been researching last night as the browser history consisted of a few Conquistador searches but mostly My Little Pony porn. He asked The Monkey if he was a *brony*. The Monkey just looked at him and said, 'What?' A statement rather than a question, and in a way that didn't invite further comment. When the flight was called, I glanced at Kev and said, 'We had better saddle up then,' he blew Pisco out of his nose while The Monkey slid off his bar stool mouthing the word, 'Cunts,' at us as he headed towards the gate. Then a couple of hours flying to Coronel FAP Francisco Secada Vignetta International Airport, Iquitos, punctuated by Kev humming the theme tune to My Little Pony from the seat behind while I gave the occasional whinny, The Monkey just smirked.

Walking from the plane to the arrivals building the tropical heat reminded me of Cambodia and I suddenly had a sense of loss that I would never see Hambone again. He had flown us in and out of the first monkey temple we had gone searching for, and he had saved my life after I had been shot. And then, in the whirlwind of collateral damage that seems to follow us around he had been killed by a hitman. Welcome to our world...

There should be transport waiting for us and a local contact who will provide us with some 'kit' and help us find the shaman – I say all this like it's going to be easy!

22 November

Well, we met our contact. Since when has 'local' meant a dude from California who looks like a 70s porn star?

Porn dude is called Pete, and apparently has been living in Peru since 1998 after narrowly avoiding getting caught in a drug bust and subsequent manhunt. Hiding in the back of a truck he had managed to get across the border into Mexico and then he gradually made his way south until he ended up in Iquitos and decided to stay. He told us that as he drove us to his house which is on the outskirts of the city. The Monkey asked him about his connection to covert British agencies and he just shrugged and told us that from time to time he does 'things' for a number of unnamed clients. 'Pays the bills and gives me a certain immunity,' he said, as we pulled up at his lodge, part of which overhangs the river and the other part backs onto the jungle. He shares the lodge with his attractive, diminutive girlfriend Maritza, who greeted us with a big smile and then jabbered at Pete in rapid Spanish, all the while eyeing The Monkey suspiciously.

While she cooked up some food for us all we sat drinking Cusqueña lager on the veranda overlooking the river and Pete explained Maritza's outburst. It seems that a few years back they rescued an Ocelot cub from an animal trader along the river. Living on the edge of the forest they decided that it would be cool to rear the cute, spotty kitten. Everything was Disney until he reached maturity and then he decided that Maritza was his mate and kept trying to pin her down and fuck her. One evening Pete and Maritza were enjoying some sexy time when the spotty bastard leapt from a roof beam and landed on Pete's back and gave him a savaging. At this point Pete showed us the scars on the back of his neck and shoulders – eeek! Pete had to go to the clinic and get some stitches and the following day they took him upriver and released him into the wild (the Ocelot, not Pete). So, what has this got to do with The Monkey? Maritza says that The Monkey has that same look in his eyes as the Ocelot and she doesn't want to get raped by him... I thought The Monkey might get indignant and kick off, but he just grinned and said, 'Fair dos.' Kev disappeared for a bit and came back smirking for Britain. When pressed he admitted, through barely suppressed laughter, that he had talked to Maritza and explained that The Monkey had a fetish for cartoon ponies, and that she was quite safe.

It took us about fifteen minutes to fish Kev out of the river. He is still having fits of giggles and may well end up back in there...

*

Over dinner Pete and Maritza (she is now okay with The Monkey but keeps giving him curious glances) explained that they run guided tours into the jungle for tourists, including the 'spiritual' tourists who usually just want the full ayahuasca experience. Pete knows of the shaman we are going to see, one don Edwardo, but thinks he is a bit sketchy, so this could prove interesting. Anyway, smashing mozzies is getting tiring so the mosquito net is calling. The Monkey's omnipresent cigar seems to do a good job of deterring the fuckers – good for him!

23 November

Ah, the joys of an open launch with outboard motor…

Quickest – actually, only way to get where we want to go, but will still take a couple of hours. So, we drink more lager as the riverside shacks of the city disappear behind us and we start gliding past jungle. We also have toys to look at. Pete has retrieved a large black waterproof bag courtesy of HM Government, that he had stashed down river. There are three Glock G17 Gen4s, a nice compact Kel-Tec KSG 12-gauge shotgun, a small collection of grenades, boxes of ammo, and tactical vests – olive green rather than our usual black (The Monkey has immediately gaffa-taped the plastic Mousetrap game dude to a shoulder tab). It's just like Christmas…

*

We have reached the compound of don Edwardo the shaman. Not at all what we were expecting, and The Monkey has asked Pete about fifty times if this is the right place. Pete keeps nodding and saying that this is where the intel told him to bring us, and he also keeps reminding us that he said he thought the shaman was a bit sketchy.

It seems that don Edwardo runs ayahuasca ceremonies for tourists coming on journeys of self-discovery. This we gathered from the full-colour leaflet handed out to us by a young local woman dressed in what can only be described as Primark's finest fashion. She had literally run from a brightly painted portacabin set back by a gated entrance, to the small bamboo 'visitor information' kiosk at the boat landing, and with a huge welcoming smile had thrust the leaflets and her ample cleavage at us. Pete spoke to her in Spanish and told her we had come to see don Edwardo and she nodded obligingly and led us to the portacabin where she proceeded to attempt to check our names off a list attached to a clipboard. As she was doing this she kept smiling and saying in broken English that no one was expected for the next ceremony for a couple of days. Pete explained in Spanish that we weren't there for a ceremony, we had business with the shaman. Ah, well don Edwardo has fucked off to Iquitos on a supply run and won't be back until very late. Oh great! She said that we were welcome to stay the night as there were no guests in the guest huts, and she would get the chef to sort us out with some food and drink while she got accommodation ready for us…

The Monkey is doing a lot of growling, but I don't think he will shoot anyone. Pete says that we might as well stay the night as don Edwardo is probably visiting the local whore houses as well and most likely won't show until tomorrow.

*

This is a weird fucking place! There is a crescent of quite decent huts and in the middle there is a wide flat area like an amphitheatre, and at the back of this there is a white pyramid covered in LED rope lights! There are also large speakers on stands dotted around the edge of the flat area. It's more like the setting for an outdoor rave than what I would have imagined a shaman's camp to be like. Pete explained that from what he knows of don Edwardo he takes group bookings from spiritual tourists and the sick hoping for miracle cures when modern science has failed them. They spend lots of money for the privilege of nearly puking and shitting themselves to death and leave with 'life changing experiences' or a 'new sense of wellbeing' – that's what the leaflet says... According to Pete, don Edwardo also has a major reputation for sleeping with gullible young ladies who show up and treat him like some all-knowing guru. Nice...

The Monkey has found a control desk behind the pyramid, and we now have club anthems blasting out through the jungle and an impressive light show. The Monkey is actually smiling and throwing some shapes – Pete looks bemused...

24 November

There is this stuff called *aguardiente* – firewater. It's made from sugar cane, and you can get it in gallon plastic containers. We drank quite a lot of it last night, apparently...

Pete says that at a push you can run your outboard motor on it. Fuck. Kev was literally blind for a bit when he woke up, he may actually have lost his nerd status through the medium of dangerously high proof alcohol!

Seems like we had a good night though, several members of don Edwardo's staff are staggering around looking very much the worse for wear. Me and The Monkey are drinking Inca Kola to rehydrate while Kev tries not to throw up...

*

Late afternoon and the shaman has finally reappeared and our headaches have faded to a dull sledgehammer. To be honest, he seems pretty much the worse for wear himself, hiding behind some big old sunglasses, with a hoodie covering the rest of his head. He stinks of dope, had to be half carried by one of his assistants, and had a mild seizure when he saw The Monkey (he does have that effect on certain people), so we are letting him have a little rest before we start questioning him.

25 November

Well, we all just sort of passed out and woke up again this morning. That *aguardiente* is shocking stuff... But at least the shaman is now in a fit state to talk...

He is skinny, has shoulder length hair and is wearing big, and I mean BIG sunglasses. Also, which has made my jaw drop, he is now dressed in a black Giorgio Armani suit and has a white, sequined glove on one hand that he swears once belonged to Michael Jackson! He claims he bought it at an auction when he was visiting the USA. Ahh! This is not how I pictured a jungle shaman!

His English is a bit dodgy, so Pete has been interpreting for us. And now for the bad news – don Edwardo has admitted, after much questioning and not a few threats of violence, that he doesn't know where the Monkey Temple is. It seems he got wind of the pendant and temple from one of his ceremony participants, a man who claimed to be ex-military and who wanted to work through his post Afghanistan PTSD, although the man suddenly left before the ceremony. But shaman boy saw a chance to make some money and advertise his business and suddenly became the leading local expert on lost monkey temples. The Monkey is livid, and by livid, I mean little blue flames on fur livid. We are going to get back in the boat before any deaths occur.

Don Edwardo has offered to do an *ayahuasca* ceremony for us, at reduced rates, but The Monkey has told him to, 'Fuck right off.' He had his fill of DMT, the primary psychotropic in *ayahuasca*, when he was a nipper in the US research facility in Thailand and doesn't want some bargain bucket Castaneda dosing him up with jungle juice.

So, in the boat for another couple of hours back upriver. What a waste of time that was…

26 November

When we got back yesterday evening Maritza was a bit freaked out. She had a visit from the local police, and they had been none too friendly. They seem to have been tipped off by sources unknown about our presence and are under the impression that we might be drug smugglers. Maritza told them we were on a weeklong trip into the jungle so at least that has bought us some time to get out of town.

*

Pete made a call to his handler and explained don Edwardo's stupidity. There was a lot of 'Yes' and 'No' on his part and then quite a bit of listening. When he had finished, he told us that it now seems likely that the temple is up in the cloud forest in the mountains around Machu Picchu and not in the rainforest basin at all. Sources had been so convinced by don Edwardo's bullshit, which had been picked up by mobile phone intercept, that they had looked the wrong way. Classic misdirect.

They still want us to go in under our own steam, which is very frustrating. Once again, the deniability thing rears its ugly head so we can't expect to get picked up by a nice Apache Longbow and whisked off to the mountains, there to reign fire upon our enemies and be back in time for last orders. We are just heavily armed tourists according to The Monkey, so we need to suck it up and get on with it…

Kev fired up the laptop. It has pictures, so he prefers using it to the sat-phone, and had a chat with JudyZ, she has a sexy Indian avatar. He filled her in on the situation and she immediately went through a few million terabytes of satellite comms chatter and found something that had a reference to the Monkey Temple. Most of the message was encrypted but being mostly code herself she just insinuated herself into it and before long it was deciphered. There is a strong possibility, read that as 100% possibility, that someone on the British team backing us is playing for the other side. Looks like this person knew we were going on a wild goose chase and steered the powers that be to make sure we were given all the necessary aid to go chasing those pesky geese. This has given the Illuminati a chance to get their own teams out there looking, and looking in the right area. JudyZ is also convinced that this same double agent is responsible for her abduction and murder. It seems she has been busy following up some leads of her own and now could link a message sent just before she was taken as having the same encryption signature as the one she just decrypted regarding the Monkey Temple. Ahh! Kev is now looking at flights to Cusco and The Monkey is hacking at a tree stump with a machete.

*

Pete has an option for us. He has a 'friend' who owns a light aircraft and does drug runs in and out of the jungle. He flies from an airstrip a couple of miles upriver and if we go with him, we can keep hold of our toys. Pete has radioed and for a price he will fly us up to Cusco. We will leave in the early hours of the morning so better only have a couple more drinks...

27 November

When The Monkey saw the beat-up Cessna, he just stood there with his hands on his hips, shaking his furry head. He looked at me and then nodded at the bullet holes along the fuselage.

Pete swears that Chico, the pilot, flies hundreds of miles every week in the very wrong looking plane. Chico, who is apparently from Mexico, just keeps laughing and saying, 'No worries.' I think he may have had a little too much marching powder...

*

Well, we flew in from the north, via a series of valleys that cut into the Andes and touched down in a farmer's field about ten miles northwest of Cusco. On the way Chico gave us plenty of advice about clubs and bars in Cusco. He also advised us to drink coca tea to fend off the effects of altitude sickness, The Monkey confirmed, saying it was mentioned in the Lonely Planet Guide, I will reserve judgment.

The farmer is a business partner of Chico, and this is obviously a regular stop. Chico was very happy with the cash that had been for don Edwardo if he had come up with the goods. We gave him a hand loading a few suspicious looking parcels onto the plane and then with a final wave goodbye he took off again into the clear blue sky.

The farmer is agreeable to driving us into Cusco in the back of his truck, which we have to help him load with sacks of potatoes. Ah, the high life…

*

Saturday night in Cusco. We have found a quiet hotel, stashed our stuff, so what else is there to do but go and party with the tourists.

28 November

It was all fun and games at Chango Club. Lots of drink, although we were very restrained (the lass at hotel check-in warned us not to drink too much for the first couple of days until we were acclimatised to the altitude. She advised drinking coca tea – there we go again) compared with the backpackers who were really letting their hair down. Lots of EDM and rock blasting out and everyone was very friendly except the couple of heavies spotted by The Monkey who were eyeballing us. They were trying badly to blend in, but they obviously hadn't been issued with the party vibe.

We left the club about 2am and made a pretence of staggering back to the hotel. We wandered across the Plaza de Armas in totally the wrong direction to our hotel and stumbled down a side street. After a few minutes, our 'friends' slipped out of an alley in front of us, blades in hand. Thing about The Monkey is that he doesn't do chit chat, so the pretend threats and theatrical 'Give us your money' lines would have been wasted even if they had got to use them. The Monkey leapt to the side and bounced off a wall and onto heavy number one, pushing him over onto heavy number two. There was a loud crack and a muffled cry as an ankle broke. Me and Kev jumped the downed guy and I hit him hard with the sap I now carry everywhere. He went still and we turned to help The Monkey, but he had punched the goon in the throat and the man was on his knees, gasping out his last. The Monkey went over to our man and snapped his neck with a cold efficiency, and then after a quick and fruitless search we dragged the bodies over to a low wall that bordered a deep ditch and rolled the bodies over. Then we backtracked and went to our hotel which is on the other side of the Plaza.

*

Took turns standing watch for the rest of the night but there were no other incidents, so we have had a bit of a lie in.

Sunday today so no trains to Machu Picchu until tomorrow. We will have to play it cool as there are bound to be police everywhere…

*

Very odd. No police, well no more than usual, and no mention of two dead bodies in any of the cafés or bars we went into. The cleaners have been to town – maybe they were here anyway to take away our remains? Well, we are staying close to the hotel and not getting shit faced, just in case. We are sitting on the balcony of a small restaurant overlooking the Plaza. Loads of touristy types wandering about and plenty of locals in their Sunday best out with the family after attending mass. The Monkey has just pointed out something that had crossed my mind – why would the Illuminati or the remnants of the now evil Green and Red Society, send two half-arsed heavies to sort us out when they know what The Monkey is capable of? Is there another player in the game who is yet to catch up, or is it just another diversionary tactic?

*

An uneventful day, it was almost like being normal people. Would have been nice to do a bit of sightseeing but that might have just been pushing things too far.

Kev has been back online with JudyZ. She has been scanning the cloud forest around Machu Picchu, but it is so dense that she hasn't had any luck. Even managing to switch to a heat map scan via another satellite has produced nothing conclusive as there are locals and backpackers dotted all over the place and it is not clear what to look for.

But we have found Fight Club in Spanish on the TV, but I can't talk about that…

29 November

Coca tea bags in the room and a kettle, so when in Rome or high in the Andes, or whatever…

Anyway, tasted like strong green tea, and if it stops us getting ill then bring it on! It makes a change to take something herbal that is not going to end up with us being naked on the roof or heading down to the all-night garage for snacks…

The train is at 7.30 so gotta get our shit together and get to the station.

*

Man, these trains get busy!

By the time we left the station there were people sitting in the gangways on boxes and sacks of produce, and at least four people crammed in the toilet with more bags and boxes. There are quite a few backpackers and other tourists who have decided to take the easy option rather than walk the Inca Trail, but mostly it is locals in multicoloured shawls and hats. Boxes of live chickens and hessian sacks with half pigs are piled up between the seats along with all manner of other produce. Sitting just down from us is a late middle age Scottish couple. He is so pale he is almost transparent, although he has got a pink glow from the high-altitude sun, and he was very put out by the locals filling every conceivable space with goods they are taking to market. He was even more put out when the sack of potatoes on the luggage rack above him got rattled lose and fell onto his lap. The owner of the sack was very apologetic, and the Scotsman didn't look injured, but he wouldn't stop bitching about it. We found it very difficult not to laugh – I know, how childish, but would you expect anything else? It's a good job the padded waterproof sack that we have stashed in the luggage compartment didn't fall on him, the shotgun, ammo and grenades might just have knocked him out.

People keep clambering around the outside of the train, moving from carriage to carriage. They are mostly selling stuff, cigarettes, sweets and other food. We had missed breakfast because of the early start so we have bought some small savoury meat pasties. Hopefully, they won't kill us...

*

The Monkey is reading a dog-eared copy of *Starship Troopers* that he found in the hotel. We are all big fans of the film and every now and then he will shout quotes out, much to the bemusement of the locals. He has just shouted, 'Come on, you apes! You wanna live forever?' That has confused everyone and made Kev blow Inka Kola out of his nose...

*

Aguas Calientes, our final stop. A village with earth-coloured buildings made of rendered concrete blocks on either side of the railway tracks, at least that's what we can see at the moment. There are restaurants with outdoor seating almost on the tracks, so we are going to have a sit and a drink while we watch the tourists amble about and try to work out our next move.

*

While we were sitting there eating banana and chocolate pancakes and drinking extraordinarily strong coffee the sat-phone rang. It was the lovely Ms Wright calling, all the way from jolly old England. I passed the phone to The Monkey, and he immediately took off into a rant about incompetent fuckwits who can't be bothered to check sources properly – you get the picture. After he had exhausted his annoyance, at least for the moment, he spent the next five minutes having a grunted conversation, at one point even taking the cigar from the corner of his mouth. When he had finished, he simply said, 'We have to meet a man this evening. He is going to be our guide and take us to the temple. Apparently, he is walking down from a village in the mountains,' he gestured upwards. All you can see is mountains in all directions.

So, another cheap hotel and another round of beers while we wait for the sun to go down.

30 November

Now this dude is a proper shaman. Don Mamani is a Q'ero, descended right from the Incas, and he is a head man of the Andean shamanic council of elders – I know, all a bit Harry Potter. He has brought his son Amaru along to interpret as he mostly speaks Quechua and I think Kev's love affair with Google translate might just be over if we had to rely on that! He was very pleased to meet The Monkey and held his paws for a long time while he stared intently at him. The Monkey doesn't usually do up close and personal with strangers – unless he is killing them – but he was very chilled and let the old man have a good stare.

The temple is on a mountain opposite the Temple of the Moon, which is about halfway up the side of Huayna Picchu, the big mountain that is always in the photos of the ruins at Machu Picchu. It has been a closely guarded secret for many generations, the last outsiders to see it were Conquistadors who were on a quest for gold (as usual) and totally missed the royal palace at the top of Machu Picchu and instead blundered on the Monkey Temple where they met violent ends or went mad and ran off into the forest. That was our potted history of the Monkey Temple from don Mamani.

Now it seems every man and his dog want to get in there, and they know the rough whereabouts if not the actual location.

Don Mamani explained how they, the shamanic elders, had been approached by various interests, all wanting to be best mates and offering sizable fortunes for the privilege. They had mostly been white business types accompanied by henchmen, although there had been a Spaniard who had turned up saying he had historical links to the Conquistadors, and a Japanese contingent who had no need of henchmen. The Monkey nodded, we had all met members of the Green Dragon Society Yakuza, and they certainly didn't win medals for charm. The elders had fobbed them off saying that there were many temples in the mountains, but they knew nothing of a 'Monkey Temple'. They had also performed some intense rituals to cloak the area with what Amaru could only translate as 'confusion', this was to keep anyone from accidentally stumbling over the temple.

Then they had all started having the dreams, admittedly under the influence of a bucket load of San Pedro cactus but when they compared the visions, they were all the same – a many limbed demon goddess had spoken to them of the Monkey God and told them that they should agree to help the next outsider who came asking for their assistance. There had been quite a bit of disagreement but they could not ignore the fact that they had shared the same dream and so they eventually agreed. The following day a lone stranger had turned up. He said that he represented the British Government, and he had a single request – guide The Monkey to the Monkey Temple. So here was don Mamani, going to do exactly that.

We are fascinated, and not a little taken aback by their 'ghost of Christmas future' experience with the many limbed demon goddess. Too reminiscent of the Monster Highs for comfort…

*

It's the morning and we will walk up into the cloud forest and find this temple. Don Mamani asked The Monkey if he could see the monkey pendant, so he dug it out of his pack and unwrapped the cloth covering it up, and as he did so the room was filled with throbbing amber light from the pendant's eyes.

Here we go again…

*

There is a path that skirts the base of Huayna Picchu which has made the first few hours of walking pretty easy. There are quite a few backpackers wandering around the trail and a restaurant, not quite what we were expecting but I guess sometimes you have to hide things in plain sight. Still, all of the backpackers seem mightily impressed that we have two real life Q'ero walking with us. You can see some of them have that look of, 'Where did they hire them? That wasn't in the guidebook!' Bless…

*

Getting up into the forest now and off anything resembling the path we were walking on, so I am going to stop trying to note this down and instead try to avoid tripping over a snake.

1 December

Yesterday turned into the weirdest, best day ever – if you ignore the bloodshed.

After walking for what seemed forever, we came to a steep slope, okay – a steeper slope, with an almost invisible track zig zagging up it. Don Mamani and Amaru have calf muscles that look like turkey breasts and barrel chests that obviously work perfectly in this altitude. Me and Kev on the other hand do not, and we puffed and blew our way after them, legs on fire and heads swimming. The Monkey just sort of loped along; cigar as always clamped in the corner of his mouth. Amaru gave us a handful of coca leaves each and told us to chew them, they were bitter but after a while the going got a bit easier.

About an hour up the heavily forested mountainside The Monkey came to a dead stop and signalled us all to do the same. He reached into his pack and produced his Glock and favourite K-BAR knife. I fished out my Glock and Kev took the shotgun from the weapons sack (he does love a shotgun!) and handed out a couple of grenades each. We waited, motionless, and after a few minutes muffled voices sounded through the trees off to our right. The Monkey motioned the shaman and his boy behind a fallen tree, and we fanned out around the edge of a small clearing and did our best to merge with the undergrowth. I watched from cover as The Monkey effortlessly climbed a large tree and from a branch about twenty feet up signalled that there was another group following the path we had taken.

The group entered the clearing and looked around in a half-soaked manner. It was obvious they were not following us, but they did have side arms and the definite bearing of hired goons. Another man followed the first five into the clearing, map in one hand and GPS device in the other. He looked like he would have been more at home in a hotel leisure club than slogging through the cloud forest. He stopped and scratched his head with the hand holding the GPS and called one of the goons over to him. As he was pointing to the map and then pointing up the slope a neat hole opened in the side of his head, although it's fair to say that the other side wouldn't have been so neat.

All hell broke loose in the clearing. The goons all opened up on the downhill slope while diving for cover. I hit the deck and hoped that Kev would do the same, and from my position I could see that one of the goons had taken cover almost on top of where Kev had been hiding. There was a moment, which Kev described later, when the goon realised he was not alone and turned to see a lanky, twenty something nerd pointing a Kel-Tec KSG at him. Kev said there was a disbelieving look on the idiot's face and then Kev blew his disbelieving head off – sort of by accident. Kev said he didn't mean to pull the trigger, he just panicked… I saw the body tumble backwards out of the undergrowth and heard the blast of the 12 gauge, the other goons must have seen and heard as well as two of them turned their guns onto the bushes concealing Kev. Bad move…

The Monkey took out one and I got the other. The remaining three broke from cover and ran back across the slope the way they had come, firing downhill as they went. Another shot came from somewhere down the slope, and we heard one of the retreating men cry out. Whoever was firing from down there had skills and was picking their targets. There was the sound of frantic blundering through undergrowth, a single pistol shot then a burst of automatic fire followed by silence. I could see The Monkey up in the branches staring intently down the slope and then he slipped around the tree's thick trunk and disappeared.

There was movement below us then three men slid noiselessly into the clearing, one from the direction of the fleeing goons, while the other two aimed assault rifles at the bushes where me and Kev were hiding, the first one continued over to the fallen tree and stood with his rifle trained on don Mamani and Amaru. Then a piece of jungle detached itself and for a moment I had a mad urge to shout, 'GET TO THE CHOPPA!' (perhaps watching *Predator* so many times has actually been detrimental to my health?), but it wasn't an alien hunter collecting skulls, it was a man in a ghillie suit carrying an AS50 sniper rifle. The ghillie suit signalled us to stand, and of course we all complied, then he had a quick panic when he realised that The Monkey was missing. He dropped into a crouch, scanning the trees and never saw The Monkey drop from a branch directly above him. But he felt him land on his back and he felt the cold sting of the K-BAR pressed against his throat.

'Guns down,' growled The Monkey, and the man beneath him sighed and lowered the AS50 to the ground signalling the others to do so too. The Monkey slid off his back and pointed the Glock at his face. 'Who the fuck might you be?' he asked, as the man pulled the camouflage hood from his suit.

Don Mamani stepped forward and stared at the man's face, then he looked at The Monkey and said, 'The Spaniard.'

The Spaniard introduced himself almost in the style of Inigo Montoya from *The Princess Bride*, as one Nicolás González, descendant of Francisco Pizarro and special agent of the Inquisition. Well, no one expects the Spanish Inquisition, and The Monkey told him that. It was totally lost on him although me and Kev giggled like idiots… Anyway, it seems that the Inquisition have a twenty-first century branch and a stake in the Monkey Temple, this based upon tales handed down from the days of the Conquistadors. It would appear that a party of Spaniards did in fact stumble over the temple but only one made it back to Cusco alive. The priests who recorded his tale believed that he had been driven mad by devils in the mountains and, because he came from a rich family, he was shipped off back to Spain. But when he was interviewed by the Inquisition certain details of his story made them sit up and take notice. Seems that the Inquisition had a hard-on for the Illuminated Ones, were well aware of what they were searching for in various ancient places around the world, and were doing their damnedest to stop them because they considered the Illuminati to be Godless heretics. The unfortunate survivor was locked away in a deep, dark, 'safe' place where he couldn't spill the beans if any of those naughty Illuminati came a-looking, and an expedition to find the temple and blow it up failed spectacularly to find anything.

Fast forward five hundred years and the Inquisition hard-on still rages on undiminished along with their need to throw a spanner into the Illuminati's finest works. Nicolás and his team had been dispatched to ensure that the Illuminati and their associates would not reach the Monkey Temple and so once again frustrate their plans of dominion. I asked how they knew about the sudden interest in the temple, and he said that the Inquisition have many sources always on the lookout for reports of the esoteric and occult and a report had been intercepted of a monkey faced pendant with glowing eyes and tales of a lost temple. He himself had been chosen because his genealogy made him the right choice to continue the work of his ancestor, the Inquisition seem to be big on that sort of thing.

Okay, but who the hell were the dickheads lying all dead and stuff at our feet? They sure as fuck weren't Illuminati, they were way too amateur for that.

Nicolás had been made aware that there was a shadowy tech company based in Germany who were also very interested in the temple and the potential ancient artifacts that they might find inside. He believed that these dead bodies were they, or at least representatives of the company. The Inquisition had found strong evidence that the company was connected to neo-Nazi groups that spanned eastwards as far as Russia, and they had a reputation for hostile takeovers. It seemed likely that it was a couple of their hired thugs who had tried to jump us in Cusco, they looked like the sort who did corporate security and were suddenly way out of their depth. Why had the Spaniards executed them so ruthlessly? They were unnecessary distractions...

Which left us... The Monkey wanted to know what 'instructions' the Spaniard and his men had been given regarding us. Nicolás shrugged. We were a bit of an enigma. The Inquisition had heard of The Monkey and they knew he had caused the Illuminati a great deal of trouble. They also knew he would be looking for the Monkey Temple which could again thwart the plans of the Illuminated Ones. So, with the old 'enemy of my enemy is my friend' adage, Nicolás had been told to work with us if at all possible, and if our joint aims were compatible.

The Monkey grinned and waved don Mamani and Amaru to the front. 'Come on then,' was all he said and off we went again, but he glanced across at me as we left the clearing and his eyes said, 'For the moment' – either that or he had wind...

*

The entrance to the temple was a proper let down. I had expected something like the one in Cambodia, all carvings and Indiana Jones shit, but this was literally just a vine covered hole in the mountainside. Kev summed it up when he said that it looked like a council drain culvert.

After a bit of hacking by Nicolás' buddies – they had brought machetes with them, the show-offs – the hole in the mountainside was revealed to be regular in shape and the walls past the opening were of dressed stone tall enough to pass through while crouching in single file. Torches were produced from packs, and we began our crawl into the bug- and possibly snake-infested tunnel. Don Mamani wasn't at all sure about going inside. For generations the Q'ero had told stories of the temple and the dire consequences of trespassing inside it. I think it was only the presence of The Monkey that eventually swayed him, and after he and Amaru had prayed and made offerings to Pacha Mama, they joined our shuffle into the mountain. The tunnel angled upwards slightly, and after a scramble over some masonry that had dropped out of the walls, we heaved ourselves out into a large chamber. Suddenly Indiana Jones had entered the building.

Giant carvings reached up to the chamber ceiling. Simian but in a strangely disturbing style that looked much older than the Inka art we had seen around Cusco, odd angles, exaggerated proportions, and a lot of teeth. In the wall in front of us, between two of the grinning stone monkeys was a doorway with no door, broader at the bottom than it was at the top. The Monkey touched me on the arm and nodded up at the lintel which was marked with a partially eroded seven-pointed star.

As we crossed the threshold, flames ignited in bowls carved into the walls of the chamber beyond and the illuminated scene made The Monkey drop his cigar.

In the floor at the centre of the chamber a black hole was spinning and crackling, its event horizon quivering with flashes of energy, and the carvings on the chamber walls seemed to move in the infernal light of the flames and the energy bursts. But what made us gawp like idiots were the two figures on the other side of the black hole. Long hair blowing in some unfelt other worldly wind the Monster Highs stood in all their naked glory, not merged together but separately whole! And in perfect unison they said, 'Hello boys!'

But before we could express our joy at this truly unexpected reunion don Mamani shouted a warning and we heard the sound of automatics being cocked.

*

The Monkey span around, gun in paw, me and Kev followed suit although with less panache. The Spaniards had their weapons pointed at us except for Nicolás whose AS50 was trained directly on the girls. One of his men crossed himself and the others followed suit without lowering their guns. 'What the fuck are you doing?' asked The Monkey. I could see blue fire starting to creep across the fur of his shoulders.

Nicolás looked at him, 'The witches!' he said, gesturing towards the Monster Highs with the barrel of his gun before addressing them directly.

'Aleksandra and Kristiāna Zukas, you have evaded the justice of the Inquisition for six hundred years and defied the word of God with your perverse ways. I am authorised by the Grand Inquisitor to execute you without trial in the name of his Holiness...' He never got to finish because a lump of rock hit him on the side of the head and sent him sprawling to the floor. Amaru, who had thrown the missile, leapt back through the entrance dragging don Mamani with him. Nicolás' men sprayed the entrance with bullets, but father and son were already behind cover. I took the opportunity to slot one of them while The Monkey went a bit special. He seemed to grow massive, blue flames dancing across him as he moved unstoppably forward. He grabbed the nearest man and pretty much pulled him apart. The second one wasn't so lucky. He managed to get a burst of fire off which made The Monkey even more angry, and he grabbed the man by his head and drove his thumbs into his eye sockets. His head seemed to boil and then just exploded.

Kev went over to Nicolás who was trying to get to his knees, blood streaming from the gash in his head. Kev kicked the sniper rifle away, but the Spaniard swung out his leg, sweeping Kev's out from under him and sending him crashing to the floor. He hit Kev with an elbow strike and quickly wrestled the shotgun from his grasp, but a perfect foot on the end of a long, shapely leg stomped it down against the stone of the floor, crushing his fingers. While one of the girls kept the weapon from his grasp the other grabbed his hair and dragged him across the chamber. Then both of them crouched down beside him as he cringed back from the ferocity in their glowing eyes.

'We offered to work with the Inquisition in their war against the Illuminati. We chose to ignore what had been done to us and our family in the name of your God so that together we could fight a foe intent on crushing humanity. Bur your inquisitors would not countenance an allegiance with women of power, women who did not "know their place", women who were neither alive nor dead. And that is why we have haunted your dreams for six centuries!' It was almost a chant, and then they lifted him between them and gave him a leg and a wing into the black hole as he shrieked.

Me and The Monkey

The Monster Highs looked at us and smiled, and in that stupid way that I have I said, 'So, you've got names then.'

*

We spent a good ten minutes in a group hug. I think it was the first time Kev had touched a naked woman, so he was incredibly happy for a couple of reasons – awkward! Don Mamani and Amaru crept out of their hiding place and just stood there bemused by the love-in. When we finally managed to peel apart there were a lot of questions all at once, mostly from me and Kev to be honest. The girls gently shushed us and said there would be time for that later, but right now we had to go. Go where? La Paz in Bolivia to be exact, and we would be traveling through the black hole. But first we helped them strip trousers and shirts off the dead Spaniards, and they belted and knotted themselves into the make-do outfits. It's amazing how they always look great no matter what.

We also found C4 charges amongst their kit, looks like they were planning on sealing the temple permanently. So, along with their weapons the charges went into the black bag of shooty and explody things.

While the girls played dress up, we explained what was happening to Amaru who translated to a mesmerised don Mamani. He nodded and held The Monkey's paws again, tears in his eyes, and then we all thanked them and said goodbye with manly man hugs, and father and son headed back to the tunnel and the cloud forest beyond with, I suspect, no small sense of relief.

Aleksandra and Kristiāna, or Aleks and Kris as they like to be called (seems rude now we know their names to keep referring to them as the Monster Highs) showed The Monkey two indentations in the altar stone at the rear of the chamber. The indentations are hand-shaped and when The Monkey placed his paws in them the black hole stopped swirling and became still. Aleks said that he should focus on where he wanted to go, in this case La Paz, and after a brief series of flickering images the black pool cleared into the image of a marketplace much like the one we had seen in Cusco. This was very much how the black hole in our spare room in Cornwall had looked, showing scenes of Area 51 or Iceland or wherever it was we needed to go. But this was being controlled by The Monkey's will – scary thought!

We bagged up our weapons and hid any bloodstains as much as we could while the girls had a snack on the Spaniards and then we stepped through the black hole…

2 December

We are sitting on the balcony of the presidential suite at the Cassa Grande Hotel, enjoying a vista of mountains and the rarefied air of the world's highest capital city. Around us is the remains of the entire room service menu and quite a few empty JD and beer bottles. Bless the UK Government intelligence services for funding us…

We stepped out of the black hole into what turned out to be the Witches Market. The hole had opened in a dark side alley, so no one noticed us suddenly materialize. Kris did that thing they do and made the alley sort of disappear, hard to explain but it's like looking at something that keeps shifting so that you can never focus on it and your mind gets confused, so you just stop looking, and then we strolled out into the late afternoon sunshine of La Paz. There were the usual mix of backpackers and tourists, so we didn't attract too much attention, although some of the locals manning the shops and market stalls selling jars with llama foetuses and magic charms gave us longer looks. I guess in a society where the supernatural is widely accepted we, at least The Monkey and the girls, are more likely to register. But whether Kris did her thing, or they chose to ignore us, there was no trouble.

The girls headed straight for a shop on the far side of the square selling women's clothes. Although they pulled off the 'dead man's' combat gear look with quite some flair, the military style of the clothes was likely to draw unwanted attention from the local police, plus they were barefooted. So I handed over the credit card supplied us by Ms Wright, and they went shopping while we grabbed a beer and some melted cheese sandwich things called jawitas. We have no Bolivian cash, but everyone seems happy to take dollars of which we have an ample supply.

By the fountain in the square's centre groups of musicians played *el Condor Pasa* on pan pipes to the obvious delight, or not, of passing tourists, while men with the look of a 'dodgy Uncle Keith' tried to sell knock off Ray Bans or obviously 'genuine' gold Rolex watches. The Monkey's eye was caught by a tough looking man doing a kung fu demonstration. He challenged the much larger gringos to take him on and I suddenly got that sinking feeling as The Monkey looked from him to me and then back again. His constant joy at getting me into fights for his amusement borders on the pathological. Fortunately, before he could propel me into some low budget version of *Enter the Dragon*, the girls reappeared. Skin-tight jeans, crop tops, little leather jackets and high leg combat style boots in dark metallic colours completed the ensembles. And they also had small rucksacks containing a change of clothes and plastic carrier bags holding the dead Spaniards' kit, these they dumped in the nearest bin.

While The Monkey had been eyeing up options for me getting my head flying kicked in, Kev had been searching on his phone for a decent hotel. With 'fuck the cost' being the motto of the day he had found the Casa Grande and booked us rooms, so with The Monkey still casting wistful glances back at the Bolivian Chuck Norris we followed Google Maps.

*

We checked in and procured some bottles of Jack and Aleks and Kris told us what had happened to them after the fight at the Brightstorm warehouse. They intuitively knew that the only way to close the rift caused by the sword and spear touching was for something with an equal energy value to enter that rift, causing it to close upon itself.

Me and The Monkey

It was either them or me and The Monkey, and they chose themselves. When they fell into the rift it had seemed to them that all their atoms had been ripped apart, vastly different from going through the black holes. And then they had sort of just floated in limbo, scattered across a multi-dimensional plain, aware but unable to do anything but observe.

To them it had appeared as if eons had passed in the blink of an eye as they watched giant entities battle with each other for control of the dimension they were in. Armies who strove to prevent change fought other armies who wanted constant change – chaos and order smashing eternally against each other.

Then there was a great rushing and they felt themselves collected and hurled away at terrifying speed while all the time they saw visions of the monkey pendant, its eyes glowing, and then they were in the Monkey Temple, ejected from the black hole as individuals again.

That had been the day before we had entered the temple and seemed to coincide with The Monkey taking out the pendant to show don Mamani. The girls had somehow known we were on the way and so had just waited for us.

We told them everything that had happened to us after losing them. They were sad that we had to blow up the house, and were most annoyed to hear that Arno Whitaker, or at least some version of him, was still running things at Brightstorm. When we told them about the British X-Files team who had 'recruited' us they said that they were only surprised it had taken so long. Apparently they have known about the special unit dealing with the esoteric for quite some time, it would appear that the unit was formed in the Victorian era as a result of certain happenings associated with the Illuminati and have been doing their best to mitigate their influence in the UK ever since. Interesting, and could explain why we have been given such a free reign...

So, what where we doing in La Paz? Aleks explained that while they were being reassembled and fired through time and space to the black hole, they had seen a part of the Illuminati's plan as if it had been projected from the future, although it appeared to them as only one possible future. They didn't need the temples anymore because, after the shaman had made the black hole for them in Iceland, they had produced a portable version. That explained why no Illuminati super troopers showed up at the Monkey Temple, they just didn't care. But what about the Yakuza types don Mamani had told us about? The Monkey thinks they are working on their own agenda because Arno Whitaker is not likely to share with a group who switch sides to suit themselves.

So... La Paz?

They may not need the temples anymore, but they are working up their plans for a new world order. One possible future seen by the girls is their full commitment to the hollow Earth nonsense that The Monkey found out about before the battle with them in Iceland. Except it seems it's not nonsense... There are massive vaults inside the Earth where they are developing stealth aircraft and supermen, and they intend to unleash these upon the world through the portable black hole technology. And one of the vaults is bellow an area a few miles outside the city of La Paz with an entrance in a place called Valle de la Luna.

Fuck me! It's all gone a bit Jules Verne!

*

So, we are taking the chance to chill out while we can. Kev has JudyZ online and she is overjoyed at the girls being back, and we have spoken to Tony and let him know, he had a little cry – girl...

3 December

Today we have mostly been sitting around the swimming pool and drinking.

The Monkey had a sat-phone conversation with Ms Wright and informed her that we had located the Monkey Temple but were now on a side quest in La Paz. She responded that she knew exactly where we were based upon the credit card usage, and why were we buying women's clothes? The connection got very bad at that point, sunspot interference I believe, and she got cut off – shame...

JudyZ has been kindly pointing a satellite at the area where the entrance to the underground lair of the Illuminati is and has found a small heat signature irregularity which she believes is our way in. That location has been transferred to our phones so we should be able to navigate to it via Google Maps. She also had a long conversation with Aleks and Kris; I think she is glad to have more females on the team again – fucking hell, this is turning into an episode of Friends!

I can see The Monkey planning to push Kev into the pool, so I think I will take the opportunity to get another bottle...

*

I asked the girls to explain about the Inquisition and they laughed grimly and told us that, as per usual, men had taken control of spirituality and perverted it. There was a lot of pent-up sexual frustration and pure psychotic tendencies all wrapped up in a big, glittery bow of dogma. Religion is a virus they said, 'A virus that affects the desperate and the needy and is fed by the rich and powerful until the virus itself is seen as the only cure. They talk about faith but all they understand is fear. Preaching about the necessity to believe as they lead those who refuse to the auto-da-fé.'

They wouldn't go into detail, but they explained that their own family had been the victim of religious persecution even before they had become ghouls. And even though they had offered to work with the Inquisition, they had been chased across Europe over the centuries. Always with a price on their heads, and always in the name of some benevolent God. At one point they had infiltrated the headquarters of the Inquisition in Seville and killed everyone that they could find there as a warning to the rest that they wanted to be left alone. But it seemed that it never ended, and if it wasn't them, then any who didn't fit the Church's norm where mercilessly hunted and killed. 'Despite what that Spaniard may have told you he would have been under orders to exterminate The Monkey and anyone with him after they had got what they wanted at the temple. The Monkey is one anathema that the Inquisition could never allow to exist.'

The Inquisition had stopped persecuting other beliefs and even those with no belief because with the advent of the modern world, with its technology and particularly the internet, they couldn't keep up with the heresy that flooded out from every laptop, smart phone, and TV set 24 hours a day. So they concentrated their efforts on trying to shut down anything that was physical, like the Monkey Temple, or like the girls themselves. There had been several 'accidents' involving witches (real ones, not posers), vampires, and some more difficult to classify sorts at festivals and gatherings all over the world. And, of course, they hate the Illuminati with a vengeance.

To them, the Illuminati represent everything that is evil. The Illuminated Ones recognise no God in any way, shape or form. They are seen to worship only technology and man as the supreme being, with the sole purpose of becoming the one single power in the world, with one mind. The Illuminati equal Satan.

They are all as fucking bad as each other…

4 December

2.30am and I have just extricated myself from the puppy pile on the bed. The girls are sleeping soundly, and The Monkey is having a bit of a snore and the occasional grunt. Don't judge, we have a lot of catching up to do…

Kev has his own room and actually managed to hook up with an American college student who is doing the South America thing with three of her buddies. We got Aleks and Kris to give them the once over to make sure they weren't vampires or something else dangerous to Kev's wellbeing (after the incident with Johno and the Newquay hen party you can't be too sure) and they gave them the green light and off he went.

I have just turned on my phone after what must be four or five days of not using it. Needed to check emails and upload blog entries and have just seen the utter nonsense in my inbox from Amazon. Looks like The Monkey wasn't just looking at My Little Pony porn when he borrowed Kev's laptop, he has also logged onto my Amazon account and been adding things to his wish list. So now, for God only knows what reason, I am getting suggestions based upon his search history that include an inflatable triceratops fancy dress costume and a life size cardboard cut-out of Danny DeVito. For absolute fucks sake Monkey!

*

Had another drink and went back to bed, man I have missed the girls!

Missed breakfast entirely and so glided seamlessly into lunch at a little restaurant just across from the hotel leaving the girls to catch up on sleep. Kev joined us and I could swear he was talking with a deeper voice. We ripped the piss out of him mercilessly and miraculously his voice seemed to go back to normal.

*

We are going to spend another night at the hotel. Aleks and Kris need some more sleep after their interdimensional jaunt, and then filling up on Spanish food… So Kev gets another evening with his college paramour while me and The Monkey play drinking games with the girls and watch subtitled *Nightrider* episodes on the big TV in our room.

5 December

We have booked a taxi to take us to Valle de Luna which is apparently a tourist attraction as well as a secret entrance to an underground Illuminati base. Well, nice to know we can get a commemorative tea towel while we are getting our arses shot off!

Leaving everything except the bag of guns at the hotel, so will check back later…

6 December

The spot identified by JudyZ was a dead end in the maze of rock formations that is known as Valle de Luna. There are fenced off areas to keep you on designated routes, and of course, the entrance was in a fenced off area. So, Kris did whatever voodoo it is that the girls do, and we clambered around the fence while tourists obliviously wandered past, cameras and smart phones recording the ancient rock formations and themselves next to said formations – but mostly themselves.

Past the fence we single-filed though a narrow passageway and out into the horseshoe-shaped dead end. For a moment I thought we had picked the wrong cul-de-sac as there were no cave entrances or holes in the ground or signs saying 'Entrance to Secret Base – Nothing to See Here', but the girls either have much better eyesight than us or they can see on a different wavelength, because they went straight up to the rockface and after a few moments the rockface parted and we were looking into a lift.

Seemed to take an age for the lift to eventually come to a stop. Aleks did some stuff to the security camera so that it would appear that the lift was empty if anyone looked, and after that it was just a case of waiting. There was of course the schoolboy humour of 'Going down?' although to be fair that was started by the girls... Between bouts of *Carry On* worthy puns we did discuss what would happen if the doors opened and we were presented with a host of armed guards pointing guns at us, you know, sort of like the end scene of *Butch Cassidy and the Sundance Kid*.

Kev took the shotgun from the weapons sack and said, 'It's a good day to die.'

We all looked at him and The Monkey was just about to say something but stopped himself when it was obvious that Kev didn't really believe it but was trying to be brave. Instead, The Monkey reached into the bag and took his Glock and two grenades and said, 'Let's try not to do that, eh. Don't want to make your girlfriend sad, do we?' Kev went rather pink and busied himself loading 12 gauge, and Kris nudged The Monkey and grinned.

Anyway, the door of the elevator slid open, Kev later said that it had a *Star Trek* door sound – he was impressed, we all just stared at him again. We had assumed the position, that is, as far to either side as we could get with guns ready, but there was no one there. No waiting welcome committee, no reception desk, no bustling minions with clipboards or armed guards patrolling back and forth. No, the lift had opened out at the end of a long, brightly lit, featureless grey corridor at the end of which we could see another door. Aleks and Kris blew their magic pixie dust and killed the cameras that were dotted down the corridor in their little black domes, and we set off at a jog.

The door at the end had a swipe card reader and keypad to one side. Aleks borrowed The Monkey's K-BAR and slid the business edge of the blade down the slot of the card reader while Kris put the palm of her left hand over the keypad and then they clasped each other's free hand. There was a loud crack and blue sparks. It was as if they had formed some sort of electric circuit, and with a sigh the door parted and stepping through, we found ourselves on a walkway set about halfway up the wall of a massive cavern. The walkway ran off in either direction and looked like it made a full lap of the space. There were stairways leading down at intervals and service ladders leading upwards. The Monkey grabbed my arm and diverted my gaze up towards the domed roof where the girls were already staring. There, suspended just below the roof was a series of long metal structures forming an immense seven-pointed star. And at the nexus, a ring made of some sort of rough gun-metal coloured substance contained the pulsing disk of a black hole. 'Fuck!' was I believe what we all collectively said...

When we had got over the fact that there was a black hole suspended above us, we sneaked to the edge of the walkway to take a look at what was below. Kev looked like he might just pass out with excitement, he does miss his fellow nerds to fully nerd out with, and the rest of us just stared at the sci-fi tableau laid out before us.

On four raised platforms sat four aircraft / flying saucers / imperial starfighters. I don't quite know what. They were all angles and flat blade-like profiles, and reminded me of stealth spy planes I had seen in photos and History

Channel documentaries, but these bristled with weapons instead of cameras. Around them clustered teams of technicians and ground crew fiddling in open inspection panels and doing stuff with high pressure hoses and cables trailing from tall scaffolds next to each craft.

There was a distinct absence of armed security, which, as The Monkey pointed out later, gave the impression that they felt very secure in their underground lair. Kris pointed off to our left and there was an archway leading off into a long tunnel that was easily big enough to be an aircraft hangar. Rectangular units that obviously served as a control centre with all of the functions needed to support such a large facility stretched back into the tunnel. Yellow light in the windows illuminated figures inside going about their duties.

On the other side of the cavern opposite the tunnel there was a row of glass tubes glowing with an eerie blue-green light, and in the tubes slowly squirmed human like shapes. This was almost identical to the tubes we had destroyed at the Brightstorm facility in Wales. The Illuminati are very attached to their idea of creating super soldiers and supermen who will rule the rest of us if they get their new world order shit together.

We moved back away from the guard rail that ran around the edge of the walkway and knelt to make ourselves less visible. Even though the girls had put their special influence on the area around us we still felt very open and exposed under the glare of the overhead spotlights. I asked what the plan was with a sinking feeling in my stomach. The Monkey looked at the girls and they nodded in unspoken agreement – we needed to fuck the place up! But we were a little low on fire power, outnumbered, and the place was very large, just a normal adventure for us!

Then Kev's massive brain kicked in and he peeked between the bars of the guard rail and said, 'Those are compressed gas hoses, and I would bet that there are oxygen tanks down there as well. It also looks like the flooring is some sort of anti-static material so they are trying to keep ignition sources to a minimum around the aircraft, either because there could be an explosion and/or they don't want electrical interference buggering up their sensitive systems.' We gave him a look that acknowledged that all those hours watching science fiction instead of getting drunk and womanising had been good for something – oh, and going to university and studying as well of course…

*

The plan then…

We would sneak down to the lower level and split into two teams. Aleks and Kev would aim for the aircraft with the intention of booby trapping at least one of them with the explosives we had taken from the Spanish team. The Monkey, Kris, and me would take the remaining explosives and some grenades and get busy with the tube thingies. Then we would rendezvous back up by the lift and get the fuck out of Dodge before everything went Kaboom!

Me and The Monkey

But what was it Mike Tyson said? 'Everyone has a plan until they get punched in the teeth.'

*

It was obvious that things were going sideways when the creature in the glass tube opened its eyes and stared straight at me...

We had been sneaking around the back of the tubes with their multicoloured wires and power units with whirring fans when I accidentally tapped the glass. It wasn't like I was ten years old and trying to attract the fish at the local pet shop, no it was an accidental tap as I was attaching a charge to the power unit. The humanoid lump bobbing in whatever soup they are grown in suddenly whipped around and thrust its featureless face against the tube, looking straight at me with unnaturally blue eyes. The gash of its mouth worked, and bubbles came out in streams as it began to bang on the glass with pale waxy hands, the veins very visible through the skin. We had seen others more fully formed, more or less human-looking, in some of the other tubes, and we had seen a few who were obviously at the start of the process, more like large pink jelly babies. But this one was just unformed enough to be totally repulsive. Of course, the thrashing attracted technicians who clustered on the other side of the tube and fussed with computer tablets, and adjusted sliders, and checked digital read-outs. I got as close to the floor as possible and held my breath in the hope that the thing would lose interest and that I wouldn't be noticed by the gaggle of lab coats. Glancing at The Monkey and Kris who were three tubes over, I saw him flick the safety off one of the automatics we had taken from the Spanish operators, and gestured for me to stay down. Kris touched his shoulder and whispered something in his ear, and he nodded. She put her hands together as if praying and appeared to blow into the gap between them. As she separated her palms, I could see a faint ball of blue light hovering between them. She made a pushing motion and the ball of light floated towards me across the space behind the tubes. As it got level with me, I glanced up and saw the thing in the tube staring at it with fixed attention. The ball of light began to move slowly up and around the tube and the thing followed it, seemingly enraptured. The Monkey signalled to me and as the tube's occupant calmly turned away and the lab coats began to relax, I crawled across to him and the three of us slipped around the side of what looked like a large generator. Kris brought her palms together again and a quick glance showed that the glowing ball had disappeared, much to the annoyance of the thing, which began a frantic search around the tube. One of the technicians appeared at the back of the tube where I had been hiding and after a brief look shrugged his shoulders while one of his colleagues at the front produced a hypodermic and injected a white fluid into a drip line that ran up and over the tube and down into the thing. It calmed immediately and went back to its gentle bobbing, like a meat lava lamp. But the technician at the back of the tube hadn't gone. He was looking down at the power unit and as we watched he squatted down with a puzzled look on his face. Next second, he was on his feet and backing quickly around the tube shouting to the other technicians – he had spotted the C4.

All sorts of fuckery happened next. The shouting, scrambling lab coats set off an alarm. A siren began to squawk and red spinny lights began to be red and spinny in their positions halfway up columns. Armed men and women appeared from nowhere and we could see the technician who had been at the back of the tube talking to one of them and pointing to where he had seen the C4 charge. And at the entrance to the long tunnel huge steel blast doors began to close, gradually sealing off the control centre and the lab coats who had skedaddled in that direction. The Monkey began to rapidly screw a silencer onto his Glock. One had been supplied with our toys and he had immediately commandeered it and put it into the pocket where he keeps his cigars.

The armed man edged his way around to the back of the tube and crouched down to take a look, and as he did so The Monkey shot him through the top of his head. He dropped forward onto his knees, chin dropped onto chest and stayed there. It must have looked to those on the other side of the tubes as if he was examining something, and so we took advantage of the uncertainty and made a break for the nearest staircase that would take us back to the walkway above. I glanced up and saw Aleks' face at the top of the stairs, they had obviously finished their mission and got back to the walkway without incident – don't you hate a show-off? Kev wasn't with her, but she indicated that she had sent him ahead to make sure the lift was waiting for us.

As we ducked behind the walkway railing, we heard the commotion as they realised the dude at the back of the tubes wasn't having a long think, possibly the fact that he had finally toppled forward and face planted had given the game away, and they dived for cover, shouted commands rang out. The Monkey looked at the girls and asked, 'Can we get up in the lift?' Aleks and Kris closed their eyes and when they opened them, they nodded, 'We can keep them from cutting the power for a short while, but we have to go now!'

I gave The Monkey a, 'Shall we?' look and then we both lobbed grenades as far out into the room as we could and ran like fuck for the door. Kris closed it behind us and fired into the number pad with a Glock, and we sprinted down the long corridor, a series of faint vibrations echoing though our feet, and into the waiting lift where Kev and the shotgun played lift attendant.

We had given ourselves plenty of time to get out before the C4 charges blew but now we wondered if that might not give them enough time to find and diffuse them. We had not heard the grenades explode, only felt the vibration of possible explosions, and we guessed that the heavy door at the end of the corridor was probably a blast door. We would have no idea if the charges had detonated, and there was still thirty minutes left on the timers. All we could do was get back to the surface and hope for the best.

The Monkey had an almost guilty look on his face when he admitted that he had set the charges to detonate way sooner than we had discussed. He then got all defensive and belligerent and said, 'What?' as we felt the sides of the lift vibrating...

Me and The Monkey

*

The lift came to a halt and after a couple of seconds the doors parted, and there waiting for us was a single figure, clad in black from boots to full face helmet. We hugged the sides of the lift as bullets ripped through the doorway. I felt stinging as shards of metal sprayed from the wall behind us. There was a moment of quiet and then a sort of change in pressure and it was obvious that the girls had done something to give us some sort of protection. The next bullet spray appeared to travel in slow motion as it entered the lift and when the bullets hit the back wall, they bounced off harmlessly. With a growl The Monkey stepped out and opened up with his automatic, and I watched as his face changed from grim glee to confusion. Poking out my head I saw why. The black clad figure had taken much of the blast but although they had staggered backwards, they were still on their feet and about to return fire, dodging from side to side with unnatural speed. The Monkey leapt through the door and out of the protective bubble, the blue flames burst out across his fur as he became larger. Then they made contact. The figure in black moving with that same unnerving speed and strength, threw the Monkey against the rough stonewalls of the passageway. There was no room for rifles so both dropped them and went for side arms and a close quarter battle ensued as each attempted to point weapons while kneeing and elbowing the other. The Monkey still had the silencer on his Glock, and it was now a major disadvantage as his adversary used it as a lever to redirect the barrel as he head butted The Monkey and pushed him back against the wall.

I kept thinking, 'Holy fucking shit! Holy fucking shit!' I had never seen The Monkey struggle against an enemy, especially when he had started to go God Mode! Then The Monkey wrapped his tail around his attacker's right wrist and let go of his own gun. He had taken a blow across the face and his tongue darted out and tasted the blood from his split lip.

And fucking boom!

The girls dragged Kev and me out of the lift as a huge tremor made it shake and the light went out. We sprawled on the ground and looking back I saw the lift car sort of twist and then disappear as it fell downwards. Kev shook my arm and I looked back at the fighting figures, and wow! The Monkey now stood around nine feet tall. The blue fire was flowing across him in waves, and he was holding the black clad figure up in the air by the throat and staring into the black reflective visor as his adversary fired into his chest repeatedly. And then The Monkey smashed the still firing attacker's head against the opposite rockface and there was a sickening crunch as the helmeted head deformed and the neck snapped.

The Monkey turned towards us as he dropped the limp figure and for a few very scary seconds I thought he was going to attack us. This wasn't The Monkey who had hung from my curtain rail throwing shit. This wasn't the Monkey who had drawn a monocle and cock on my face when I was asleep. This was a creature from another time, another place, and it was very fucking scary...

The girls walked straight up to him, and each took one of his massive paws, all the while they chanted something in a language I couldn't understand and as they did so he gradually began to return to his normal size, the fire flickering out. Then he staggered and collapsed, and all the time I could hear Kev muttering that this was just like the Hulk! We quickly checked him for bullet wounds but there were none, even though he had been shot from point blank range. I hoisted him up over my shoulder while Kev and Aleks dragged the black clad body over to the lift shaft from which smoke slowly drifted up. Aleks removed the shattered helmet from the body and even though the head was now distorted and bloody it still resembled the thing in the tube, intense blue eyes staring lifelessly. Then they pitched him down the shaft and forced the doors closed, leaving what appeared to be a simple rockface.

We began to make our way through the passageway leading back to the tourist routes of Valle de Luna and it was only then that we became aware of the line of people on the other side of the fence all pointing camera phones. Yay for covert ops! I glanced at Kris, but she shrugged and said that it would be too late to do anything now, we just needed to cover our faces as much as possible and get out of there. The tourists wouldn't have seen much but they would have heard the gun fire...

*

So, back at the hotel.

The Monkey is unconscious, so we are letting him sleep it off. Kev has been on to JudyZ and it seems we are social media sensations – not influencers, more side show. She is going to see if she can do something to mitigate the damage.

I need sleep, and food, and a drink, but mostly sleep. Maybe just one JD...

7 December

Keeping a low profile. The camera phone footage wasn't best quality because of dust and smoke, and we are not hugely identifiable...

JudyZ has done some tech magic to help draw attention away from us. She has Deep Faked the footage using Nicholas Cage's face on everyone and uploaded all of the clips back to social media and YouTube. It is getting way more hits than the original footage and she has leaked out a story that it could be filming for a new movie, so with a bit of luck Joe Public will think it is just a stunt. She has also picked up a large underground heat signature from the site of our latest havoc, so it seems we might have had some success after all.

*

Me and The Monkey

The Monkey is still sleeping, and I think it is best in this case to let sleeping monkeys lie...

8 December

Kev met up with his American girlie last night for more desperate romance. She asked him if he knew anything about the Hollywood blockbuster, possibly featuring Nicholas Cage, that was being filmed nearby, but he said that he hadn't heard anything. I think secretly he was gagging to show off a bit but wisely kept it to himself...

*

The Monkey has finally woken up. He was totally confused as he had been having a very real dream in which he and David Hasselhoff had been fighting time-travelling Nazis. He punched me in the head as he was coming around, which I could have done without, and shouted something about, 'Not letting them get the blue ones!' After picking myself up off the floor I asked him what 'The blue ones' were, and he just looked at me as if I had gone mental, and then asked me why I had been on the floor – I give up... He did say that in his dream he had discovered a way to exist in two places at once and grabbed the hotel notepad and started writing. After about thirty seconds he gave up and with slumped shoulders said, 'Bollocks! I've forgotten.' I shouldn't have laughed, but I never learn and so I did, and I'm still holding a towel full of ice to my fat lip...

I decided that while he stood under the shower trying to not get his cigar wet, I would broach the subject of him going next level God Mode. He says that he doesn't remember much other than extreme rage after the black clad dude smashed him in the mouth but he seems to recall having very uncharitable thoughts about the two meat puppets (his choice of words) standing by the lift doors – this was undoubtedly me and Kev. I told him that Kev had gone on about it all being a bit Incredible Hulk and he just laughed, although I think he quite enjoyed that. As to whether he can go to that level of nuclear on demand he is not sure. He said it felt as if a switch had flipped but he can't say for sure if he can flip that switch whenever he wants. His comment of, 'Will be interesting to find out though!' was not reassuring...

*

We have ordered most of the room service menu again and several bottles of Jack while we wait for Aleks and Kris to get back from their own quest for food. They have located a morgue and gone to feed their hunger – probably won't be putting that on TripAdvisor.

Kev has just come in with a big sad face. His girl and her friends have all left to get an evening flight up to Quito in Ecuador and the next phase of their South American odyssey. Ah well, nothing that lots of hard drinking and manly piss taking can't cure – probably.

The Monkey is a bit concerned about the super soldier thing that he fought. He says that it seems he is more than capable of upping his game to cope with them, and Aleks and Kris have their own scary response to imminent danger, but he is concerned about me and Kev. He thinks that either of us would have been toast if the black clad cock-womble had got to us first. After seeing him throw The Monkey around I think that is true. We need to be a bit more careful, and The Monkey is very keen on us getting some more magic weapons like the Spear of Lugh that got sucked into the vortex. He wants to have a chat with the girls and find out if they know whether it got destroyed or if we might be able to get it back, or if they can point us towards something else similarly devastating.

9 December

The girls got back about 2am and wanted to sleep, as they always do after a big meal. They are very much like snakes in that respect, sexy, sexy, partially dead snakes...

Before The Monkey would let them drift off into a corpse buffet coma, he insisted on asking their opinion on gaining more magical weapons. And much to our surprise they said that when they had been in the other dimension, the one with the warring god type beings, they had seen the spear and the sword being used in the eternal conflict that was waging. So, they hadn't been destroyed when they had touched as we, well at least I, had imagined. They said that they really needed to sleep but believed that we may be able to get the spear back as it was created in this world and I have a connection with it, having used it in battle. Well, lucky me...

*

There is no chance of Aleks and Kris waking up before this evening so I guess we will spend another night here. Could be worse, and it gives our unwanted social media stardom a chance to die down a bit. On the subject of which, Kev has been talking with JudyZ online again and she seems to have done a great job discrediting the footage and spreading false trails. But I think in his enthusiasm Kev may have badly misjudged the situation. He had a little boasting session about his hooking up with the American girl and JudyZ went very monosyllabic on him. I think he has drastically underestimated the connection that has formed between the two of them. It has been a bit like online dating over the past month or so and he has just outright admitted to being unfaithful. Kev has next to zero experience with females, having spent his twenty something years lost in sci-fi, computers, physics experiments, computer games, and watching porn. JudyZ is obviously a fellow nerd and so has a lot of that in common with him – except maybe the porn – but being a ghost in the machine must fuck with your head eventually, and I think the emotional connection she has been getting from him helps to keep her going. I truly hope he hasn't fucked that up.

I tried to chat to her, but she didn't want to engage and in the end The Monkey had a more business-related conversation with her regarding activity around the Valle de Luna site, and she was okay with that, and they had quite a long keyboard conversation. She also told him that she had spotted some activity around the Monkey Temple back in Peru and picked up some comms chatter which would indicate our UK beneficiaries have boots on the ground there. There is a good chance that somewhere in our kit is a GPS device that has led them directly to the location…

*

On the balcony again with our old friend Jack. The Monkey has sparked up a larger than usual cigar and is rescuing the Mouse Trap dude from his tactical vest. It didn't hold up too well to The Monkey supersizing so the vest will be going in the bin. Mouse Trap dude got a bit melty around the edges, but he is still in the game.

Kev is angsting about JudyZ; he is going to need to rebuild some bridges, poor sod. And the girls have just woken up, yay! Time to open another bottle…

10 December

We went through the kit that had been supplied to us and found no sign of a GPS or other tracking device. We were just about to have a rethink when The Monkey dug his wrecked tactical vest out of the bin and did a bit of unstitching with the tip of his K-BAR. And there it was, hidden in the back of the neck seam, a GPS chip…

We are going back through the black hole in the Witches Market and if, as we suspect, British Intelligence are there setting up shop, The Monkey may have a few words. Surprisingly, he is quite sanguine about it. He says that we shouldn't be surprised that they had us tracked and that he would have done the same thing.

Kev has been talking to Tony back in the UK and apparently JudyZ is pissed at Kev and has been, metaphorically, bending Tony's ear. I hope she doesn't lose focus when we need her. The girls say they will have a chat with her when we get back to Peru. In the meantime, we need to get our arses back through the black hole to the Monkey Temple and hope that the spooks don't get in the way of our attempt to get the spear back, I'm sure they won't want us having that weapon of mass destruction, not when they could keep it for themselves…

11 December

Going back through the black hole was easy enough, a few stares again from the local stall holders, but the girl's voodoo had held, and we got back into the alleyway without causing a riot.

More panic at the other end though. We stepped back out into the Monkey Temple to find that the British arm of the X-Files had set up in there. They jumped out of their skins when we suddenly appeared in their midst, and I think we did well not to get shot!

As we looked around the assembled armed men and women it was obvious that this bunch had combined the idea of scientific rigour with extreme violence – they were spec ops nerds. And there in amongst them, doing her best Lara Croft, was Ms Wright. I get the feeling that when she had spoken to The Monkey a couple of days ago on the sat-phone she hadn't really been in the UK. The little tease…

She invited us into the outer cave for a debrief and we introduced Aleks and Kris as our 'associates', although Ms Wright had a very suspicious look to her. They had set up folding tables and camp chairs, and in a corner a small generator whirred away powering the computers on the tables and the work lights on tripods dotted around the space. There were two armed men by the tunnel entrance and when she indicated that we should sit down we all dragged our chairs out into an arc so that we didn't have our backs to them. Ms Wright sighed and said, 'Really?'

The Monkey just looked at her and replied, 'Really.'

For the next couple of hours, we had an in-depth Q&A session about how we had managed to travel through the black hole (which they have decided to designate as an 'energy portal' because technically it is not actually a black hole – potato potato) and get back again. They had seen it had been focused on the marketplace for a couple of days and when it did not change, they decided to chance it and were preparing to send a team through when we had reappeared. The energy portal had gone black again after we came through so they were obviously wondering how we knew where we would end up. The Monkey grudgingly explained that he could make it focus where he wanted it to open, it was all down to his need. Ms Wright wasn't at all pleased with that answer as she wanted some mechanistic process that they could easily replicate, she tutted and the spec ops nerds who had joined us made copious notes.

The girls had been quiet up until then, but Aleks glanced at The Monkey and then leant forward and said, 'It can be learnt. The Illuminati have managed to attain the skill and if you are truly in opposition to them then you will need to up your game.'

At this point Ms Wright glanced at a rack of grey metal hoops that we could see through the entrance to the temple cave, she quickly looked away again when she realised we were all looking as well, and changed the subject.

So, we then got onto the topic of, 'What the fuck did you get up to in La Paz?' The GPS tracker had worked until we descended into the earth and had briefly flicked to life when we had resurfaced, but The Monkey's blue flame had put paid to that. Ms Wright had seen the social media posts, both original and doctored, and one of their satellites had picked up the heat signature coming from underground that JudyZ had spotted. The Monkey gave them a potted account of what had happened, although he skirted around most of the detail as, at the moment, he trusts Ms Wright and British Intelligence as far as he can throw them.

Eventually Ms Wright was at least partially satisfied and there was an almost imperceptible relaxing of the guards by the entrance. I wondered what their orders were if we didn't play ball...

*

They have taken our backpacks and the weapons bag and put them 'for safe keeping' in a pile by the generator. There is a camp set up in the cloud forest just above the tunnel entrance and we are to spend the night there, and then tomorrow Ms Wright wants The Monkey to demonstrate focusing the energy portal and to start teaching them how to do it. We have other plans...

Tonight, we are going to use the energy portal to get back the Spear of Lugh from some hell dimension, and then we are getting the fuck out of Dodge.

12 December

Ah, it all seems so easy. Open a doorway to another dimension. Summon a possessed spear. Close doorway. Live happily ever after... My friends, you should always read the small print because now I have a metal arm!

We snuck back into the temple at around 0300 hours, to use The Monkey's military parlance. Of course, there were guards outside but the girls used some sort of sleepy night night juju on them, and we walked straight past the now snoozing hard men. The inner chamber with the black hole, sorry, energy portal, was lit with the dim glow of computer monitors and some LED striplights that had been placed around the chamber's walls. Kris had explained to us that The Monkey needed to open the doorway into the dimension where the spear was, and the only way he could do that was if he allowed the girls to merge consciousness with him so that they could guide him. Kev got all excited and started going on about, 'Vulcan mind melds,' and shit. He came very close to getting a slap from a hairy paw.

When the doorway was open, it was my job to summon the spear. How the fuck do you do that? Well according to Kris, because the spear is of this dimension and because I was the last person to wield the thing in battle in this dimension, it should come rushing back to me like some demented homing pigeon. So far so good. Then The Monkey would need to collapse the doorway to stop anything following the spear. Great, what could go wrong?

As I write this I am looking down at my left arm. It is shiny and silver. I have a fucking metal arm! But I get ahead of myself...

The Monkey, with the girls stationed one on each shoulder, focused the energy portal. It cracked and sparked with what Kev later told us were plasma arcs around its event horizon – whatever that means. We hadn't seen it do that before and as the swirling black surface cleared there was a vision of total insanity. A vast plain stretched away from us, the surface of which seemed to be in constant movement, like the ocean, except this was rock. Towers of what looked like crystal rose from the surface and they slowly rotated, shining out beams of light like lighthouses in a mad man's nightmare. All across this immense scene swarmed figures battling each other, some seemingly tiny, and others immeasurably vast, their forms becoming lost in the boiling cloud mass that blotted out the sky. This was a Hieronymus Bosch painting on steroids, brought to life.

I stood on the edge of this doorway into a lifetime of therapy and was at a loss. I glanced back at The Monkey, but he seemed to be in a trance, lost in the mind wrenching lunacy before us, and it was Aleks who responded to my ineptitude by telling me to, 'Reach out, summon the spear!'

So, I reached out and lost my balance, tripping almost across the threshold. And I would have gone if Kev hadn't grabbed my right hand as I frantically reached backwards to save myself. Again, Aleks shouted, 'Summon the spear!' and without a clue what I was doing I reached out my left hand into that other world and called out, 'Here speary spear,' while imagining myself holding the Spear of Lugh – what a dickhead...

There was a tearing in the clouds obscuring the sky of that other dimension and a strange sigh seemed to come from the warring figures. A shape of demonic fire roared between and sometimes through them, howling as it came, and then suddenly the spear was in my hand. I started to pull back my arm and a giant armoured figure crashed through the boiling clouds, rushing towards me at terrifying speed. I heard Kris yell at The Monkey to close the doorway and then there was a flash like lightning as the portal closed but my arm wasn't free. Kev pulled back with all his scrawny might and I landed next to him on the floor of the chamber, my arm feeling strangely cold.

They all gathered around me as I lay there, the girls keeping a respectful distance from the spear, and The Monkey helped me to sit up, an unusually concerned look on his hairy face. I looked down at my left arm, as I am looking down at it now, and I started to giggle. My arm had been turned into living silver metal. I passed out.

*

When I came to, we were all in a cluttered living room and everyone was staring at me. Tony the nerd was there as well, and he was staring at me. I passed out again.

*

It's now early evening. The girls have spent a long time with their hands on my head doing something to calm me down, and I am thinking straight again – at least for a bit.

The Monkey refocused the energy portal again after I fainted, and dropped us into Tony's living room, he said it was the first safe place he thought of. So now we are sitting in a semi-detached house in Slough, drinking tequila. And have I told you, I have a metal arm?

13 December

I have been awake for a couple of hours having slept for nearly twenty-four. I keep staring at my arm. There is no pain, just an odd coldness. I have sensation in it, I can feel pressure and something akin to tactile sense. There is a ragged demarcation line across my upper arm where the metal and the flesh sort of blur into each other, Kev says it looks very much like the pattern of a plasma arc – like fuzzy lightning.

I can still use my arm and hand pretty much as normal, but after a few experiments we soon realised that I can crush house bricks to powder with zero effort and The Monkey's attempt to stab me with his K-BAR resulted in the blade just sliding off. If I hold the spear in my metal hand an intricate pattern appears, illuminated within the metal, and the lines of the pattern glow amber. It is very cool looking, but I think I am in a state of shock.

The girls keep telling me in their soft hypnotic tones that I will be okay. Kev and Tony are looking at me like I'm a character from Mortal Combat, they constantly want to touch the arm and point testing thingies at it while they mutter to each other and make notes on their laptops. As for The Monkey, the little bastard has started humming the theme from *The Six Million Dollar Man* with that piss-take look on his face. He has been out and bought a dozen bottles of Jack, half a dozen extra-large stuffed crust pizzas, and managed to score some hideously strong skunk from a hoodie who was hanging around outside Dominos. I have to admit that I am hungry...

14 December

You know what pisses me off? The fact that I spent hundreds of pounds getting that tattoo sleeve and now most of it is shiny metal. I could have just wrapped my arm in tin foil, would have been a whole fuck load cheaper and less painful!

Yes, I am still ranting on about my appendage upgrade. I am coming to terms with the fact by constantly rationalizing that the new arm is like something a superhero would have, and it does look very cool. But I liked my old arm, AND I lost my watch! Kev and Tony keep checking it out and I heard one of them whisper something about 'Thanos'. I have had to tell them in no uncertain terms that it is not an Infinity Gauntlet, and that if I snap my fingers half the creatures in the universe will not disappear. The Monkey overheard and has been daring me to try – he really can be a nihilistic fuckwit...

*

Aleks and Kris have taken a laptop up to one of the bedrooms so that they can talk in private with JudyZ. They are going to use a voice comms program that Tony and JudyZ have recently worked on and allows a proper chat rather than just typing. Tony mentioned again that during his last few conversations with her after Kev spilled the beans about his American adventure, she did not seem pleased. Ouch! There is a whole load of confusion going on there. Disembodied young female nerd forms attraction to hormonally charged young male nerd who then gets his freak on with a physical female – against all the odds I might add – and when disembodied young woman finds out she feels jealousy and betrayal. Ah, a story as old as time...

Fuck me, this skunk is strong...

*

The Monkey is sitting on the coffee table going through the weapons bag. Kev had the foresight to grab it from the outer chamber of the temple along with our backpacks and threw them all through the energy portal while the girls dragged me through, and The Monkey fucked about with the portal so they couldn't follow us. Kev also liberated one of the grey metal hoops that Ms Wright had gazed lovingly at. I seems to be made of a similar material to the large black hole in the roof of the Illuminati base and expands when twisted outwards. He had seen one had been set up on a stand by the techs in the temple, and he made a wild, but it turns out, educated guess that it was some sort of portable energy portal, the sort of thing that we suspect the Illuminati may have developed. Seems Ms Wright and her colleagues needed a functioning black hole/energy portal to sync up their new bits of kit, hence why we were press ganged, but they still have no idea how to point the things and go somewhere without getting turned inside out. Well now we have one, and between staring at my arm and trying not to white-out from the skunk, Kev and Tony are trying to figure out how it works.

The spear is propped up in the corner of the room, and I must say that the demons from the other dimension have done a lovely job fitting another shaft to it. We had a nice man who makes replica medieval weapons fit one before, and it was functional but plain. This bad boy is banded with intricately patterned filigree work in a polished bronze and has rune-like markings all along its length – nice! The spear head has been smoking ominously and we have had to make sure it doesn't touch anything as it keeps leaving scorch marks. The Monkey has asked Tony if he can get in touch with Prof Brian in Bristol and ask him if he knows anyone who might be able to decipher the runes. It's a bit of a long shot as the spear shaft comes from another dimension but the markings look familiar, sort of like the ancient Irish Ogham alphabet…

15 December

As much as Prof Brian bid us farewell with the fond hope of us never darkening his door again after the zombie monk and associated carnage that happened in Scotland last time, he still couldn't help himself when Tony emailed a teaser photo of a section of the spear shaft over to him. He responded almost immediately, his nerd radar locking onto something interesting, and he promised to try and help as long as there were no massacres. Tony said that we couldn't promise but we would do our best. So, he now has photos of all of the shaft (that definitely sounds wrong…) and he is going to put his puzzle-solving cryptographer's hat on and see what he can come up with.

The JudyZ and Kev thing – that is a problem that might not be so easy to solve…

Kris and Aleks talked with JudyZ for a couple of hours yesterday and when they emerged, they didn't look very happy. They think that JudyZ is on the verge of a breakdown. This is hardly surprising news when you stop to think about it, but of course, we hadn't stopped to think about it with everything else going on. JudyZ was a young Hindu woman who had split from her family because they were trying to get her into an arranged marriage, whereas she wanted to become a hacker and use her powers to stick it to the man. But then, in the act of helping us, she had been brutally tortured, and her consciousness had fled her body and eventually taken up residence in an orbiting satellite. Whatever her hopes and dreams had been I bet they didn't include that! And now, the dude she had been chatting to most, and flirting with, has gone and cheated on her (as far as she is concerned) and she feels even more alone and separate from who she once was. She has a good chunk of the world's communications at her virtual fingertips so she can see the joy and sadness of all of us down here without ever truly being a part of it. It sucks...

*

I was in the living room trying out my new arm in a *Call of Duty* death match when Kev came running in and grabbed the TV remote changing the input to the Sky box. I thought The Monkey might kill him, but the look on Kev's face made him hold back. Kev stabbed the buttons until he hit a 24-hour news channel and then dropped to his knees as we all stared at the screen. Tony came in and I looked at him for some sort of explanation and he just looked over at Kev and said, 'It was just on the radio.'

There on the screen was the smoking remains of a passenger jet set against the backdrop of jagged mountain peaks. A news crew wandered amongst the wreckage as the reporter explained how the plane had seemingly just flown into a mountainside after taking off from Quito airport in Ecuador killing everyone onboard. The scrolling text at the bottom of the screen gave the flight number and the casualty count. The Monkey looked at me with a, 'Sad but so what?' look on his face and then Kev, without taking his eyes off the screen said, 'She was on that flight, the American girl and her friends. She showed me her itinerary, and you know what I'm like, I memorized the flight numbers and times.' His shoulders sagged and Tony awkwardly knelt by him and put an arm around his shoulders.

The girls came into the room; they had been asleep upstairs. They both had very wide eyes as they took in the scene and the TV screen. Aleks looked across at us and said, 'We had a dream that woke us. A dream in which Judy had done something terrible...'

16 December

As the news reports came in it became more and more obvious that something extraordinary had happened to the plane. Aviation experts gave their expert opinion, and Ecuadorean air traffic control said that everything had been fine until immediately after take-off when it had become very far from fine. We asked Tony if it was possible that JudyZ could have caused the crash and he said that, technically, yes it was. There would be a GPS system on the aircraft to help it navigate and Tony thought that JudyZ could have influenced it, and by influenced it he means fucked it up.

We sat with Kev into the early hours of the morning. Poor bastard is in a state of shock. We can't confirm our suspicions yet but we haven't been able to make contact with JudyZ so the signs aren't looking too good. Aleks eventually did some voodoo stuff to Kev and made him drift off into a deep sleep, she thought it would be kinder and more effective than The Monkey's drugs and booze approach, she is undoubtedly right.

*

Kev is still out of it, so we are going to let him keep sleeping. The news has still been mostly arguing aviation experts, aircraft manufacturers, and anyone with skin in the game trying to shift blame away from their area of responsibility. And still no JudyZ. Kris has tried but even the girls' supernormal abilities don't seem to be able to reach beyond the Earth's atmosphere…

There have been a few calls from Ms Wright on the sat-phone this afternoon since we turned it back on, The Monkey has ignored them for the moment. He says he wants to know how the portable black hole works before he is prepared to give too much information away to British Intelligence regarding where we are and what is going on. He was rather hoping that Kev and Tony could come up with some answers, but it may be a while before Kev is back in the game even if it turns out that JudyZ had nothing to do with the crash. I think he intends to have a fiddle with the ring (once again – wrong!) to see if he can work something out (just gets worse…), and I believe it will be me and Tony who get to be his glamorous assistants. Oh joy…

17 December

In between calling me Robot Boy and the Bionic Man, The Monkey managed to stop taking the piss long enough to actually get the portable black hole working. Colour me surprised!

If you hold the grips on either side of the ring and pull outwards, it opens up like the iris of a camera. Tony thought it would require some power source to get it cooking, his guess was fusion. The Monkey had other ideas, he said that he thought they had taken the rings to the Monkey Temple to give them a jump start from the permanent one there, and with his hands holding the grips on the grey metal ring he summoned up his blue fire and *voilà*, what Ms Wright termed an energy portal. He focused on a place for the portal to open and there was the image of the local Domino's Pizza – hardly ambitious but a positive test. He shut the portal again just as the hoodie who had sold him the skunk, and must be a permanent fixture outside the establishment, turned and saw The Monkey grinning at him through a hole in the air like the Cheshire Cat. He dropped his can of Red Stripe, and his stupid face took on an even more stupid expression just before it disappeared.

*

Finally got in touch with JudyZ. She claims sunspot activity had cut her off and has only just received our messages. She also denies any knowledge of the plane crash, and in fact, was mortally offended that we should even think that she had anything to do with it. She says that the solar flares blacked her out from not long after Aleks and Kris talked with her until just now so there is no way she could have messed with the plane's GPS even if she had wanted to, and suggested that it was those same solar flares that might have caused the plane's navigation to fail. Tony just shrugged and said that it is possible, but The Monkey is wearing that look on his face again.

JudyZ has asked to talk to Kev and so we have handed the laptop over to him and left them to it.

18 December

Kev is still upset although he is no longer blaming himself for bringing down the wrath of JudyZ on the American girls and their fellow travellers. JudyZ has managed to convince him that she couldn't have done it because of solar activity, and she wouldn't have done it even if things had been fully operational. She had been a bit pissed at Kev's macho boasting but not enough to commit a jealous act of mass murder, he needed to get over himself – is how it seems to have gone.

Aleks and Kris on the other hand are not so sure, and they reckon that we need to be a bit wary of our eye in the sky until she seems to be emotionally stable again. They pay a great deal of attention to their dreams and the one that woke them up had been particularly portentous...

*

I am getting used to my new arm. Still possibly in a state of denial but it doesn't freak me out as much when I catch sight of it in the mirror. And the girls seem to think it suits me, like I should always have had it. Maybe they are just trying to make me feel good...

19 December

It may seem harsh, but in the words of Tropic Thunder it's time for Kev to shave his head and get back on the monkey bars. Prof Brian is driving up from Bristol, much against his better judgment I think, because he wants a first-hand look at the new spear shaft. He is intrigued and his puzzle-solving ego is a little stung as he can't quite work out the markings and their message. He has shared a couple of the photos that Tony sent him with the researchers who helped decipher the runes on the stone we brought back from Chernobyl, but they are as stumped as he is. They all think it is Ogham, but the language is not any form of ancient Irish/Celtic that they recognise. We haven't mentioned that it was actually made in a demon dimension – not yet at least – but the girls seem to believe that there is a common root for all of the things we consider magical, even extending across dimensions, and that it should be possible to translate the markings on the spear shaft.

At some point soon The Monkey is going to have to have the difficult conversation with Ms Wright. They are going to want their portable energy portal back and we aren't going to want to give it to them. They have been remarkably laid back about our fun and games so far, it would seem that they have known more about us and for a lot longer than we would like to believe. The Monkey is intrigued by some comments that the girls made about it being a surprise that it has taken them so long to get all over us. Kris has said that the X-Files bunch who are shadowing us have been around since Victorian times and were started as an operational unit in direct response to the activities of the Illuminati. How do the girls know this? Same way they know about the Inquisition and a bunch of other weird stuff, I guess. Aleks said that The Monkey should ask Ms Wright when he next speaks to her, she may well have more answers than she is letting on…

*

Prof Brian, still in the same old jacket, reassuringly. Poor sod tried to run back to his car when I opened the door and he saw my arm upgrade, but he is now firmly ensconced in an armchair with a cup of tea laced with Jack and a chocolate Hobnob. Tony looks a bit concerned for him, but The Monkey just keeps saying he will be fine, even though he can't take his eyes off my shiny appendage. Ooo-er missus!

He has calmed down enough now to appreciate the spear, although I am having to hold it as it does seem to be more 'alive' than it was before and we don't want it smashing through him in its demonic blood lust, that would be very bad form. He is fascinated by the way it makes my metal arm glow with intricate designs and he thinks that they might be the key to deciphering the markings on the spear shaft. I did explain that the arm thing and the spear weren't a 'come as a pair' deal, but he just raised his eyebrows and said, 'Tell them that!' indicating the patterns flowing out from the spear and up my arm.

I think it is going to be a long night with the Prof making notes, sketches, and taking pictures. Good job I have the other hand free to eat junk food and drink beer. Tony has found his box set of *Lost*, so we are settling down to watch that. The Monkey hasn't seen it before and is intrigued, I just hope that doesn't descend into violence as the series progresses…

20 December

Well, that ended as expected. The Monkey was so upset by the way *Lost* developed that he punched Tony and made him put on *The Expendables* to make up for it.

*

I woke up in the chair, partially slumped across the table, drooling. I know, dead sexy… The Prof had literally sat there all night long writing, drawing, and looking stuff up on his iPad. He has also taken a whole series of photos all the way around the spear. He has an idea that he might be looking at the patterns in the wrong way and he wants to go back to the Uni and get the images scanned into a software program that will allow him to manipulate the designs in 3D space. He believes he is beginning to see something emerging from the web of lines and Ogham-type markings. We fixed him up with lots of strong coffee and a bacon butty and then he headed off, too excited to even stop and have a couple of hours sleep. It's only about an hour and a half drive back to Bristol so hopefully he should be fine. I can hear The Monkey in the kitchen shouting that I should stop worrying, that it's not like we are engaged or anything just because I let him look at my shaft – furry wanker!

Kev has reappeared and although he is a bit quiet, he and Tony are looking at the energy portal ring. Hopefully doing something will keep his mind off the crash…

*

Couldn't be put off any longer so The Monkey pressed speed dial and got a rather exasperated Ms Wright on the sat-Bat-phone. She was majorly pissed at us for running off without saying goodbye… Well, no actually, she was simmering with cold fury at the fact that we had nicked an energy portal, used the black hole in the Monkey Temple for something that had made all of their computer equipment go berserk, and made our get away without the Tell, Show, Do session that she had planned for The Monkey. All of that added up to a lot of marks on the naughty list.

The Monkey let her get it out of her system, in fact agreeing with her that yes, we are a bunch of cunts. But when she began to go on about us 'having an agreement' The Monkey dug his heels in. He told her that as far as we were concerned the 'agreement' was that we would locate the Monkey Temple in exchange for my house being rebuilt and them leaving us alone as much as possible. It seems though that you should always read the small print, even if nothing has been printed and you didn't know you were entering into a binding contract which you would need a team of lawyers and a microscope to comprehend.

Ms Wright explained that as far as Her Majesty's government were concerned, we had taken the shilling we had been offered, and we had agreed to not only find the temple but also to aid in the acquisition and use of any and all ancient technology found therein. And, in exchange for this we would be granted certain requests and privileges, one of which was not being locked up in a black site for the rest of our days. The Monkey kept his calm and blew a large cloud of cigar smoke before answering. 'It's time you told us the truth. Why is there a connection between your unit and us? You could have tried to shut us down or brought us on board at any time, it seems obvious that we have been on your radar, so what gives?'

With the speaker phone on we all heard Ms Wright stop in her verbal tracks. She didn't talk to anyone else, but we got the impression that she had been given the nod by someone in the room with her. 'Okay, we need to talk and get our cards on the table. Maybe then you will see that we are not the enemy.'

Me and The Monkey

*

Me and The Monkey are off to London in the morning. Aleks and Kris will be coming with us but not into the actual meeting that Ms Wright is setting up in her Whitehall office, they will be our get out of jail card should we need them, and lurk in the neighbourhood undetected by the spooks. Ms Wright is flying back from Peru this evening, not cattle class I should imagine, probably on some slinky private jet, and will be waiting for us at 2pm sharp.

I have borrowed some gloves from Tony to cover up my shiny new hand, He only has knitted ones in a sort of Nordic pattern. Oh well, it is December so shouldn't look totally out of place. Fuck me! It's nearly Christmas! You never know, if we don't get shot or drugged or renditioned we might be able to do a bit of Christmas present shopping…

21 December

Winter solstice – the shortest day of the year. Hasn't felt like it…

Been an interesting day if nothing else. We are back in the Hilton Doubletree by the Tower of London, scene of our last London visit when we first located the spear point. There is a nice rooftop bar where The Monkey can get away with lighting up a cigar while we drink and stare at the view out towards Tower Bridge. The girls don't feel the cold and The Monkey has his own cladding, so it is just me in the North Face puffer jacket missing the warmth of South America…

*

After some fun and games at the security check where the metal detector did a song and dance and I had to give them a peak at my metal arm, not moving the fingers of course, we were escorted through featureless corridors and into a largish office with a Georgian sash window that faced into an inner quadrangle, and here Ms Wright was waiting for us.

The greeting was on the frosty side, but then that was only to be expected. Ms Wright sat behind a modern office desk bristling with tech, the large computer screen off to her left. The room was comfortable, well, as comfortable as an office can be, and the pale green walls held clusters of pictures and several maps. Ms Wright invited us to sit in the two executive looking leather chairs in front of her desk, but The Monkey's sharp eyes had spotted something, and he went straight over to one of the collections of illustrations and photographs. He stared hard, pointed a hairy finger, and demanded, 'What's this?'

I went to join him and could see that his attention had been caught by a brown, faded photograph showing a group of men, all wearing dark tweed suits and a variety of top or bowler hats. Standing in the front and centre of the group was a monkey wearing a very dapper tweed suit and a bowler hat. He had quite bushy sideburns and a more scarred face, but other than that he looked very much like The Monkey, right down to the cigar clamped in his jaw. They were on a roof top, a decorative balustrade running along the edge behind them. In the distance there were tall buildings and the dome of St Pauls, and in the sky floated an airship with a military insignia emblazoned on its side (I didn't think that there were airships in Victorian England!) The inscription along the bottom of the photograph read 'Esoteric Investigation Department – 1885'.

The Monkey walked back to the door and opened it to look at the sign, it read EID 19. We both noticed the armed men who had appeared since we arrived and were now stationed on either side of the door. They had a certain look about them and The Monkey closed the door and looked back at Ms Wright, 'SAS. We should be honoured.' Ms Wright gave a tight smile and said that after our disappearing act in Peru she wanted to make sure we hung around long enough to have a serious chat. And what about the photo? She gestured again for us to sit and this time we did, and after asking if I was warm enough with a nod towards my Nordic mittens, she began her explanation.

Wayne's World style flashback...

Things had happened that could have made the good folk of Victorian England a bit nervous, a bit twitchy, if they had known about them. Objects appeared that seemed to have no human origin, at least no known human origin. Secret organisations working on the fringes of governments and in league with powerful business interests began to further exert their influence across the nations of the world. There was a moment when the very future of freedom hung in the balance, when power seemed about to pass to new rulers of the world. Things needed to be dealt with and covered up for the good of the Empire, dealt with in a subtle manner. Instead, agents of the Queen's Secret Service had foiled the plans in a night that had caused huge destruction across parts of the city of London. One of those agents was known as The Monkey. The Monkey sat back in his chair and grinned, 'I like him already.'

Under a royal warrant, and answerable only to her majesty Queen Victoria, another secret department was formed, this one with a very specific remit – occult organisations and conspiracies, weird things that could not be easily classified, and anything that your everyday cop couldn't just hit with his truncheon. Not exactly Ms Wright's words, but that's what it boiled down to. And so, EID was born and continues to this day, dealing with the things that can't be classified elsewhere, the things that no one else knows how to deal with, or to be honest, wants to deal with.

So, The Monkey in the photograph? He and his partner, William Chapman, had seemingly singlehandedly fucked up the nefarious plans of the Illuminati and for his sins he was made commander of the new department. Yes but, 'The Monkey' – did no one see the blindingly obvious similarity? The Monkey and Ms Wright both looked at me as if I was in need of some meds and maybe a little quiet time. She continued with a sigh, 'Over the years the department has become aware that certain characteristics keep reappearing in connection with our work. Let's just say that after seeing the energy portals we aren't ruling anything out, and, of course, there is Mr Arno Whitaker, who I believe you have met. He, or someone very like him, does seem to pop up with astonishing regularity where the Illuminati are concerned.'

The Monkey gave me that 'told you so' look. He has already proved that he has lived a previous life as a US Airborne Ranger and has been convinced that there are other past lives lurking around as well. He is going to be insufferable until something else grabs his attention...

The Monkey asked why her office was marked up as EID 19, was it just the room number or were there more EID units? Ms Wright didn't get a chance to answer. A late middle-aged man, bearing quite a similarity to the actor Edward Fox, stepped into the room through the door in the corner behind her. His pinstripe suit was obviously expensive even though it did make him look like a dodgy bookmaker from a 1930s Ealing comedy. He closed the door behind him and stood by the corner of Ms Wright's desk. He looked searchingly at us for a few moments, as if trying to decide whether we should be party to any more knowledge, and then with a small shrug said, 'The other eighteen EID units were eradicated in the line of duty. We are the latest to have the honour of carrying on their work.' The Edward Fox look alike stepped forward and held out his hand while introducing himself as Commander Malcom Grayling. We both ignored the proffered hand, and he drew it back, a touch of pink visible above his shirt collar.

Over the next three-and-a-bit hours we were double teamed by Commander Grayling and Ms Wright. They asked us some general questions regarding the black hole in my house in Cornwall, our trip to Cambodia, the fire fight at the loch in Scotland, and the wreckage we left on an industrial park in Wales. They knew a lot already, and it seemed as if they were just making sure by rechecking their information, seeing if we were being truthful. There was an awful lot that they didn't know about, the raid on Area 51, our jaunt to Chernobyl, the battle in Iceland, and JudyZ living in a satellite. We, of course, didn't offer any of that good stuff up... Then we moved on to the subject of the black holes, or energy portals as they have now been designated. Ms Wright specifically wanted to know how The Monkey had created the one in our spare room. I think she thought we were taking the piss when we told her that it had come about because The Monkey was trying to stop it raining by summoning an Aztec god... She gave up on that after the third attempt, convinced I think, that we were just being evasive. Then she got down to the real crux of the matter and wanted to know exactly how to control the destination of the energy portals. It seems that their boffins have managed to stabilize the ones looted from a Brightstorm facility, one of which we are the proud owners of, and using the energy portal at the Monkey Temple they have managed to sync them up. But and not being personal, it's a big but, they still haven't mastered the focusing thing. After losing a couple of their team in the void they are desperate to get some training, and it looks like The Monkey is their go-to guy. He is not best pleased. His temperament does not really run to playing teacher, and I am worried that there could be some violence involved. We explained to them that the Illuminati had managed to develop the skills to use the energy portals through recruiting a shaman. Once again, we got some sceptical looks, but we carried on regardless and The Monkey explained that it seems to be a combination of will and necessity that creates the conditions to focus the gateways. He glanced over to me, and I shrugged. 'Okay,' he said, 'I can set up the first energy portal for you and show you how to focus it, then you will be able to use it to control the other portable ones. After that you are on your own.'

The Commander and Ms Wright looked very relieved, and equally pleased. I think the relieved part may have had something to do with the SAS lads outside, if we had not agreed there could well have been some unpleasantness on the cards. Although they weren't to know that everyone would have died except The Monkey, and maybe me...

It was now time for us to ask some questions. First up, if they already had control of the black hole that was now somewhere in the fenced off wreckage where my house had been, why did we have to go all the way to Peru to find one halfway up a mountain in a cloud forest? The Cornish black hole as we are now calling it, is apparently too unstable to be of any use (don't see any connections with The Monkey there...), but the one at the Monkey Temple, well that is proper justified and ancient. Okay... Next question, was EID responsible for the kidnapping, torture, and death of a British citizen at the disused airbase local to where we lived? Apparently not. They knew nothing about the incident other than what they had learned from Barty, and to be honest, he didn't really know anything. So, if we told them that there was a good chance that someone in their organisation was a double agent for the Illuminati and could have been responsible for the kidnapping, torture, death, would that surprise them? The Commander kept his reserve, but Ms Wright had a bit of a fidget at this news asking if we had any proof. We told her that our 'source' had alerted us to some encrypted communications that confirmed we had been sent to the wrong address in the jungle when we should have been looking in the mountains for the temple and that they had engineered it. They had also done some digging and were convinced that the same double agent had been involved in the kidnapping, torture, death. She asked about the reliability of the source and The Monkey just said, 'One hundred percent.'

I decided to ask a question that had been bugging me, why had they just agreed to the terms that The Monkey had set before we were shipped off to Peru? There had been no negotiation, no haggling. The Commander stood facing the wall of pictures, hands clasped behind his back gazing at the images. After a while he reached out and touched the photo that had attracted The Monkey's attention and simply said, 'For services rendered, and services yet to be rendered.' I looked at The Monkey and got a strange sense of *déjà vu* – ah fuck...

*

We ended the meeting with The Monkey promising to give them a 'How To' session with the energy portals, I think mainly so that we could get out of there. We are to go to another location tomorrow where everything will be set up. Ms Wright had asked about the portable energy portal that we had borrowed, but The Monkey just told her that we would be keeping that one. She had begun to remonstrate but the Commander had shaken his head and said, 'It's okay Caroline, let them have that one,' and so she had grudgingly let it go.

*

We left the Whitehall headquarters of EID and met up with the girls. And then? And then, as if all of this was the most natural thing in the world, we went shopping...

*

Drinking and looking out over the London skyline it all seems surreal. I seem to be the only one who is a bit gob smacked by the knowledge that another version of The Monkey was responsible for the formation of EID, and that we seem to be playing out pre-ordained roles. Aleks and Kris simply nodded when we had told them about the photograph and The Monkey has taken it all in his stride. Kris held my metal hand, taking off the mitten, and said, 'Look, look at your hand. After all that has happened so far can you really be that surprised?'

I must admit that if I honestly think about it, I am weirded out not so much by the revelations as by the odd familiarity of it all, as if I had always known but somehow forgotten – that sense of *déjà vu*, the glitch in the matrix. Kris reached over to a bag on the floor beside her and took out a slim box. 'This is an early Christmas present from us,' she said, and opened the box to reveal a pair of black leather gloves. She took out the left-hand glove and I let her pull it over my metal fingers, covering the hand in a snug, expensive looking fit. I flexed my hand and the feeling that all this has happened before, like watching the same movie trailer on YouTube looping constantly, washes over me. I order another drink...

22 December

When I woke up this morning the feeling hadn't gone. I have often wondered why the crazy shit that happens seems so normal, even the death and carnage, and why no one seems to bat an eyelid at a talking, cigar-smoking monkey. Since finding myself to be the unwitting prize in a game of Othello I seem to have become able to rationalise away the most bizarre things, but are they bizarre? I am having trouble remembering life before The Monkey. Maybe I am lying strapped to a bed in a psychiatric hospital somewhere, pumped full of drugs and living this crazed fantasy in my head? Maybe I am sitting in the corner of my living room constantly talking to a soft toy monkey and a couple of blow-up dolls in a schizophrenic fantasy delusion brought on by too much booze and psychoactive drugs? Or maybe I am just full of shit and need to come to terms with the fact that my best friend is a god, I sleep with the living dead, and I have a shiny metal fucking arm. Have I mentioned I have a new metal arm?

It is easy to get lost in the forests of the mind…

*

Breakfast, that always cheers me up. The Monkey has made them go and get a new box of Chocolate Weetos. He has already had two bowls but a family of five have come into the restaurant and the three kids have finished off the box. There was murder in his eyes until Kris suggested he ask for some more. I hope they give them straight to him as he likes a good sugar buzz to go with strong coffee when it is early, and I don't want to be the one who has to pull burning children out of the toaster…

Okay, drama sorted. They showed up with the Weetos and a box of Lucky Charms so now The Monkey has a wild, sugar crazed look about him and is a bit less hostile although not any more forgiving. As we walked out of the restaurant, he used his tail to 'accidentally' spill a jug of fruit juice all over the table of the family and when one of the kids looked at him, he drew a finger across his throat and pointed at the kid who burst into tears. I can almost see the bills for therapy.

We are now in the hotel lobby waiting for a car to take us to somewhere where The Monkey will do his demo. The girls will follow and lurk in the vicinity again and if all goes according to plan, we will meet up again mid-afternoon and get a train back to Tony's…

*

The car took us to a nondescript building somewhere between Euston and King's Cross. It was down a back street in one of those odd, typically London areas away from the main traffic routes that seem far too green and quiet to be in the centre of the capital. We knew that the girls were following in a taxi at a discreet distance. They are able to home in on us and although they don't know what is happening, they seem to be able to sense our emotions, even at a distance, and so can tell if we are in trouble or not. Nice…

We were escorted into the lobby of the building which seemed to be one of those places with temporary office space to rent or hire by the hour meeting rooms. The pretty receptionist nodded to our escort and picked up the phone as we made our way to the single lift at the end of the lobby. We were patted down in case we had smuggled in a bazooka or something and I had to explain once again that I have a shiny metal arm. While I was doing that, I noticed The Monkey doing what he always does, checking out exits, windows, possible ambush points, the snack machine, and then we stepped into the lift and one of the men inserted a key onto a keyhole on the panel and pressed and held the B button as we began to descend. There was lift music, I would love to be able to say it was *The Girl from Ipanema* but I think it was a mangled synth pop version of a Pet Shop Boys tune, maybe *It's a Sin*. Anyway, the lift carried on descending for quite a bit longer than the number of buttons would suggest and we refrained from the Carry On humour of the lift ride in La Paz and stared at the bull necks of our escorts until it came to a halt.

As the doors opened, we were greeted by what looked like a very large underground garage. There was none of the grand scale and almost antiseptic sterility of the Illuminati's underground base, not in good old Blighty! Brick arches led off into deep shadows and the seemingly low ceiling made you feel you should duck even though it was at least eight feet high. You hear stories of tunnel systems running under London that were used during World War 2 and my immediate thought was that this is part of that system. One end of the long room featured a row of floor to ceiling dark grey metal cages that filled a couple of the brick arches. Behind the grey mesh we could see racks of equipment and bundles of cables hanging neatly on hooks, and there was rack mounted on a trolly that held a row of the energy portal rings.

Running along the centre of the room was a row of waist high metal work benches and behind them sat a dozen men and women all wearing the same sort of paramilitary overalls as the EID techs in the Monkey Temple in Peru. Perched on the edge of one of the tables was Ms Wright in a very businesslike dark blue trouser suit. She had obviously been talking to one of the senior looking technicians and as we made our entrance she stood up and turned to us. 'Good morning gentlemen. We are all incredibly pleased to have you here with us to share your knowledge of the energy portals.'

It was almost like The Monkey was the guest lecturer at some prestigious event and the expectant looks on the faces of the assembled techs showed more than a little awe. He, of course, did his best to ruin the moment by belching loudly and saying, 'Ow, too many Lucky Charms. Right come on then. I don't have all fucking day.'

From that point onwards I played the part of Debbie McGee to The Monkey's Paul Daniels. He was presented with a version of one of the portable energy portals the EID had liberated from Brightstorm; this was their own version and they seemed rather proud of it. Same rough grey metal construction but with a few of their own modifications – this one could be opened with one hand.

The Monkey explained, as best he could, that in order to focus the portal to a specific location you had to 'see' that location in your mind, or at least an approximation of it, and then you had to want to go there. He struggled with verbalising that bit as he said it was more of a physical sensation similar to falling, like when you fall in a dream, but that once you had experienced it, it became progressively easier to call up again. One of the techs asked if that is how the one at our house in Cornwall had worked, and without giving away our destinations he replied that, 'No, that one just opened up where it wanted to.' This was all interesting stuff for me as well. I had never discussed the actual method of using the black holes with The Monkey, every time the subject had come up, he had just said, 'Nerd stuff!' and pointed at one of the nerds, who, to be honest, were just working on theory, most of which they had invented themselves.

The Monkey opened the energy portal as if he was opening a flick knife. Some of the techs looked a little shocked at the cavalier treatment of their shiny, and extremely powerful, toy. Others were trying hard to conceal that they thought it was very cool the way it just sprang to life – a two-foot diameter disk of swirling black energy, with a little crackling blue frosting around the rim. The Monkey expanded the energy portal by pulling it apart; it had the same sort of iris configuration as the one we had 'borrowed'. He looked around for somewhere to stand the portal and one of the techs excitedly held up a hand and told him that it would stand up on more or less any surface because of a gyroscope thingy built into it, (I think he may have used a more technical description). So, The Monkey placed it on the floor and low and behold it stood there, pulsing away malevolently like Satan's arsehole after a big night of demonic fist fun. Next, he asked for some suggestions as to where he should focus the portal and they eventually agreed on Ms Wright's Whitehall office as a safe, witness free target. So, The Monkey made it happen and through the portal we could see the office with the photos on the wall.

Now it was my turn to be the glamorous assistant and The Monkey got me to step through the portal, and then come back again to demonstrate that there were no ill effects. Then a couple of the techs volunteered to make the round trip, and like excited kids they crossed the narrow gate to infinity. The Monkey asked me to focus the portal onto a location. I must admit that came as a bit of a surprise as I had never considered doing it before and I gave him a, 'What the fuck?' look, but he explained to our audience that I was a virgin the same as they were and if I could do it then they should have no problem. Thanks for that!

I stepped up to grip the edge of the portal and he manoeuvred me to one side so that I was holding with my right hand and not my metal hand. I must have given him an obviously quizzical look because he nudged me quite hard and told me to concentrate on somewhere I knew, somewhere where there wouldn't be many people. So, after a couple of seconds thought I pictured the cliff top at Bedruthan Steps not far from my house in Cornwall. I figured that at this time of year there was little chance of ramblers and the particular place I chose was a bit too near to the edge for dog walkers. The portal remained black but then I had a distinct feeling of falling in the pit of my stomach and a view of wintry grey sky and cliffs overlooking a churning sea took form. He gestured me to step through and I was buffeted by the wind and the smell of the ocean as I did so, standing on the short grass and looking right and left across the gorse. Then I stepped back through into the underground room in London and realised that I had a sudden longing for home...

Each of the techs were brought up in turn and each stood and willed the portal to open up in a location of their choice. It took a while for some of them to get it but eventually they all were successful, and then The Monkey turned to Ms Wright and said, 'Caroline,' gesturing her towards the portal. All eyes turned on her expectantly and she smoothed the jacket of her suit, possibly to dry her hands, and stepped up. Touching the edge of the portal she looked at The Monkey apprehensively and he smiled, a not particularly reassuring smile, more of a dare. Set her jaw and turned to face the portal, after a few seconds her office appeared and then the image flickered and was replaced with what looked like a laboratory. A frown crossed her face and The Monkey moved towards her, but before he could get to her, hands reached through the portal and dragged her through. We saw her struggling with two large men in military style uniforms and then, just before the portal went black, we saw a grey-suited figure with a face like a grinning clown in a melted fun house mirror, and as the image faded Arno Whitaker waved goodbye…

*

All hell broke loose. The techs all produced guns and went from a University Challenge team to armed and extremely dangerous in a heartbeat. Our two bull-necked escorts sprinted from their station at the lift doors and backed us at gun point away from the energy portal. I could see The Monkey getting angry and it took the quick intervention of what I guessed was a senior gun-toting tech to make the escorts back down.

They all began shouting questions at us as if we knew what had happened, and when we said that we hadn't got a clue they wanted us to open the portal to where Ms Wright had been taken so that they could go in all guns blazing. The Monkey went to Def Con 2. He did that enlarging thing that now seems to happen every time the god in him comes calling. Blue fire started up on his fur, and as he held up his paws, they grew quiet, awed at this new version of The Monkey. 'It's not that simple,' he said, and then explained that whatever had happened hadn't been controlled from our side and as he had no idea where Ms Wright had been snatched to there was no way he could just open up the portal at that location. One of the techs started talking rapidly about modifications they had made, one of which was a geo location recorder built into the frame of the portal, it should theoretically record the location of anywhere the portal focused upon – theoretically because this was the first time the portal had ever been focused. There was a flurry of activity, and a tablet computer was plugged into the outer rim of the portal. A whole bunch of screen tapping followed and a large screen on the wall mirrored the tablet. On this we could see geographic data from the test runs we had taken the techs through. All well and good until Ms Wright's go. The coordinates for her office appeared and then the next set of coordinates were just garbage. Shoulders slumped and calls were made.

We sat down on the far side of the room as it was obvious we weren't going to be allowed to go anywhere for a while and The Monkey turned his face away from them and whispered, 'I think she did that on purpose.' I almost blurted out, 'What the fuck!?' but his paw on my wrist cautioned me to silence. 'Yes,' he whispered again, 'I got the strongest feeling that she made the portal change locations, and if that is correct then we need to get the fuck out of here ASAP.'

The Monkey nodded over to the rack of energy portals next to the wire cage and he signalled for me to go and stand behind the techs and look interested. Out of the corner of my eye I could see the escorts watching but I stood there and made a concerned face and nodded as they tried to work out what the scrambled location could be. The Monkey slipped across the room with his back to the racking and used his tail to lift out one of the portals. He raised his eyebrows and jerked his head back slightly to beckon me over and I sidled towards him. One of the escorts frowned and started to close in on us, but The Monkey did his flick knife impression with the portal and pulled me through with him and as he did so he pushed my left arm against the rim and there was a blue flash and the portal disappeared leaving us standing in Trafalgar Square amongst some very confused looking tourists.

*

It didn't take the girls long to home in on us and we all made our escape carrying bags of Xmas shopping to Paddington Station to get the train back to Slough. We had avoided too much hassle at Trafalgar Square because as luck would have it there was some sort of Dynamo Magician Impossible or similar thing going on there, and we were just one element in the overall extravaganza, not a very interesting element by the way people quickly turned away from us to watch something shinier...

Me and The Monkey grabbed some Yo Sushi while we waited for the train and as we sat watching the little colourful plastic bowls going around, we explained to Aleks and Kris what had happened in the basement. When The Monkey told them about his suspicion that Ms Wright had purposefully directed the energy portal to open at Arno Whitaker's location, they both nodded as if it was no real surprise. They have never said anything, but I get the impression that they think there is more to Ms Wright than meets the eye. We are all in agreement that there is something not right about the whole incident and that getting out of there was the best move we could make. The Monkey is not a fan of having his balls in a vice and electrodes on his nipples if they had decided that we were somehow responsible. No, they would definitely have to buy him dinner first to see that kind of action...

*

Back at Tony's now and we have relived the whole story for the nerds and JudyZ who Kev hooked up on a Zoom call, her disturbing sexy avatar talking to us all from space. She is going to monitor as much comms chatter as she can and has once more changed the routing of the sat-phone so that if, and you know it is bound to happen, we get a call from EID they won't be able to get a lock on our position.

I asked The Monkey why he pushed my metal arm against the rim of the portal as we went through, and he explained that he has noticed that when I get my 'Six Million Dollar Man' arm near the hardware of the portals there is a burst of the plasma energy that gave me my shiny arm in the first place. He figured that it would cause the portal to short circuit and close, and he was correct. Great, so I am also a human circuit breaker. Do you ever feel like you would be at home on the shelf of a hardware store? No, you probably don't – good for you...

We need to make a plan of action because whether Ms Wright engineered her seeming abduction or the Illuminati have suddenly got very good at homing in on the energy signals of the portals, we are going to have to convince EID we were not involved and we all have a need to piss on Arno Whitaker's parade before he pulls on his big boy pants and fucks us over. That was a metaphor car crash, but I am tired, and The Monkey has suggested a drink to help decompress, so I guess any planning will happen when we sober up. Kev is phoning for a delivery of Chinese food while the girls look like they might pop out for a snack. The Monkey is taping the Mouse Trap dude to the webbing on a new tactical vest he picked up in London and throwing M&Ms at Tony as he tries to get together plates and cutlery for the impending feast.

Ah, it's a scene of domestic bliss…

23 December

Lots of tinsel. I don't remember there being that much tinsel. The Monkey obviously thought it would be hilarious to mummify as many of us as possible in the shiny, itchy stuff. That will teach us to pass out before he does, although we never seem to learn that lesson. I am guessing that the girls helped as they are remarkably tinsel free and seem to find Tony's thrashing about in festive bondage highly amusing. I must have lucked out as just my legs were wrapped and there was a large red ribbon bow stuck to my forehead, although I did have 'WANKER' written across my chest in spray snow. Kev hasn't woken up yet, but he looks like he has fallen into the web of some fabulously gay spider…

*

The sat-phone had been switched off and almost as soon as The Monkey switched it back on a call came through from Commander Grayling. The Monkey put it on speaker phone and as we all gathered around to listen, he asked if the Commander had us on call back. The Commander was justifiably pissed and shouted that we were a shower of dangerous juvenile fuckwits, then he kicked off by demanding absolute assurance from The Monkey that we had nothing to do with Ms Wright's abduction. With a great deal of swearing The Monkey explained that the last thing we would do is collaborate with the Illuminati. He went so far as to reiterate that we were responsible for blowing up one of their bases in Bolivia, and that so far we seem to have done more damage to the hopes and dreams of the Illuminated Ones than EID have managed in a very long time.

The Commander got very angry at that and shouted stuff about good men and women dying and us being lucky amateurs. The Monkey let him finish and then stepped back in with, 'Alright then, what the fuck are we going to do about it?' He made it plain that we would keep going after the Illuminati in our own 'amateur' way whether EID liked it or not, and that we had made a deal that we weren't about to break because, well, we just weren't like that!

Grayling blustered and, 'I have never been so blah, blah, blahed,' and I could imagine him punching a passing manservant if it had been a century earlier. 'Why did you flee the basement after Ms Wright was taken?' he demanded. This was the awkward bit, not made any easier by his use of the word 'flee' which made us all smirk. The Monkey had to explain to him that we had intel that there was someone working with the Illuminati from inside EID, and that he had sensed that Ms Wright had opened the portal into the Illuminati facility herself. This provoked yet another burst of outrage and statements of unequivocal support for Ms Wright, including a comment that made Aleks and Kris sit up straight. The Commander had been citing the amount of commitment shown by Ms Wright and the personal risk she had put herself in, and then he said, 'And she has family pride at stake in all of this, she is the great, great, great, great grandchild of one of the founder members of EID, there is no way she would betray something that her family has such close ties to.'

Okay, so he doesn't believe it could be Ms Wright acting as a double agent, and although The Monkey was convinced she had changed the portal destination he couldn't say for definite that it couldn't have been someone else's doing. So where does that leave us?

The Monkey has refused to go back to Whitehall and told Grayling that they should be very cautious of an attack by the Illuminati if they did indeed manage to intercept the portal's energy signature. Either way there could still be a mole in EID and The Monkey doesn't want to be there when that all goes tits up and Illuminati super soldiers start dropping through their own energy portals and massacring everyone. The Monkey prefers to instigate the chaos, mayhem, and massacres at a venue of his choosing...

The Commander rang off saying he would be back in touch and that he would prefer us not to do anything without his say so – yeah right! He must have been very fucked off to find out that the sat-phone signal had been bounced through so many places that we might as well have been on the moon. I bet he was livid at having to stand down the black helicopters and snatch squads he had on standby to pick us up. It's almost like he thinks we have never been in serious trouble before...

*

Well, the house is decorated like there has been an explosion in Santa's grotto. The Monkey has more of a grasp of the concept of Yule tide celebrations this year. Previously he just threw things around and wrecked the tree, and of course last year he constructed Satan's roof ornament. But as he is evolving, he has more of a sense of what human's think is suitable for the Xmas ritual. This, of course, mostly means that he sits in the middle of the room directing the rest of us to plaster the walls with the cheap decorations that he picked up in industrial quantities after he saw the, what he described as 'pitiful' number of decorations that Tony dragged down from the loft. The Monkey does seem to live by the maxim that more is definitely better, or perhaps he is working on the premise that the amount of static electricity being generated by the tinsel will short circuit any attempt that EID might make to electronically track us.

To be fair, he is happy to attach anything at ceiling height, although that usually means standing on Kev's shoulders. If Kev knew that we were not laughing at the balancing act as they stagger around the room, but at The Monkey resting his balls on Kev's head with that evil grin of his, then our lanky nerd might not be so accommodating. Ah, the ancient tradition of the Christmas 'tea-bagging'. I'm sure it's mentioned in a couple of medieval carols…

24 December

So, with the house looking like a Vegas stripper's G-string, we have raided the local Sainsbury's and filled the boot of Tony's car with more food and drink than I think is legally permissible for a vehicle of that size. We now have enough festive supplies to put us all into a coma, and even with everything else that has been happening, it's starting to look a lot like Christmas!

Both Kev and Tony have promised to go and have family Christmas dinners with their respective parents and so we will be left to our own devices for a good part of tomorrow. But this evening? Well, it is Christmas Eve, so a *Die Hard* marathon, beer, shooters, party food, and possibly a Mortal Combat tournament. All of course washed down with bottles of Jack and some more of that super skunk. Aleks and Kris need to get some sustenance so they are popping out early to dig up an old friend and they should be back to join in before we are too battered.

The Monkey is sporting a very fine purple camo waistcoat he picked up during our shopping spree, and a monocle for some reason. I can't help thinking that he looks like a ventriloquist's dummy. That might just get me stabbed, Christmas or not! I will have to hold that particular comment in until I am sure he is pissed enough to not do me serious damage…

25 December

That got out of hand in a most unexpected manner!

We had finished *Die Hard 2* and were having a little refreshment break, when Kev and Tony started up a long running (apparently) debate as to whether the Second Council of Nicaea would have considered *Die Hard 2* to be a proper Xmas film. This was something that had seemingly been hotly debated over the years by nerds on the internet. The Monkey asked what the hell the Second Council of Nicaea was, and Kris told him not to worry as it was just theoretical geek nonsense and anyway the Council had happened in 787.

Well, the debate between our two nerds continued through the next couple of movies and then came to a head when Tony mentioned something about 'Jingle all the Way'. There was a lot of staring and then they began a pathetic, drunken wrestling match during which the phrases, 'Take that back you bastard!' and 'Fuck you!' were used in abundance. The tree fell on them, and I thought The Monkey would wet himself laughing. The girls began egging them on as they battled in stoned slow motion, but in the end I had to pull them apart when they began to get a little too close to the spear. Even drunk I could see the terrifying and fatal consequences of that bad boy falling amongst them.

They were both a bit bruised and both very hot and sweaty, but when separated they laughed and began sharing a massive bowl of nachos. We stood the tree back up, a little deformed but not too wrecked and the night before Christmas continued...

*

The nerds have gone to their respective parents' houses. They both look very wounded and collapsed in the back of the Ubers they had booked. I doubt there will be much Christmas dinner eaten there, but that's not a problem as we have plenty here and aren't intending to have it until late this afternoon anyway. We will do the present thing when they get back, although I can see The Monkey eyeing the pile of presents in the corner of the room with a predatory look.

I am going to phone my relatives and wish them a merry Christmas and hopefully by the time I have finished the painkillers will have kicked in and my head might not feel as if it has been used as a *piñata*...

*

We have spent most of the day just lying around eating Quality Street and having the occasional Jack – just to take the edge off you understand. I tried to start a conversation about Ms Wright, but The Monkey doesn't want to go there today. He is still angry with the presumption of EID that we have to be 'on team', almost as if we owe them something. Aleks said I should just leave it for the moment. She has a feeling that Ms Wright is not in any immediate danger, even if she is not enjoying the festivities. I pushed a bit as to why Aleks and Kris had got real interested when Greyling had mentioned that Ms Wright had family connections to the origins of the EID? She gave me one of her cryptic smiles and said that it would be best to wait until The Monkey was in the right mood and then we could discuss all of that. I am sure the girls use their voodoo on us when they don't want to talk about certain things. I happily wandered off and started preparing veg for this evening's feast and it is only now, about two hours later, that I am wondering why I gave up so easily. Bloody sexy witches!

*

The nerds are back and as predicted they didn't overindulge at their parents, which is good as I think I may have overdone things. Given that the girls eat people and not people food (although they are quite keen on dessert) that means there are four of us to wade through the giant mountain of food that has somehow materialised. I have changed into tracksuit bottoms too so that the elastic waist can gently expand along with me. *Bon appétit...*

Me and The Monkey

*

I may die...

Why does it seem appropriate to make four different types of stuffing? And at what other meal would you think it reasonable to have every known root vegetable from the western hemisphere? Although I won't have a bad word said about wrapping as many food items as possible in bacon, that was just pure genius – as long as my heart doesn't give up, I will declare myself King of Xmas Dinner!

We are now opening prezzies. The Monkey is massively excited and is sitting in the middle of a big pile of wrapping paper. I got him a couple of books on ancient Tibet and China with some myth and legend stuff in there that should keep him happy, and the Complete Michael D Echanis Collection (special forces hand to hand combat for those of you who don't know – and to be fair, why should you?) as he lost his original copies when we blew up my house. I also got him a diamond file and strop so that he can keep his K-BAR in top form, and some throwing spikes.

I opened the large present that he thrust at me, and there it was, the inflatable T-Rex costume that had popped up on my Amazon list. I just looked at him and he really wants me to put it on, but I have said we need to do the rest of the presents first. At least the cardboard Danny DeVito isn't here! Oh, and another smaller gift is a tin of Brasso, for my new arm apparently – cheeky cunt!

We got the nerds some geeky stuff from Forbidden Planet that they are very excited about, including a T-shirt each. Tony is now sporting one with 'Particle Physics Gives Me A Hadron' emblazoned across some sciency stuff, and Kev is proudly showing off one that has a floppy disk saying to a distraught USB stick 'I Am Your Father'. I know ladies, try and contain yourselves...

Aleks and Kris are now the owners of vintage tarot cards that came from a shop in Covent Garden, and a skull carved with occult symbols. The bloke in the shop was none too forthcoming when The Monkey mentioned how realistic the skull looked and the girls seem very impressed with it, and they know a thing or two about dead stuff... They had also asked us if they could get some new clothes as part of their present, and of course we said yes. So, while we had been down in a basement teaching weaponised nerds, they had found a goth/industrial/fetish clothes shop and got their signature look back. We wrapped the clothes up in reindeer paper and stick-on bows so that they could join in the unwrapping fun. Just taking them out of the paper and holding them up has made Kev and Tony go very quiet and a bit red and sweaty. The girls had already given me my leather gloves, but they also gave me a really cool Viking style silver bracelet with wolf heads. They gave The Monkey a very nice leather cigar case that will fit perfectly in his tactical vest and a new Zippo lighter engraved with something that looks like Thai characters, I can't read it, but it made The Monkey smile.

And the nerds? Well, they got us some expensive booze (they know us so well) and they got the girls a couple of CDs – yes, apparently people still buy CDs. So, we have Rammstein playing in the background with sone Nine Inch Nails to go on next – nice!

*

I am sitting watching *Home Alone 2* dressed in my inflatable T-Rex costume. It could almost be a scene from a Dickens novel. Merry Christmas one and all...

26 December

The Monkey has his head buried in the books I bought him, so I decided to mention to Aleks all of my odd feelings when we were in London. I explained about the sense of unreality that was bothering me and how this 'normal' that we live in is actually far from normal – I think... First off, she asked me about the circumstances that had led to me and The Monkey being best mates. I explained to her my drink and drug-fuelled odyssey in Amsterdam after splitting up with my ex, and how, after spending several days experimenting with DMT I had spotted him and his previous companion in a bar, and thinking I was still hallucinating, I had wandered off. Then, of course, they had followed me to the coffee shop, and I had ended up playing Othello and winning The Monkey. She nodded as if all that made perfect sense and said, 'That was the nexus, the point at which you changed realities. The DMT opened the doorway and then The Monkey saw you and pulled you through.' Wait, what?

So, this is not my dimension. It is similar but not the same, and the more I think about some of the inconsistencies the more I realise that no, I am not in Kansas anymore... What about the me who should be living here then? Aleks said that as we had never bumped into each other the chances are that he has been pinged off into my dimension, or more likely that he is face down in a canal somewhere. Not sure how I feel about all that... Aleks went into the kitchen and came back with a Sara Lee chocolate gateau and two spoons. It was still fairly frozen, but she insisted that we eat saying that when we face the infinite multiverse the only way to deal with the mind-numbing terror of possibilities is to eat – preferably something with chocolate. She's right, it does help.

She has now been explaining that The Monkey has this sort of field around him that makes everything just a little bit crazy most of the time and bat shit crazy the rest of the time. She described it as an 'entropy aura' that produces chaos, and extends across the boundaries of the worlds, this is where his god powers are drawn from. She seems to think that I am holding up remarkably well given that I have been dragged from my own dimension and spent so long in the presence of a demon god who has a special knack for fucking with the normal! Coupled with all that she thinks I am still suffering with PTSD and the constant possibility of violent conflict hasn't done anything to help that. Good point. And when I look at Kev and Tony, I can see how fragile they are despite the bravado.

Then I asked why she and Kris had looked so interested when the Commander had told us of Ms Wright's family connection to the EID? She gave me a searching look and then with a sigh decided to confide, at least a bit. She explained how she and Kris had known the founders of EID. I laughed at that as it was obviously founded in Victorian times, but then she reminded me that they were ghouls who had been around for quite a while – fair point. Continuing, she told me that alongside the other monkey in the photograph there must have been a man who was that monkey's friend and accomplice, not just in the forming of EID but in a great deal of other shady goings on. She stopped and looked at me, and when I just stared blankly back at her Aleks put her hands on my shoulders and said, 'It was you. It was you in a different life doing what you have always done for who knows how long?'

Slowly dawning realisation...

Like The Monkey I have lived before and known The Monkey even across many dimensions. I sat down hard and Aleks squatted down in front of me and held my hands. She stroked my left hand; I could feel the sensation somehow through the metal. 'Even this isn't new,' she said. I didn't know whether to laugh or laugh hysterically so I just said, 'So what about Ms Wright?'

'Yes, Ms Wright...,' she then proceeded to tell me that they, she and Kris, think that Ms Wright might be my great, great, great, great granddaughter from another life. What the absolute fuck! I didn't even have kids in this life and suddenly I'm a great, great, great, great grandfather! Aleks explained that it wasn't exactly like that. Ms Wright wasn't my blood relative, but we were cosmically related. Argh!

As if all that wasn't enough, The Monkey had wandered in unnoticed while we were talking, and from his position leaning against the door frame he joined in. 'Well, that puts a different slant on it doesn't it, grandad. We had better find out where she is and get her back.'

Bollocks, another nickname, and another mission...

27 December

I was digging around in the packs this morning and found the cigar tube containing the monkey finger. I had forgotten all about it. Funny that, as it is part of an ancient demon god and possesses enough of its own juju to warp space and time apparently. But hey, it's been a bit frantic of late...

Anyway, excuses aside, I popped the top off the tube and emptied the finger onto the tabletop to check it was okay after being run around South America and in various shootouts. The fucking thing went mental, spinning around like a ballet dancer on crack. It pointed to my left then did a 180 and pointed at the spear leaning against the wall, and then it spun to the right and almost left the table. For a couple of seconds, I didn't know what was exciting it so much, so I picked it up and walked to the doorway, and there, in the backroom was the energy portal where the nerds had set it up to do tests. They had their backs to me as they tapped away on their keyboards and didn't notice me walk across the room, mummified finger held out as if I was trying to divine water. The portal wasn't operating but the finger was aiming at it like it was true north. I held the finger close, and blue fire shimmered across the gnarly patches of fur that still cling to it. I felt a strong pull and put out my other hand to steady myself, and that's when my metal hand gripped the rim of the portal. There was a lot of blue plasma, and I could vaguely hear shouting coming from Kev and Tony and from the girls who were upstairs as I was thrown backwards into the piles of cables and technical stuff that they have accumulated. I got shakily back to my feet, the smell of ozone filling the air, and realised that I was surrounded by the girls, the nerds, and The Monkey who was holding the monkey pendant in his paw and it was glowing like a bastard. He looked from the monkey finger to my arm and then to the now swirling energy portal and asked, 'Okay, Metal fucking Micky, what have you been up to?'

As he had explained in London, my metal arm seems to have a very profound effect on the energy portals. It seems able to kick start them to life and The Monkey's suspicion that it has a direct link to the black holes in the temples could be well founded. Between the pair of us we seem to be capable of stirring up quite a bit of activity in these black hole things. I asked why he thought the monkey pendant had kicked off and he gets the feeling that all the black holes in all the locations around the world came to life when I held the portal with my metal hand. What that means in the long term I have no idea, but The Monkey is thinking that we might just be able to use this energy to locate Ms Wright. The nerds are in agreement. I heard the term 'quantum fluctuation' mentioned and I immediately blanked out; the rest of the conversation just a buzz of jargon. I watched as The Monkey's eyes glazed over and we let Kev and Tony argue between themselves as they ran algorithms on their laptops, or something, while we grabbed a bottle of Jack. The Monkey says it is the only way to deal with complex physics and existential problems – I'm sure he is right...

*

Kev and Tony are still deep in debate and hard sums, but we have had an interesting chat with JudyZ. It seems she has been monitoring various transmissions and has picked up some hidden signals. She says they are in the 100 to 400bps range and under -20dB. Not a fucking clue what that means but she described them as an audio watermark, there, but not to be focused on. So, sort of like a subliminal message? Sort of, but no. Okay, clear as mud...

The upshot is that these are messages being passed by the Illuminati, and they tell an interesting story. Seems that their underground bases are only a small part of their plan for a new world order. There has been a shift in their thinking and the messages hint at some sort of population amalgamation, not just goose stepping around and blowing shit up, although they are still moist for their supermen soldiers. Not entirely sure what all this involves but they mentioned something, or someone called 'Adam' in connection with Arno Whitaker's Brightstorm and the mad scientists that infest that particular corporate hell. JudyZ kept picking up mentions of a virtual world, and believes, based on a couple of obscure technical references, that it may refer to an artificial intelligence they are working on. As a computer genius whose consciousness now inhabits an orbiting computer system, she is fascinated by what they may be developing.

She is going to collate the messages and send us a transcript although she has admitted that they aren't the easiest signals to intercept as they keep changing the beats per second and the decibels, so she doesn't always spot them amongst all the other signal crap that bounces around out there.

This would never have happened in the days of the ZX Spectrum…

28 December

Prof Brian has been on the phone, and he is very excited. He ran the photos of the patterns on the spear shaft and my arm through some pattern recognition software that pieced all the bits together into a manipulatable 3D shape. These were then stretched out flat and a friend of his whose reason for getting up in the morning is to interpret the designs and glyphs in sacred temples has been sketching out the lines and filling in the gaps. Once this was complete, they showed it to the dude who had created the 3D mapping software and he made some tweaks and spun it back into 3D form once again. Anyway, to cut a long story short, they all got major hard-ons and called another colleague who is a quantum physics boffin, and he reckons that the patterns are actually a map of a wormhole… Sorry, that wasn't much shorter, but the upshot is, I have, in conjunction with the spear, a road atlas of one of the most powerful forces in the universe attached to my body. 'A picture of infinity', was how the boffin described it. This would explain the profound effects my arm has on the black holes and portable energy portals. The nerds now think I am some sort of divine being. I am not sure what to think. The Monkey just lit another cigar and said, 'That could come in handy,' and I don't think there was even a hint of irony…

The Prof is going to transfer over the video files and images they have recorded so that we can see what they have got so excited about, there is one still recording apparently, and it is taking an age as it is massive. Ah well, plenty of time to get a drink and a curry then. I will try not to get chicken Dhansak on my black hole A to Z…

29 December

Nice, shiny 3D imagery from Prof Brian! Looks like something from Tron only much cooler. Tony and Kev are entranced by the whole physicsy wormhole thing, but me and The Monkey just think it looks like the visuals during a DMT trip. It's amazing how the Ogham-like markings sort of blend together when everything is rolled up in this way. It took me a little while to realise that the tube I was looking down was actually outside in, all of the patterns flipped into the centre rather than running around the outside. It's sort of like looking through a kaleidoscope and actually makes more sense, in a very odd way! The patterns from the spear shaft mesh with the ones from my arm perfectly, both of them producing this map thing. The Monkey has the feeling that I could probably throw the spear though one of the black holes like a guided missile, have it fuck stuff up, and then have it return to me like the boomerang of the Armageddon. He has that look on his face, you know, that one of pure malevolent joy, and he really, really wants me to try it out. I am doing my best to avoid the topic. The girls, who are the one calming factor in The Monkey's cosmos, have gone home to their house in Exeter. They left early this morning in a car they hotwired, saying they needed to pick up a few things and promising to be back tomorrow. So, in the meantime I am putting my foot down with regards to hurling the spear blindly through the unfocused energy portal 'just to see what happens...'

30 December

You know when you make loads of promises and are definitely going to do exactly what you said, and then you get very drunk and bow to peer pressure and lots of chanting of, 'Throw it! Throw it!'? Yeah, well that...

Fuck knows where it went and what chaos it caused but I caved in and amid much drunken giggling threw the ancient weapon of mass destruction through the portal. There were a few heart stopping minutes when we thought it might not return, but then it came shrieking back to land squarely in my metal hand. It was dripping with some sort of dark, sticky blue liquid which we can only think was some alien creature's blood. The Monkey said we should lick it, like some rite of passage, obviously not from the blade – that would be mental. So, we did and then we all jumped around drunkenly celebrating and drank some more until we passed out. I am a bad person...

*

The girls have come back in their own car, the red Lancia Delta with the heavily tinted windows. They looked at us with that look they have that seems to just know something has happened, as we lounged around trying to look nonchalant while demons with hammers attempted to knock out our eyeballs from the inside, and our mouths tasted like dead things from another dimension. Kris gave me a kiss and for a moment I couldn't decide if it made her hungry, excited or just confused. Anyway, they are back now so hopefully I won't fall prey to The Monkey's irresistible charms – not!

The girls had gone to get their ouija board, and they want to do a session to try and find out if Ms Wright is still alive. It won't locate where she is but could let us know where she isn't – amongst the dead. As I seem to have a connection to Ms Wright, they want me involved, so I am drinking espressos to try and rid myself of the urge to hide under the duvet until the demons fuck off.

*

Well, after a lot of, 'Is there anybody there?' (not really, but it makes me laugh that the girls frown when I say that) both Aleks and Kris have concluded that Ms Wright is still amongst the living. They are now setting up the table with their tarot cards and the monkey finger. Kev and Tony are both fascinated by the fact that what Tony has been heard to describe as, 'A load of mumbo jumbo', can provide solid, verifiable answers to questions. There have been discussions about whether the objects used are somehow reaching into a quantum level and therefore are able to draw in knowledge from the universe around them. Things like Morphic Fields get mentioned and as usual me and The Monkey just glaze over. It's not that we are against the sciency stuff, we just find it difficult to summon up the enthusiasm and zeal in which the nerds frolic joyfully. The girls are very patient with them and seem happy to explain, plus they make the nerds go pink and that amuses them. The girls have explained to them that when they look at a tarot spread it is not all in one dimension. They found the 3D scan of the spear and arm patterns intriguing as they are convinced that they occupy the same dimensional space. This sort of makes sense to the nerds who gaze fascinated while trying not to look at cleavage.

After an hour of moving cards into different layouts and watching the monkey finger twitch in different directions they think that they know where Ms Wright might be. So I held the rim of the energy portal and the girls focused hard on it while The Monkey took up position in front with his Glock pointed. The swirling came to an abrupt halt and the portal focused on a vista of white stretching as far as the eye could see. It was so white it was almost painful, but The Monkey's keen eyes picked out a grey shape amongst the banks of snow, Kev fetched the binoculars, and the grey shape took form as the doors of a bunker set into the hillside. Tony looked at the data readout from the portal and gave us the thumbs up so that we could break the connection, then we gathered around the computer monitor.

Greenland – we will need to go shopping for some warm pants...

31 December

So, camping supply shop for parkas and thermals and boots, at least for me and The Monkey. We hopefully won't be spending much time in the elements, especially as Kev has informed us that the temperature there is around -17°. But we are going to need to open the portal to outside the bunker so that we can then orientate ourselves inside with a second jump, and we don't want to freeze to death while doing so! Aleks and Kris, who will be going with us, have decided that rubber miniskirts and fishnet vest tops are probably going to be enough. Ah, the not quite dead, they make it look so simple...

We got ski goggles as well, in a sort of metallic orange. We don't really need them, but they make us look like aliens and it's funny!

The Monkey called up the Commander on the sat-phone and told him we were going to get Ms Wright back. He blustered a lot as usual and demanded to know where she is and how we had found her location. The Monkey told him that it would be better if we handled it as there were possible international implications. Greyling went a bit quiet at that and was just about to kick off on some long-winded reason why EID should be involved when The Monkey wished him a Happy New Year in advance and hung up. Well, at least we told him.

Kev has pointed out that the Greenland thing ties in with the research that The Monkey did before we went to Iceland. All that Thule Society stuff and the hollow earth theory. Well they do like their underground lairs, these Illuminati bastards so I guess we will see.

*

We are going to go through the portal tomorrow so tonight is going to be a much quieter New Year's Eve for us. No mad party or dangerous fireworks, just cleaning guns, drinking Jack and wearing ski goggles...

1 January

No Bono, all is not quiet on New Year's Day...

The girls have brought some of their books of magic back with them. When I say 'books' I am really doing them a major disservice. These things are ancient and deserve the title of *grimoires*, the sort of book that you expect to be made from dried skin – possibly human – and to contain a trapped demon. They got into a huddle with The Monkey last night and I watched as they leafed through page after yellowed page of sigils, talismans, and charms, all drawn in a brownish ink that I can't help feeling is very old, very dried blood. The Monkey's knowledge of magic is now quite prodigious, and after his success with the black hole in my house in Cornwall it can definitely be described as more than a working knowledge.

After a couple of hours of searching and discussing, which I must admit I zoned out of, they agreed on two arcane symbols, both involving seven pointed stars. I watched in fascination as Aleks and Kris took a paw each and drew the symbols, one on each palm, with glass styluses that they dipped in some sort of silver liquid that looked like mercury. The designs sat on The Monkey's skin and then as we watched they seemed to be absorbed through the surface leaving a dark shadow image. The Monkey curled his lip back in a soundless snarl, his eyes narrowing, and it was obviously not the most pleasant experience. The girls chanted quietly as they worked and held his paws still until they had finished. He flexed them, looking at the designs embedded under his skin and then rubbed them together as he blew out a large cloud of smoke. He glanced up at me and grinned, 'Like the worst case of pins and needles ever,' he offered. I know The Monkey's threshold for pain – that must have hurt!

And what was the impromptu body art session for? Well, the girls also know a thing or two about magic and the symbols on his paws should allow The Monkey to home in on whatever his intent focuses on, and allow him to bring this monkey god power into tighter control without having to go all massive and special. Should be interesting next time he knocks one out though, he will have to be careful that he doesn't blow his dick off...

*

Today the nerds aren't going with us. There has been a bit of protesting from Kev, but The Monkey said they were needed to work with JudyZ and be our early warning if anything unexpected turned up in the vicinity of our intended raid. Tony looked relieved, he is definitely more brain than brawn, and after what happened to Dave in Iceland, I think he finally got the message that if you fuck up there are no do overs. Kev has already proved his worth in a shootout, but I think he was secretly relieved to sit this one out. It has been a bit frantic of late...

Me and The Monkey have pulled on our new thermals, parkas, and snow boots, and polished the sticky fingerprints off our goggles. The girls came down looking like sex on legs, as if they were off to a goth club, and we did some final weapons checks and made sure that the sat-phone was routing through JudyZ so that we could maintain contact. We decided last night that I wouldn't take the spear. The Monkey wants this to be a quick in and out and the spear has the tendency to go on a killing spree once released. So, unusually for my furry friend we are going for subtle understated...

The Monkey is setting up the energy portal and Kev has just given me a couple more grenades, 'For good luck!' In the words of the great explorer – oh, I can't remember his name, but in his words, 'Smoke me a kipper, I'll be back for breakfast!'

*

As shit shows go, we have been involved in worse...

The energy portal put us right outside the big grey doors of the bunker. The girls had already been doing their thing before we stepped through so we were confident that we would be nothing but a random blur to anyone watching.

The Monkey pulled the portal through after us and then we edged along the side of the bunker, and he placed his palms on the surface. I don't know what I expected to happen, maybe a high-tech 3D representation of the inside of the structure, complete with little digital people wandering about, all projected in glorious technicolour. No, none of that. After a couple of very cold minutes just standing there keeping an eye out, The Monkey drew back his paws and said, 'One floor down. Two corridors across. Third room on the left,' as matter of fact as that.

He checked with JudyZ that she couldn't see anything in our immediate vicinity and then he focused the portal and we stepped through into a featureless grey room with a bed bolted to one wall, a toilet and sink to another, and a small table and chair against a third. And sitting on the chair was Ms Wright in a less than stylish orange boiler suit. She jumped as we bundled through the portal. The girls had stayed on the other side, just in case, and they watched through the shimmering hole in the air. Ms Wright looked at us and at them and stood up exclaiming, 'It's about fucking time!' and marched towards the portal.

That was when the sirens went off. Ms Wright pointed to the black dome of the camera in the corner of the cell and The Monkey gave it the finger as we stepped back through. Aleks pointed behind us and it was only then that we realised Ms Wright was not with us. We could see her in the cell, but something was preventing her using the portal. She dragged up the left sleeve of the boiler suit to reveal a thin metal band around her wrist. She raised her hand to the portal, and it was repelled, like the opposite pole of a pair of magnets. 'Shit,' said The Monkey. 'Shit,' said the girls. 'Shit,' said yours truly.

The Monkey stepped back into the cell, and we all followed him. The sat-phone was shouting at us that vehicles and men had started to appear outside and were forming a cordon around the bunker entrance. The Monkey pulled the energy portal through, and we could hear boots running down the corridor outside the cell. Kris was looking at the metal band on Ms Wright's wrist and shaking her head. It looked like it was made of the same rough, grey metallic substance that formed the rings of the energy portals and it had no obvious opening. The boots were outside the door and The Monkey began to flicker with that ghostly blue flame as he drew his Glock. Kris grabbed my left wrist and tugged the glove off my metal hand, then she yelled, 'Grab it!' indicating the metal band. I closed my hand around Ms Wight's wrist and the unwanted jewellery, and my own hand lit up with the strange runic patterns. There was a moment of eerie stillness, and I could literally see everyone's hair stand on end, then with a brilliant flash of blue, plasma like light, the band disintegrated. Ms Wright cried out and fell but was caught by Kris. The door began to open and Aleks called out to The Monkey to open the portal. He did his flick knife trick, and we could see Tony's living room, and before the first black clad trooper entered the cell, we were all standing on a nice Ikea rug surrounded by Xmas decorations. I didn't need to be reminded, and as The Monkey pulled the portal through, I touched it with my metal hand, and it swirled into black infinity along with anyone stupid enough to try to follow.

*

Ms Wright is still out cold. The shock from me disintegrating the metal band seems to have scrambled her brain, but the girls have given her the once over and reckon she will be fine. So, we have checked in with JudyZ and she says that the whole area around the Greenland bunker turned into a wasp's nest. They couldn't have really believed that we would just hang around at the scene of the crime like serial killers reliving our exploits, could they? The Monkey thinks it is more likely that they had a quick panic in case a platoon of EID stormtroopers dropped in unannounced and they had a fight on their hands. He thinks they are of course still smarting over the Bolivian base we wrecked, and it's not that long ago we had the firefight in Iceland and then the showdown at the Brightstorm plant. They must be on a permanent red alert – how sad.

Well, if we can't talk to Ms Wright at the moment, we might as well drink. I asked The Monkey if he was going to let Commander Greyling know we had rescued Ms Wright, but his response was, 'Nah, fuck him!' So, I guess that will happen tomorrow maybe? 'Maybe...,' he said, downing his second Jack and reaching for the bottle.

The nerds are nervous about someone following us and have put the energy portal in a ring of disks that make a sort of net around and over it, a bit like the one they created to help seal the original black hole in my spare room. They have been working on this one for the past couple of weeks without telling us. They seem to have developed a good deal of paranoia. Probably just as well someone is taking this seriously. The Monkey has fired up Mortal Combat and is waving the second controller at me. I can see myself reflected in his metallic orange skiing goggles, and there is a massive spliff in place of his usual cigar. Ah, another refined, intellectual evening ahead...

2 January

Well, when Ms Wright came round, she was not in a good mood. She wanted to know why I had punched her, and after we convinced her that I hadn't punched her she wanted to know why we had drugged her. Again, after much promising that we had done no such thing she calmed down a bit, but she was still convinced that we had done something to her that made her pass out. Then Tony, ever the scientist, did a quick lap of her with his homemade bug detector. Years of hacking computers and being nerd bad boys had made him, Kev, and the late Dave, nervous individuals when it came to the possibility of Big Brother surveillance, and one of their earliest creations had been a very capable scanner. Anyway, it went ping just over the back of the lovely Ms Wright's neck. Closer examination revealed a half inch scar which Ms Wright explained was where, about six months ago, she had a small sliver of steel removed after she had been caught in a grenade blast during a firefight. The Monkey, with his usual tact, pinned Ms Wright down, and as she struggled, dug into the scar with the tip of his K-BAR. After a few very shouty, very sweary moments he pried out a metal object just slightly bigger than a grain of rice. He handed it to Tony and stepped away from Ms Wright as she thrashed around trying to hit him before stopping to clamp a hand to the back of her smarting neck.

Tony and Kev disappeared into the back room where all their science stuff is kept and were soon back to inform us that yes, it was a tracking device, and no, it was no longer functioning as it looked like it had been massively short circuited. That was undoubtedly the cause of Ms Wright's blackout, the surge of power from my metal arm that destroyed the band on her wrist had obviously done a number on the tracker and being so close to her head it had switched her off as well. The shock of knowing that she had been bugged calmed her down enough to not want to immediately shoot The Monkey in his fuzzy face. In fact, her mouth moved up and down and nothing came out for the first thirty seconds, and then she looked at no one in particular and said, 'Cunts!'

We put a dressing on her neck, it wasn't a deep wound fortunately, and gave her a stiff drink, and she told us how one of the EID medics had taken out the sliver of metal under a local anaesthetic. The Commander had been present, in fact he had insisted on being there so that he could debrief her on the operation in which she had been injured. We all looked at each other with a, 'That's not good,' look on our faces and Ms Wright gave a loud groan and held out the glass for a refill.

She asked me how I had removed the band from her wrist, and I thought, 'What the fuck,' and rolled up my sleeve to show her my arm. Once again, her mouth moved up and down soundlessly, and she reached out and tentatively touched it as if she couldn't trust the evidence of her own eyes. 'You didn't have that in Peru,' she stated, 'I would have noticed that!' I explained it had happened when we had made our getaway from the Monkey Temple, although I left out the part about the bloodthirsty spear, which, by the way, I have moved into a bedroom.

The Monkey at this point decided that it was time she answered some questions: Why had she opened the portal to her Whitehall office and then changed the location to the Illuminati base? Well, she hadn't 'changed the location', it had just happened. She, like all of the others in that room had been novices at using the portals and there was no way she was capable of just leaping around the globe, especially straight into an enemy organisation's base they had spent months searching for! Kev pointed out that it was highly likely that the tracker in her neck had been used to drag her through the energy portal to a location not of her choosing. The Monkey nodded his agreement and moved on.

Why had she said, 'It was about fucking time,' when we had appeared in her cell? She had been expecting, or rather hoping, that there would be a rescue mission, and she believed that it would be coordinated by EID and that The Monkey would have been recruited to be part of it. She knew that her own techs would have been using the location tracking system they had developed and so she expected the rescue to be almost immediate. When we explained that her techs couldn't track where she had gone, and that we had fucked off sharpish she asked for another drink. Kris told her that we had located her position using magic, and she gave a slightly hysterical laugh and downed that drink.

She sat, drunk, with her shoulders slumped in a resigned manner. 'I have been fucked over, haven't I?' It was more of a statement than a question, and we couldn't disagree. 'If you hadn't decided to come looking, I would still be in that cell, wouldn't I?' Once again we couldn't give her a more positive answer. But what had happened with Arno Whitaker?

He had gloated a lot when she had been captured and even walked her through part of the base in a sort of cartoon super-villain manner. But then he had got bored and told the guards to lock her up. She believed he had been waiting for a quick rescue attempt and when it didn't happen, he just lost interest. As she was being led away, she heard him talking to an assistant about getting ready to leave for Denver, and then she was prodded through a series of featureless corridors and stripped, dressed in the boiler suit, and the metal band was fastened around her wrist. She didn't see Whitaker again.

*

Ms Wright is very drunk now and not at all impressed with EID She may have left a none too polite message on his answer phone and I think that we will be having words with Commander Greyling in person. And Denver? What the fuck is in Denver?

3 January

Interesting conversation with JudyZ...

Denver airport is massive, far larger than it ought to be, and she has picked up some interesting thermal scans from a geological satellite that she got pally with. Looks like there are structures underground that very much resemble a city grid layout. Tony did a bit of web-based searching in his favourite dark web conspiracy sites and found that there have been rumours, dare I say theories, regarding the airport since its opening in 1994. These include Masonic and occult symbols found on structures around the area, and unexplained disappearances of individuals who have gone for a poke about.

But that will have to wait for a bit as we are going to drop in, unannounced, on Commander Greyling...

*

The shifty, conniving, two-faced fuck! But I get ahead of myself...

Caroline, I feel we know her well enough now to drop the 'Ms Wright', suggested we open the portal into the Commander's office. As she knows where his office is located, she took the lead and with a little coaching from The Monkey put us inside the door. He was absent and so we did a quick sweep of the rather grand room in case there was anything interesting lying around. Nada... So, we called Kev to come through and he used a disk cloning gizmo to copy the entire contents of Greyling's computer from the boot up, by passing any security measures and passwords. It is still encrypted, but at least it can be worked on at leisure.

Caroline told us that Greyling has a house in the country, Buckinghamshire to be precise, but she didn't think that he would be there with all of the shit that would be flying around EID and the other related secret service departments. No, he would be somewhere closer to the office so that he could coordinate. Therefore, the logical place to look would be his London apartment. Did she know where it was? Yes. Had she ever been there? Once. Right then, it could be a bit hit and miss but we would open the portal there. We stepped back through to Tony's house and then had to wait while The Monkey did something rather hefty in the Commander's In tray, he followed us through with a stupid grin on his face saying, 'I've been saving that one up.' Are all Gods like this? So, Caroline focused the portal into a surprisingly modern apartment with large windows overlooking the Thames.

Music was playing, and we could hear movement in another room. Aleks and Kris moved to cover the front door in case there were any bodyguards stationed outside. The Monkey sat on the arm of the sofa and examined his cigar. Caroline stood by the doorway into the other room with the Glock we had given her held ready. And me? I stood by the window and admired the view – it was quite spectacular…

The Commander's spider sense had obviously been tingling as he came out of the room with revolver levelled – at me as it happened. Caroline stepped in behind him and put the Glock against his temple and the revolver miraculously lowered. He put it on the cupboard next to him and it was only then that he looked around and said, 'Hello Caroline.'

I thought for a second that she was going to shoot him in the face. The cold look in her eyes, the anger and betrayal, but she pushed him further into the room and told him to sit down. He did look slightly surprised to see Caroline, but he smothered that, and his expression changed to superior with a touch of gloating.

'What exactly have you been up to, Malcolm?' Caroline was deeply upset at the betrayal by someone she trusted entirely.

Greyling sat there for a few moments looking at her and then launched into his explanation. 'Jenkins in the lab found some code in one of the energy portals we took from Brightstorm. It was a sort of beacon that alerted the Illuminati when the portal was being used. We reengineered it so that it would send an alert to them when a person focused a portal, and we put it into the chip in your neck. We knew it was only a matter of time before you used one of them.'

'So, I was bait? Fucking bait!' the Glock shook as it was pointed once again at his now sweaty face.

'High profile bai… We knew that they would want to get hold of you, and we – I – thought that we could track you and storm the Illuminati base, but that didn't work out.' He looked around the room seeking agreement from us that it hadn't worked out and as if we were in on his plan. 'I had suspected that The Monkey would not want to play ball with the Department, and we thought that your abduction could be used as a bargaining chip to instil some sense of duty, or if that failed, make it seem that he had been complicit in the kidnapping and force him to work with us out of fear of imprisonment. The Monkey scowled at him, and he blustered on. 'We didn't think he could do it, so when I got your message that The Monkey and his team had freed you, we suspected that it was a little on the convenient side and that The Monkey must be working with the Illuminati and that you had been turned.'

She shook her head, 'You vastly underestimate The Monkey.'

'Yes, I see that now...'

It was then that Aleks warned us that someone was coming. Caroline looked at Greyling and asked, 'Who did you call, you dickhead?' and as he looked shamefaced at her I saw The Monkey's eyes go wide and he shouted 'Sniper!' as he leapt across the room and knocked me to the floor, the red dot no longer on my chest. One of the large windows shattered and a bullet hit the wall opposite. Then there were men swinging in through the other windows and the door crashed open.

The girls took out the first three black clad figures who rushed in through the door. There was a flurry of action and the small Karambit knives they like to carry hidden at the back of their waistbands diced their victims. The Monkey bounced off me and kicked the side of the knee of one man who had just rappelled in. He gave a groan and dropped, and The Monkey shot him through the neck. I sort of reacted instinctively, and as I got back to my feet I lashed out with my left arm and hit the second man who had come through the windows. The effect was as if I had hit him with a sledgehammer. He sort of crumpled and at the same time was hurled back through the broken window where he just dangled, bled and slowly slid down his rope.

Red laser dots danced around the room as bullets hit the walls and Greyling made a lunge for cover. But the ever-resourceful Caroline pistol whipped him across the forehead, and he went down. Kris shouted that there were more men in the hallway outside and that unless we were going for a full-on bloodbath, we might want to think about leaving. So, we made the decision to run away and live to fight another day.

We had no choice but to leave Greyling, and we jumped back through the energy portal which had been pulsing quietly in the corner. As The Monkey closed it, we saw at least another dozen black clad men enter the room looking around for us and seeing only the rapidly closing portal. One fucker with quick reflexes got off a shot and the bullet came flying through into the house and it wasn't until Kev shouted that we realised Tony had been hit.

It is a through and through on the outside of his right arm. Nothing serious, as The Monkey pointed out, although Tony doesn't seem to think so. We have cleaned it up and put a field dressing on it, and The Monkey has sympathetically told him that he will have to wank with the other hand for a while. He doesn't think that is as funny as the rest of us do...

*

Caroline thinks that Greyling is going to be difficult to corner after this, especially as she contacted a close associate at EID who told her that the Commander had put the entire department on red alert after her abduction, with the inference that she may have been turned by the Illuminati and that The Monkey and the rest of us are in on it as well, and that has only just been rescinded in the last hour. Her associate said that he and most of the other tech officers in the department didn't believe the story that Greyling had put forward, believing it was an attempt to cover his own arse after putting the chip in Caroline's neck. And after talking with him she thinks that the tactical assault team who burst into his apartment are part of the EID heavies that are recruited from ex-military. They are a blunt instrument, the sort of soldiers who just shoot where they are pointed and do it very well. They would have been allocated to him as a matter of course if they thought he may be in danger. So, they weren't Illuminati goons...

The Monkey is very sanguine about the whole incident. It has confirmed to him that Greyling is not working with our best interests at heart, whatever side he may be on, and given that he was happy to throw Caroline under the bus he is a right ruthless bastard. The Monkey is happy to wait for another day to get revenge as there are bigger fish to fry.

*

The Monkey opened the energy portal into the back room of the shop in Phnom Penh where we had acquired our toys to go and play in the Cambodian jungle what seems like a lifetime ago. He thought we needed some better weapons. Mr Guns R Us was sitting at his desk with a teenage girl draped over him when The Monkey stepped out of a hole in the humid, incense filled air, and he almost had a coronary. He dumped the girl off his lap and as she fled the room screaming, he fell to his knees, repeatedly touching his head to the dirty black and white lino and frantically muttering prayers. It would seem he thought that The Monkey had returned to take his soul for some reason, and it took The Monkey a good ten minutes to calm him down and explain that he was there to do some shopping not soul extraction. He looked at The Monkey's shopping list and immediately his business head took over and you could see the dollar signs behind his eyes. His henchmen burst through the door, obviously the screaming girl had told them that their boss was in mortal danger, but they came to a rapid halt when they saw who it was had dropped in unannounced. Boss man waved at them irritably to put their guns and parangs down and then sent them scurrying off to fetch the items on the list.

The Monkey shouted through the portal and asked me if I wanted anything special, so I stepped through as well and nodded a greeting at the sweating Mr Guns R Us. I said that I had quite liked my Sig Sauer P320 and would be happy with another one of those. The Monkey translated, and he nodded vigorously and shouted through the open door at his goons. As they began to bring the goodies in, I could see boss man glancing nervously at the portal, and when I changed position and looked back at the flickering window in the air, I could see the girls lounging on the sofa playing on the X Box; they waved and smiled and the boss man weakly waved back, the colour draining from him.

We did a quick check that everything looked good, but as The Monkey said later, 'There is no way that dude is going to shortchange us,' and we passed the kit back through the portal to Kev who poked his head through with an interested look on his face. Gold coins changed hands, The Monkey thanked Mr Guns R Us, and we exited stage mid-air.

*

We are sitting around the massive TV which Kev has screenshared his laptop onto, looking at satellite images of Denver airport. The Monkey wants to pay Arno Whitaker a visit and for once we know where he might be. Tony is humming the Dr Who theme tune, this is a direct consequence of pain meds and Jack Daniel's. The girls have joined in, and Kev is doing the bass part while The Monkey slaps out the beat with his paw on the tabletop. I am writing this while trying to add some high notes, and Caroline, well, she is just sitting there looking at us like we have just all got off the special bus…

4 January

JudyZ has provided us with a satellite heat map showing an underground railway passing across the complex. We will get ourselves above that, then the plan is to work our way down the levels, trainline first, then the structures beneath. We will go in the early hours although it doesn't matter as the airport is 24/7, but maybe the time difference giving us cover of darkness on the ground there will help.

Aleks and Kris have brought their own personal firearms from home, so an H&K MP5, and a Desert Eagle XIX will be accompanying The Monkey's Glock, my Sig, Caroline's Glock, and Kev on the Kel-Tec KSG, 12-gauge. Sort of an extremist jazz ensemble, except that I will also be taking the spear which elevates us to the status of Wagnerian opera meets death metal. We also now have a tactical comms kit called Morpheus, which will allow us to talk to each other, just like in the movies! Tony will be minding the fort with his poorly arm, and from a position safely out of the cone of fire that could come through the portal, checking in on us and providing updates from our 'eye in the sky'.

Great! Early start so only a couple of drinks…

*

Should have guessed that it was going to get weird when we stepped out of the energy portal and the first thing I saw was a massive blue horse with glowing red eyes. Yes, that wasn't in the fucking pre-match briefing, was it! I did wonder for a moment if The Monkey had thought it funny to spike my coffee with acid, you know 'just to make things interesting', but when he said, 'Look at the size of that bastard!' I knew it was real. Of course, the other option was that somehow we had fucked up the location and stepped out into a demon dimension but Tony's voice came over comms and we could see him grinning through the portal. 'Oh, yes. That's quite famous. It's thirty-two feet tall.' Thanks Tony, thanks for that…

The girls did their cloaking thing, and The Monkey rubbed his paws together in a workmanlike fashion and held them over the nearest section of runway. Caroline was stressing about being seen by security and I suddenly realised that we hadn't explained the unique abilities that Aleks and Kris possess. In fact, she hadn't seen the spear until I carried it in before we stepped through the portal, and she stared open-mouthed at the way the runic patterns on it lit up and caused the ones on my arm to glow. I gave her a brief explanation (as much as I understood) about what the girls had done to make us invisible (I may even have used the term *Alakazam* – don't judge), and she stared at them with a sort of dawning realisation that they aren't just our Goth gangster molls.

The Monkey pointed over to our right and then he held the rim of the portal and focused it down into the train tunnel he had located. Once again, we all stepped through, and found ourselves standing on a train track in a tunnel lit by yellowish lights spaced out every fifty feet or so. Kev half-jokingly asked The Monkey what the chances were that we would get hit by a train and The Monkey frowned and said that maybe we should hurry the fuck up. We all agreed, and he did his X-ray paw thing again and located our next jumping off point.

This time we stepped out into a passageway between two tall structures. At first, I thought he had completely ballsed up the location but as my eyes adjusted to the light and scale I realised that far above the top of the structures, through a layer of mist, was a ceiling. (Afterwards Kev said he thought that the mist, which was almost thick enough to be clouds, was probably caused by the moisture from the air conditioning units on the buildings.)

We gazed out of the end of the passageway at a surreal scene. Stretching out in front of us in a sort of shallow natural bowl was what could pass as a small city. Not an underground base like the one we had messed up in Bolivia. This was probably a mile across and populated with ultra-modern buildings and open areas with formal plantings of trees and lawned areas. Walkways joined some of the buildings together, and a monorail crisscrossed the city. A few people wandered around in the distance and others seemed to stride about more purposefully. Checking through a monocular we could see armed men and women dotted around but they almost seemed to be there for show rather than serving any specific purpose.

Caroline asked The Monkey where he thought we should start looking for Arno Whitaker and after a minute or two of staring across the subterranean structures he pointed a hairy finger and said, 'How about there?'

*

Using the energy portal to travel short distances is very handy when you don't want to get caught out in the open. The Monkey's suggested starting place was the tallest building, smack in the centre, as far as we could tell, of the complex. It seemed to be at the lowest point of the bowl and had multiple angled sides. Kris took one look at it and said, 'It's a pentagon.' And there at the top, like a mad homage to the Lord of the Rings was a massive eye, carved into the face of the tower.

So, in an enemy city, teeming with people who obviously didn't know it was night on the surface and were getting on with whatever world domination stuff they had on their To Do lists, where should we pop out of thin air in their most impressive building? How about the roof? Thanks for the fucking warning!

The top of the building narrowed to a stubby pyramid shape with the top sliced off. And that sliced off bit was where we found ourselves next. Okay, there was a wall around the edge, and no real chance of falling off. But Christ on a bike! It seemed high! The rock ceiling above us was still a long way off and from our new vantage point we could see the complex curving away from us, following the arc of the bowl shape. It was clear that this was all brand spanking new. It is a serious endeavour, and evil, totalitarian bastards or not, you have to hand it to them – they know how to build a secret underground lair!

We knew this point would come and so we split into two teams. Team A – me, The Monkey, and Aleks; Team B – Kev, Caroline, and Kris. Then we did a final comms check on our shiny new Morpheus kit and The Monkey parked the energy portal behind a cooling vent. Tony gave us a thumbs up through the mid-air window and told us to be careful.

We knew that to cover more ground in a large building we would need to search in teams floor by floor, but it seemed odd after just 'stepping' from place to place through thin air, almost primitive. The doorway to the stairwell was unlocked and so we began our descent. At the first landing Team B took the door to that level and we carried on down to the next.

Opening the door took us into a corridor that was very art deco. Everything had that sort of 1930s look to it, as if we had stepped onto the set of the movie *Metropolis*. Going from door to door along the corridor we checked each of the rooms. Nothing but bland office space. No secret plans spread out on tables. No filing cabinets with the words 'Top Secret' written on them. Just a series of work cubicles with desktops and turned off computer monitors. There was no sign of life, and as Aleks pointed out, maybe they kept similar hours to the surface dwellers after all. The Monkey asked Team B if they had found anything, and Caroline described much the same as we had found.

Back to the stairs and down again. This floor was a little different. There were more open spaces, meeting rooms that had movable partition walling between them. In the third we found a large dry wipe board covered in symbols and lines radiating out to circles in which had been stuck different coloured Post-It Notes. An Illuminati brainstorming session? Seems even evil empires need Post-It Notes... I used my phone to take pictures of the board and then, after The Monkey had taken a moment to draw a massive cock and balls across it all we headed for the stairs again. As we did so Kev came on the comms to tell us that they had caught someone and were taking them to the stairwell.

*

Poor bastard was shit scared. He was some low-level janitor type dude who was just doing the rounds when Team B jumped him and bundled him out to the stairs. I seriously had doubts as to what sort of relevant information he could give us, but Caroline sat him down on the stairs and looked him straight in the eye until he began to squirm. Then, with her gun held just in view, she asked him if he knew where Arno Whitaker was. To our complete surprise he began to nod frantically. He seemed only too happy, in exchange for not being tortured or shot, to tell us whatever he thought we wanted to know, and in a rush, we found out that Whitaker was at some sort of rally for the Illuminati faithful (senior ranks) which was happening at 'The Temple'. So, was that why this building was empty? Apparently, there were people still working on the lower floors but all those on the higher floors had left. And where was this 'The Temple'? Well, if we would take him to the windows looking out of the front of the building, he would show us.

So we took him back to the floor we had just checked, and he led us through the meeting room with the Post-It Notes. He kept glancing at the dry wipe board, obviously aware that we weren't supposed to see what was on it but equally perturbed by the huge cock and balls scrawled across it. He stopped in front of the large expanse of glass that looked over the complex and pointed to a short, squat pyramid structure on the other side of the open space that surrounded the building we were in. 'That's The Temple,' he told us, and it was obvious as we gazed out that the space was laid out in a geometric design that radiated out from beneath us and joined various structures spaced around its edge. And did he know how many people would be there? 'At a rough guess, maybe five thousand.'

Well, fuck...

The Monkey glanced at Kris, and she nodded and put her hands on either side of the hapless janitor's head. His eyes rolled up and he crumpled to the floor. Caroline began to protest but Kris held up her hand and told her that he would be fine and wake up in about eight hours feeling hungry. The Monkey just grunted and said, 'I thought she was going to kill him,' the disappointment evident in his voice. Kris tutted at him and then laughed as he headed back towards the stairs yet again. I followed with Caroline who looked a little taken aback. 'I'd like to tell you that he didn't mean it,' I quipped, and realised too late that it had just made things worse. *C'est la vie*...

*

So, into The Temple of Doom – disclaimer, no one shouted 'Kali Maaa!'...

A bit hit and miss getting in there as we weren't close enough for The Monkey's magic SatNav paw to do its stuff. Consequently, the portal opened at the back of the entrance lobby, and we had to close it quickly when we realised that there were about two dozen people milling about, some of them armed guards. The Monkey recalibrated, by that I mean focused a little up and to the left, and this time the portal showed us an empty room that looked like an audio-visual suite. Lighting consuls, a sound desk, and a couple of large projectors lined one side of the room beneath a row of tinted glass. And looking out of that glass we could see down onto the floor of the temple, like a giant convention centre with rows of chairs facing away from us towards an elaborate stage. I glanced over to the left and could see another row of windows the same as the ones we stood behind. Dim figures moved behind them, illuminated by control desk lights and monitor displays, and it was clear that we had lucked out by landing in the AV suite that was not being used for the production crew of tonight's extravaganza. And extravaganza it appeared to be. The stage rose in three dais, the centre one being the highest. Behind them were seven columns supporting a curved lintel that wrapped around the back of the stage. In the middle of the lintel was a septagram, a seven-pointed star, and in its centre an eye in a triangle stared out across the congregation. On the central dais stood a figure in a yellow hooded robe, its back to the audience and its arms raised up towards the eye. We could hear a muffled noise and Kev slid one of the windows open a crack so that we could hear.

Chanting. Chanting from the yellow clad figure and an answering chant from the thousands of throats in the audience. The noise grew to a crescendo, almost a roar, and then it died away to an eerie silence. The yellow robed figure turned towards the hushed masses, and the hood framed the strangely melted features of Arno Whitaker, that psycho clown grin that is perpetually on what passes for his face seeming to stretch from ear to ear. He opened his arms wide again with perfect theatrics. Spotlights hit the dais either side of him and from the shadows at the back of the stage two figures stepped into the light. They had that look about them, the way they moved, the way they held themselves. They radiated danger, a sort of controlled, studied calm sat upon their faces, but it looked, even from that distance, as if they were acting. And their faces! The genetic bastard children of Arno Whitaker stared out with cold, reptilian intensity over the wildly applauding crowd. They nodded in acknowledgment of the adoration, but whether the audience knew it or not they would never have anything in common with this superman and woman.

Whitaker hushed the crowd again and addressed them, once again the Southern Baptist preacher working the crowd, the snake oil salesman whose audience had already given him everything, including their souls. We watched fascinated as he extolled the virtues of the 'coming race', those who would lift humanity from the tyranny of struggle, and lead the world into a new age, an eternal utopia. Where had I heard this shit before? Hmm, let me think...

The Monkey looked at me and smiled that smile. 'How's your throwing arm?' he asked.

'Why don't we see,' was the best I could come up with – of course now I can think of much cooler, wittier responses, like, 'Oh, I think he will get the point.' Actually, that's pretty much it... Fuck, I need a scriptwriter. Anyway, Kev slid the window wide open, and I took the leather hood that the girls had conjured up for me off the spearpoint and watched as the runes on my arm mingled with the runes on the shaft. And then I threw the fucker...

The spear likes to scream. It has no stealth mode, no silencer. And it has flames blazing off the head, like a Ghost Rider comic book (not the shitty Nicholas Cage movies), but in the form of a stick with a deadly pointy bit on the end. Maybe it was the shrieking and burning that gave the game away? After all, last time Whitaker had met the spear it had touched the magic Viking sword that had chopped into him and produced a vortex of antimatter-type stuff that had whisked that version of him off into oblivion, so I am guessing that he probably viewed it quite negatively... Anyway, he jumped backwards off the dais and at the same time the female super clone, with incredible speed and agility, leapt the eight or nine feet from her dais to the central one and put herself into the spear's path. Amazement, the first emotion we had seen on her face, as the spear didn't stop when she grabbed it. Instead, it smashed into her chest like a bullet train during rush hour and split her in half.

The crowd went wild, and not in a good way. They were staring up at our row of control booth windows, pointing and shouting their outrage. Kev said something about *Invasion of the Body Snatchers*, and yes, it was a bit like that, but without the gnarly trees and Donald Sutherland. The Monkey shouted that Whitaker had disappeared and that maybe we should abort. I thought it unlike him, but then I realised that the enraged acolytes were all flooding in our direction, and we could hear doors crashing and running feet somewhere in the passageways beyond our closed door. Caroline pointed and I could see the male clone kneeling by the remains of his sibling – would that be the right term? He looked up at the windows and sprang to his feet, then he came at a run, knocking mere mortals out of his path. He looked pissed off.

Ah, the spear. Never one to be shy, it had looped back and was now tearing through the crowd, who, to be honest, never saw it coming. Blood and fire. That tang of iron in the air that is becoming uncomfortably familiar. Oh, and so much screaming. The Monkey held out the portal as if we were all performing dolphins and we dutifully jumped through. I stood in Tony's house staring through the gap in space at the chaos happening in the auditorium as The Monkey stepped through and nodded to me. I held out my metal hand and within seconds the spear came tearing through the windows and the portal to land perfectly in my grip. The Monkey grinned and turned to close the energy portal but there, pale blue eyes staring with hatred, was the clone. He had made it past all of the others and into the control booth and was coming through into Tony's house! The Monkey grabbed him by the hair, pulling him further in, and then he closed the portal. There was a flash and the smell of burning meat and roughly one half of the clone dropped onto the carpet, mouth emitting a sickening groan as the eyes glared at The Monkey before glazing over. We all just sort of stood there staring while Tony said, 'Fucking hell!' quite a few times...

*

So, that was our big night out. Not lying, I have had better.

We missed getting Whitaker again, and almost got home invaded by one of his supermen-clone-soldier things. The Monkey thinks he will have gone to ground, and he is not too happy that we fucked up a prime chance...

There will need to be some explaining done for the benefit of Caroline as well. She has seen a few things that have raised some questions. The girls' mystical powers for one thing, and of course, the spear. She is also rather concerned by the fact that Aleks and Kris want to eat the portion of the super clone that came through the portal. She has persuaded them not to as she wants the boffins at EID to take a look at the remains. Yes EID. She had come up with a cunning plan to get them back on team. But now we all need sleep so explanations and plans will have to wait.

Oh, and Tony's wound has almost healed! The girls think it is possibly due to the alien demon blood we drunkenly licked off the spear. Who knew?

5 January

Today has been a day of answering questions, Caroline's questions...

Over quite a lot of Jack we told her much of what has happened over the past twelve months. She got to hear about Cambodia, Area 51, finding the spear, our little jaunt to Chernobyl, Iceland, and the Brightstorm facility. Some details were left out or conveniently forgotten. She still doesn't know about the Green and Red Society's involvement, or JudyZ. We still need a few aces up our sleeves. I think what we told her might have been more than enough anyway. By the time we had finished she was wide-eyed and had laughed several times in a semi-hysterical fashion.

She then wanted to know if Aleks and Kris were related to the two Eastern European women mentioned in the EID archive reports from the late 1800s. The girls smiled that cat-like smile they tend to do before doing really bad things and in perfect unison replied, 'We are those two women.' At this point I really thought Caroline was going to have a seizure or something. The Monkey seemed to be enjoying himself, but I suggested that we have a break and get some food so that Caroline could let this new information sink in without something snapping.

*

After a lot of Chinese food, we used the power of MSG to get back on task.

Caroline had recovered enough to explain that she had come up with a plan. Said plan was meant to get her back in with EID and get the rest of us off the hook for being suspected Illuminati henchmen. The plan would involve the remains of the clone, currently stuffed into Tony's chest freezer, her team at EID who still supported her, and Commander Greyling. That bit didn't please The Monkey. But Caroline believes that even though Greyling acted in an underhand manner, in fact pretty much threw her under the bus, he was still acting in the interests of EID and against the Illuminati. The Monkey has yet to be convinced but he is willing to give it a try as long as he gets to turn Greyling inside out if he turns out to be a wrong 'un. Caroline told him that he could do as he pleased with her blessing if she was wrong about the Commander.

*

So Caroline has gone off to another room with the sat-phone to start the ball rolling. The girls have popped out to do a spot of grave robbing. And me, The Monkey, and the nerds have settled down in front of the TV for a *Mad Max* marathon session.

What a lovely day!

6 January

Seems that when the girls came in late last night, they found Caroline still awake and plotting. So, they sat down and had a chat with her about The Monkey, me, and the past. Anyway, Caroline keeps looking at me funny and none of them will let us in on the conversation. The Monkey doesn't seem bothered, although that could be because we were very drunk last night and are feeling it this morning – correction, it's just gone twelve-thirty, so this afternoon.

Watching *Mad Max* last night inspired Tony to dig out his old Scalextric set, and we raced the cars round and round while the movies played as accompaniment. We built barricades on the track and smashed the cars through, and then we packed the cars full of cotton wool doused in lighter fluid and they sped around like tiny fireballs until there was nothing left of them. I asked Tony if he minded the destruction of his childhood toys. He said that he had only played with it about half a dozen times as he preferred his junior electronics kit and chemistry set, and that his dad had only bought it for him because he didn't think his twelve-year-old son was macho enough. Ah, dads. Imposing unrealistic expectations on their sons since the dawn of time…

The living room smells of burnt stuff and there are pools of melted plastic welded to the large figure eight track. The Monkey has burnt a patch of fur on his chest, and we think it happened when we were trying to send the cars off a jump, and he bet us that he could catch one in his mouth. Fortunately, he missed…

*

Lots of coffee and a fry up – much better!

The ladies still won't fess up to what they discussed. Kris came and sat on my lap and stroked my hair telling me, 'There are some things you don't need to know, at least not yet.' I'm sure she has done that mind voodoo thing again because I am finding it hard to care about it at the moment.

What about Caroline's plan I hear you ask? You are a bunch of nosy bastards, but here is the gist of it…

She managed to get through to one of the senior tech team on the sat-phone. She explained to him that we had procured a lump of flesh that EID would definitely be interested in having a look at. Like all the mad scientists we have met so far, he got a bit hot under the collar about the prospect of getting a specimen of prime Illuminati super soldier meat to run some tests on. But there was a condition. Ms Wright wanted to know whether the Commander could be trusted or if the EID had been totally compromised. Her contact, a Lieutenant Steve Collingwood, said that after the shootout at Greyling's apartment there had been a summons from 'on high' which had stopped the witch hunt he had begun to instigate around the department. He had been called to see 'The Boss' and asked to explain himself. Who is The Boss, I asked? The Monkey looked at me through a cloud of blueish cigar smoke and reminded me that, 'EID has a royal charter. Who do you think The Boss is?'

Greyling had been made to explain himself and had obviously been believable enough as he hadn't ended up in the Tower (do they still do that?). Anyway, he has been told to calm the fuck down and offer olive branches to Caroline and The Monkey, and I guess, by default to the rest of us as well. That seemed to be enough for Caroline and she has arranged to meet Lieutenant Collingwood at the research facility they share with the MOD's biological weapons department at Porton Down.

She then phoned Greyling on his personal number and informed him that she knew about his meeting with The Boss, and told him about the frozen clone she was bringing in. She also told him that we had discovered a major Illuminati complex and that if he played nice all of this wonderful information could be his.

The Monkey is still of a mind that we should, 'Shoot him in the face. Just in case,' but, along with some reassurances from Aleks and Kris, is willing to go along with the plan. As long as we don't get stitched up because the Commander is actually an Illuminati scumbag, we should have a working relationship with EID that doesn't involve rendition and black sites.

Well, that's the plan anyway...

7 January

We can't go to Porton Down today as they are apparently having an issue with some undead. Caroline explained that they had rounded up half a dozen zombies who were wandering around the Scottish Highlands. After extensive testing they were discovered to not be contagious but were quite disruptive, and they seem to have broken out of containment and into the MOD section, and there is a chance that they could have been throwing anthrax at each other.

We didn't have the heart to tell Caroline that we were, at least partially, responsible for the zombie outbreak that had made the news. That bit of info is probably better kept to ourselves until we get the current drama out of the way! She says that we will know later on today what the potential contamination risks are and when we can meet up with Collingwood and Greyling.

So, while the rain has stopped, we are going to get in some knife throwing practice in the back garden...

*

Bounce backs are a bitch. To be fair, Kev was very lucky. The knife went through the front of his trainer, right between his toes, and didn't even scratch him. Jammy bastard! He did go and put on some steel toe cap boots, but his very next throw came bouncing back and hit him in the shin. It was just a nick, but he called it a day and went back in the house to the sound of The Monkey's laughter. Such compassion...

*

Okay, so Caroline has found out that the stupid zombies had rampaged through the kitchen before stumbling into the MOD section, and the substance they were throwing around turned out to be custard powder looted from the kitchen shelves. Ah, those zany undead...

Consequently, we will be able to do the meeting tomorrow, barring any more zombie buffoonery. So we might as well get shit faced. The Monkey has managed to procure some more of that mental skunk, and we have Dominos on speed dial for when the munchies kick in. Caroline is looking at us like we are teenage delinquents. Maybe we are.

8 January

Porton Down is an uninspiring array of low prefab buildings surrounded by miles of security fencing and barbed wire and set in a featureless expanse of Wiltshire countryside near Salisbury Plain.

Me, The Monkey, and Caroline arrived there in a borrowed VW camper van, the defrosting chunk of clone wrapped in plastic in the back. I had noticed when we were parcelling it up on Tony's kitchen floor that there were what looked suspiciously like two bite marks out of the remaining arm's triceps. Speaking of which... We were, as usual, shadowed by Aleks and Kris, this time in their Lancia. They had also brought the energy portal with them, and a collection of weapons.

The security at the gate stared at us hard and we were invited to step out of the van and into the gatehouse for a thorough search as other members of their team went through the interior with a dog, and others walked around the exterior holding mirrors on sticks beneath the vehicle. The dog had a moment when it came to the clone, but they had obviously been warned that we would be bringing 'something unusual' with us so we were eventually waved through with an escort to take us to the EID building and plastic ID cards they printed off at the gatehouse with our photos on them. The Monkey seemed pleased with the crazy face he had pulled for his, and he clipped it to one of the pockets of the shabby vintage Vietnam War olive green tactical vest he likes to wear when we are not going on a mission, to keep his cigars, zippo, and other assorted crap in.

It took about five minutes, at a very slow pace, to drive to the EID building. It was, if anything, shabbier than the other buildings we had passed. They all had that 1950s Cold War look about them, and it seemed the only exterior modernisation had been the occasional lick of paint. The fact that it was dull and misty didn't help, and the whole thing felt like an episode of *Quatermass* or maybe Tom Baker era *Dr Who*. We pulled up outside and a couple of EID heavies came out to greet us. They were, quite possibly, even more hostile than the MOD boys, and went through the whole checking routine once again, although they did nod to Caroline, and she even greeted them by name. when they were happy that we weren't tooled up they notified the tech guys, and they came out in hazmat suits to collect the chunk of clone from the back of the van. It felt suddenly as if we were dodgy meat vendors, you know the ones, they appear at markets and lay-bys and sell vacuum packed meat of dubious origin. One of the hazmat suits stopped next to Caroline and had a brief chat and I guessed that it was probably Lieutenant Collingwood. As they carted the clone inside on a gurney we were allowed to follow them. I once again had to explain that I had a false arm when the metal detector we were shepherded through went ping, and after a brief examination during which I kept my hand immobile we were shown into a much more modern looking conference room.

Sitting at the head of the large table was Commander Greyling. I found it hard to read his expression at first but when he greeted Caroline, I decided it was relief that was coming to the surface. There were others around the table, six men and three women, and even those not in uniform looked at the very least ex-military. They had left empty chairs for us halfway along one side of the table and The Monkey immediately sat in the chair nearest Greyling. I grinned to myself knowing that if it all went south the Commander would be the first to die.

'I would like to begin by apologising for the heavy-handed way in which the Department has treated you, and for any bad feeling that this may have caused. Some rash decisions were taken, which although they were done out of good intentions I can see now were ill advised and could have been handled with more subtlety.' The Commander's little *mea culpa* received some nods from around the table although Caroline looked on stony faced and The Monkey just grunted and blew smoke rings. One of the men sitting opposite, in an expensive tailored suit, glanced at Greyling and then fixed his hard, calculating pale green eyes on the three of us.

'A line needs to be drawn under this incident. Ms Wright's loyalty to EID is without question, and we very much want you and your associates to work with us to put a stop to the Illuminati threat once and for all.' His lips smiled but it never reached his eyes. I got the feeling that he was MI6 or something of that ilk, and he seemed to be speaking with the backing of a higher authority.

*

Over the next few hours those around the table asked us seemingly endless questions about what we knew regarding the Illuminated Ones and their secret bases and plans. Our latest discovery was one of the lures we had dangled in front of them to get Caroline back into their good books and to prevent us being hunted as domestic terrorists, so we had already agreed to be forthcoming about that. We told them about the Greenland bunker where they had held Caroline. They had suspected something in the Arctic Circle, but they had no clear evidence. As we talked, laptop keys were tapped and messages sent. A projector hanging from the ceiling was fired up and a satellite image of Greenland appeared on the wall behind the Commander. The image zoomed in and tracked across the white wasteland, and with my usual lightning speed I realised we weren't looking at Google Earth but a real time satellite feed. We had given them the GPS coordinates that Kev and Tony had given us, and as we watched the tracking stopped over an unimpressive white mound amongst the rest of the white. Then, as the image zoomed in further, there was obvious movement around the area of the mound and whited painted military vehicles came into focus given away by their shadows. There was much nodding of approval and more keyboard tapping. Then we dropped the bombshell on them. Denver Airport. Ah, a great deal of consternation at the thought that we had already gone on a raid into the UK's major ally and the world's only superpower. Greenland is a little close for comfort, but it is largely uninhabited and using the energy portals in an attack wouldn't be like a traditional land, sea, air assault. But Denver! Fuck!

The Monkey told them to collectively grow a pair. Now they knew where the base was it would be no different to attacking the one in Greenland. They could send forces directly into the underground city and, as long as they kept the attack purely subterranean, the powers that be in the US of A would be none the wiser. There was still plenty of talk of international incidents and acts of war against the continental United States, and I could see The Monkey gearing up to tell them that we had already committed acts of war in Area 51, and done a lot of shooting in Iceland, as well as just recently in Bolivia, but before he could drop that particular revelation Mr MI6 raised his hand and said, 'Covert, isn't that what we are good at? If The Monkey has already been causing havoc in their underground city and no one here has heard about it then it is quite probably not common knowledge within the US administration. I am guessing that you only know if you are part of the club. So, Ms Wright, if your energy portals are as good as you say, what's to stop us just dropping in our tactical squads and then getting out without those on the surface being any the wiser?'

There was, of course, much toing and froing as to whether the President should be advised, and his permission asked, but even amongst those erring on the side of caution there seemed to be a strong desire to, 'Keep it in the family.'

Caroline shared the photos I had taken of the dry wipe board and Post-It Notes, and this set off another round of keyboard smashing. She had already told us that they have a special department for deciphering intelligence of this sort, and so we took it for granted that it would be electronically winging its way to GCHQ.

The Monkey tapped the table with his coffee cup and brushed biscuit crumbs (he had commandeered the plateful) from his tactical vest as they all gave him their attention. 'You do understand that we have already stirred up the hornet's nest, and by that, I mean blown stuff up and shot people, don't you? They may just be expecting another visit from us and therefore have put their lairs into red alert mode. It could mean walking into a trap going back in there so soon.'

One if the uniformed officers gave a little cough, I suspect to cover up a laugh. 'We are exceptionally good at what we do, thank you. All our assault groups are backed up by serving special forces not like the hired hands you met at the Commander's apartment.' He smiled a rather ingratiating smile and I saw The Monkey's toes curl into fists beneath the table although he smiled back and then took a deep draw on his cigar. 'You will be briefed in due course when we have had chance to digest the intel you have presented us with and work out the logistics. It will be good to have your expertise when we launch the assaults.' The emphasis he put on expertise was just a little too much and I saw Mr MI6 glare at him before The Monkey could throw his coffee cup. The uniform shut up and there was an uneasy silence until someone passed The Monkey another plate of biscuits…

*

What about Arno Whitaker?

Commander Greyling held up a dossier, quite a thick dossier, and it was passed around the table until it got to The Monkey. He opened the cover and there, on the top sheet was the grinning, vaguely fuzzy face of Whitaker. 'That is the information we have on Arno Whitaker,' was all the Commander said. But once again the smartly suited spook took charge.

'You can take that file with you and study it at your leisure. I'm sure you will find some very interesting information in there. But there is something else you need to know, something that is not in the file, and something that must not be repeated outside this room. We have all signed the Official Secrets Act and we are aware of the penalty should we disclose this information.' He took a deep breath and looked around the room. Greyling fidgeted nervously. 'Having said that, I am going to trust you with this information as I am well aware that at least for you,' he indicated The Monkey, 'the Official Secrets Act would be of little consequence.'

The Monkey inclined his head in agreement and said, 'So, what do you know?'

Mr MI6 took a deep breath and began a story of *Fortean Times* weirdness with the simple question, 'Do you know who Dr John Dee was?' We nodded and then we got this...

The Queen and therefore by default the Government, have their own occult source. This source is a descendant of Dr John Dee (for those of you who don't know, Dee was the court astronomer, and advisor to Elizabeth I. He was a mathematician, alchemist, and scholar of divination, the occult, and Hermetic philosophy. He may also have done a bit of spying for Queen Liz). Dee went mad after he found out he had been duped by Edward Kelly, an Irish chancer who convinced Dee that he was a channel for Dee's angelic messages and then ran off with his wife. In his madness Dee kidnapped a serving girl from the local tavern and performed a ritual over her which summoned an angelic spirit into her body. He then raped her and kept her locked up in his house until she had delivered the child. As the boy grew, Dee instructed him in the rituals of Enochian magic and necromancy. Elizabeth found out and she imprisoned the now teenage child in her palace and forced him to perform the same occult functions, with an even greater degree of success, as his father had, she also had Dee's notebooks appropriated in which he recorded how the child had been conceived. A secret pact with her chancellors and newly made secret service ensured that as the boy grew into a man he was kept for the service of the Crown. When James I came to the throne Dee was disowned and it is believed he died in poverty in London. When the son was older, he was made to perform the same ritual as his father had to produce another son. This continued, in secret, through the following centuries, each child held captive in the Tower and becoming incrementally more knowledgeable and insane. And it continues now.

The fuck!?

Me and The Monkey

Yes, the descendant of Dr John Dee is held in hidden rooms in the Tower, prophesying for the Queen and her Government.

But, as if that isn't bat shit crazy enough, Arno Whitaker is a twin born of one of these rituals!

It was 1841 and it was the first time a twin had ever been born because of the ritual. When it was obvious to his mother that she was carrying twins, she arranged for one of them to be spirited away and smuggled to America where she had distant family members. And thus began the story of Arno Whitaker.

Mr MI6 ended with, 'The rest of it is in the file.'

*

I sat there gawping like an idiot, and to be fair there were a few stunned faces around that table. It seems some secrets are too dark to be shared even with those who are supposed to be protecting the country. I glanced at Caroline and the shock on her face was plain to see. The Monkey relit his cigar and sat back in his chair. 'You really are a bunch of cunts,' was his profound view. Mr Spook just opened his arms wide in a, 'Well, what can you do?' sort of gesture, and Greyling, who had obviously been in the know, looked down at the table shaking his head.

At this point, and much to the relief of most of those around the table, there was a knock on the conference room doors and after a brief pause one of the armed guards stuck his head in and announced that, 'The lab boys are waiting outside.' The Commander asked for them to come in and two very intense military nerds, one of whom I guessed was Lieutenant Collingwood by the way he grinned at Caroline, entered the room. Almost before they were asked, they began talking excitedly, and one of them used a tablet PC to link to the projector and began scrolling through images as they took it in turns to speak. They were very excited because the tissue samples taken from the clone had proved to have a very unique make up. They were unlike normal human tissue in their ability to withstand damage and both techs were convinced that the cells would be capable of regenerating if the clone was still alive. They would have to wait for the DNA results to come back but they were 99% sure that they would be a match for the base sample they had been given.

Base sample? What did that mean?

Mr Spook glanced at the dossier in front of The Monkey and said, 'When the remaining twin died, they kept him in a jar. The Victorians were very keen on that sort of thing.' Holy fuck, what a fucking freak show!

*

We left in the VW van without Caroline. She has decided that now Greyling in on a leash, so to speak, it is safe for her to go back to work. And there is a lot of work, mostly generated by our recent adventures.

We had given them as much information as we could about the Greenland base, not much, and everything we could about the complex beneath Denver Airport, which was a bit more. Kev had taken some photos with his smartphone, and we shared those with them as well. There was a good deal of expletives used when they saw the scale of the complex, and it was going to take a good few sleepless nights for them to come up with a workable assault plan, despite what the uniformed dickhead had believed. But hey, that's why they get paid the big bucks!

Before we left there was a whole lot of, 'Wanting to make sure you are on-team,' and, 'Of course we can count on you to take part in the operations, even on a purely advisory level,' bullshit. We nodded and promised to phone, and then, like it was some one night stand we fucked off with no intention of it turning into a marriage. Perhaps the occasional drunken fling, but nothing more.

Caroline thanked us for rescuing her and then gave us one of her serious looks, 'Will you be in touch?' she asked. With her, yes. But the others might find us more difficult to reach. Would she be okay now that 'The Boss' was involved? 'Yes, that has dramatically changed the dynamic,' she gave a little satisfied smile. Good…

She watched us drive through the gates of the EID section and we watched her in the rear-view mirror as she turned and went back inside.

*

Once out of the main gates we drove North until we met up with the girls at Stonehenge and then we drove another couple of miles to some woodland and dumped the VW there. We are under no illusions that it would have had tracking devices hidden all over it while we were in the meeting, and as we had 'borrowed' it from the West bound car park at Leigh Delamere services on the M4 we didn't really give a fuck where we left it. Yes, we are caring like that… Back to Slough and Tony's house in the Lancia – man, those window tints are dark!

9 January

Last night we filled everyone in on the meeting, the nerds were very excited to hear all about Porton Down, and I felt like we had pissed on their parade when we told them how bleak and old it looked, but they just thought that was even cooler; strange lads…

Of course, we told them all about Dr Dee and his descendants kept secret in the Tower. Like they really thought that we weren't going to spill the beans on that. Maybe they have more faith in us than is wise. The girls were very interested in that little revelation. It seems that they met Dr Dee back when he was in Germany for a while. They also met Edward Kelly, who they describe as, 'A bit of a lad'. They had heard rumours of a son who had been taken into the care of the Crown, but after Dee was kicked out of the royal court there was nothing more.

Then we got a bit drunk, unusually, and watched a whole season of *Breaking Bad* again until we crawled into bed...

*

Spent the day looking through the Arno Whitaker dossier. Welcome to the *Twilight Zone*. Some of it we already knew from the research that Tony did before our trip to Cambodia, but most of it is very new...

11.47pm, 31 October 1841 and baby Arno was squeezed out and then spirited away from the Tower straight after his delivery. According to the established protocol if there was a multiple birth the first out would be the one that was kept if it seemed healthy, and the others would be taken away and smothered, the same applied if the child was female. He was passed to a waiting steam launch at Traitors' Gate and taken to a cargo ship docked at Wapping, where an uncle of the mother would take him and a wet nurse hired for the journey, across the Atlantic to America.

The ship made land in New Hanover, North Carolina, and then Arno and wet nurse were transported to St Clair County, Alabama. Here his upbringing was taken over by distant cousins of his mother and for the next few years he was just a kid doing kid things.

When he was twelve years old, he had a fit, some sort of grand mal seizure, and when he woke from it, he began to have visions. He was soon leading sermons in his local church and those in the area, and his visions became increasingly more prophetic. At around the age of sixteen he began handling snakes during the church meetings, leading to a vast increase in congregation numbers but also condemnation from some of the region's more orthodox churches – quite possibly because he was stealing their members.

His grand mal seizures continued, although infrequently, and he was heard to talk about a twin brother who was locked up in a castle during some of the fits. It was quite possibly a seizure when he was nearly eighteen that caused him to be bitten on the face repeatedly by the rattlesnakes he was handling at the Tuesday evening service, 14 June 1859. He was pronounced dead by the local doctor who was attending the church that evening. The multiple bites caused excessive swelling of his face and neck, and nothing could be done to save him.

Two days later he rose from the dead, or more accurately, clawed his way out of the grave. It was an exceptionally hot June and he had been buried quickly to avoid any further decomposition, especially given the level of necrosis that was reported around the bites. Anyway, he was back, probably looking like roadkill, but hailed as a miracle.

Funny thing is, on his return to the living, he stopped having seizures and visions. In fact, he was no longer interested in the church and seems to have locked himself away, disappearing from the records until he joined the Confederate Army and took part in the Battle of Shiloh at the beginning of April 1862. The photo that had been in the notebook given to The Monkey by the old lady in the grand house on the edge of Dartmoor, the one of the Confederate cavalry officers sitting outside a tent, is not present in the dossier, but there is a copy of one featuring a cavalry officer on his own. It is one of those posed photographs taken in a studio, the sort where you would have to sit still while the image was burned onto the photographic plate. It looked like the sitter had been shaking his head very rapidly from side to side so that his features, except for that grin, were a blur even though everything else was in perfect focus. A twenty-year-old Arno Whitaker in his uniform, looking remarkably similar to the last time we had seen him even with the one-hundred-and-sixty-year difference.

The dossier then goes into detail regarding how he came to the notice of the fledgling EID. There appears to have been a deserter in the Illuminati ranks who wanted to spill the beans in return for a guarantee of safety and a large payment of cash. He told a tale of how a young man from one of the American Southern States had come to the attention of, and been recruited by, the Illuminati. This young man with his badly scarred face had exhibited amazing regenerative powers after being gravely wounded at Shiloh, and after reports from the field surgeons were passed to certain interested parties, he had been taken under the Illuminati wing. The deserter didn't live to enjoy his money. It seems that the guarantee wasn't all it was cracked up to be and he was found eviscerated in the Whitechapel district of London. Almost a copycat version of the Jack the Ripper killings the report said. A very grainy photograph that looked as if it had been taken in an abattoir added to the gory detail.

Then nothing until his name was mentioned in a series of documents passed back and forth between two bonkers European aristocrats in 1908. The documents (the dossier only contains an outline) were a proposal for the formation of a single Pan European state in which all the nations, including bordering countries who could be co-opted, would be encouraged to interbreed, and form a sort of docile, mongrel race of serfs who would be controlled by the aristocracy. Sounds familiar, right? Arno Whitaker appears to have been involved in planning talks with the two aristocrats and mention was made of the possibility of enlarging the plan to encompass all the nations of earth. Several attempts were made to engage the crown heads and governments of Europe, and there were positive noises being made from several quarters, although a branch of the Catholic Church that still called itself the Inquisition (yes, them) spread dissent amongst the ranks by claiming it was a global plot by the Jews to take over. Scapegoats once again...

And then? And then the war to end all wars tap danced its way across the hopes and dreams of mad aristocrats, totalitarian secret societies, and a generation of young men who died in the mud of a foreign field. A company that later became Brightstorm was linked to poison gas manufacture and distribution to the highest bidder, and strangely to treatments for the Spanish flu that gleefully added to the death toll of that decade. Oddly, a large portion of the information regarding the Great War has been redacted in the reports...

Fast forward to that in-breath between the World Wars...

Whitaker is noted as having been seen at Nazi Party rallies in Berlin, and parades celebrating Stalin in the new USSR. Once again, copies of grainy photographs show the grinning waxworks effigy that is Whitaker standing with senior officers and party members of both groups. It is mentioned that there doesn't appear to be tacit support from the Illuminati for either brand of extreme political thought, with Whitaker there, seemingly, just as an observer. As The Monkey pointed out, he was probably taking notes...

And then World War 2 happened. The war to end all wars was eclipsed by industrial scale death and destruction that just goes to prove that humans really are their own worst enemies. Whitaker is mentioned late on in the conflict as having been an advisor on the Manhattan Project with the newly rebranded Brightstorm producing parts, and as one of the prime advocates for using the bomb against Japan even though they were on the verge of surrender. Again, The Monkey observed that it was a perfect opportunity to test out something in anger that would never be countenanced under any other circumstance.

With the Cold War, Brightstorm became a favourite supplier of the industrial/military complex, and Whitaker was to be found touring hot spots all over the world. Photos of him in Africa, Indo China, and Latin America show the extent of his input into global conflict. There is a particularly disturbing (given the genocide that followed) photo of him in a Parisian night club with Pol Pot. They are shown laughing in the company of several scantily clad young French women, Whitaker's face, as usual, out of focus and grinning like a Halloween pumpkin.

There is brief mention about his involvement in 'antiquities' as a collector, and patron of several expeditions, but there is no mention of the one on the Cambodia/Vietnam border in the 1970s that in many ways resulted in where me and The Monkey are today.

Then when the Cold War ended, Whitaker was very busy meeting with all sides during the Yugoslavian conflicts, plenty of flirting with Middle Eastern dictators, and a few dalliances with genetically modified food and DNA sequencing. And mention of a contract to work with the US military in Thailand and experimental drugs used on monkeys – most of this had black lines through it. The Monkey narrowed his eyes as a little blue flame rippled across him and he snarled, 'There are no coincidences...'

Next in the pile of papers are up to date reports regarding Brightstorm and the Illuminati master plan. But and it is a big but, the information is sketchy at best and a large amount of it has been redacted – which makes us very suspicious...

What about the fact that Arno Whitaker would appear, to anyone paying attention, to be approaching two hundred years old and doesn't seem to be aging? Well, the dossier does make note that at conveniently regular intervals Whitaker seems to disappear only to be replaced by a 'son' who has been waiting in the wings until his 'father's' passing. The fact that we watched him turn inside out during the fight at the Brightstorm plant when the spear and sword touched together is quite another matter. That whole incident, which the EID apparently 'cleaned up', has black lines running through it in the dossier. We saw Whitaker on TV not more than two weeks later talking to press at a trade show, and definitely not inside out! The last remaining good guys from the Green and Red Society had told us that they believe Whitaker has a series of identical clones in waiting, and that a constantly updated version of his consciousness/memories is stored on a computer and can be uploaded to a clone as needed. Well, we have first-hand experience of the Brightstorm cloning technology and I can believe all of that to be true.

*

So, that's what we now know about Arno Whitaker, which is more than we knew before, and confirms that he is indeed a creepy mutant clown...

I asked The Monkey if we were really going to join in with the EID in a mass assault on the Illuminati bases in Greenland and Denver, already suspecting what the answer would be. 'Fuck that!' was in fact the answer I suspected, and the answer I got. No surprises there then. So, what were we going to do?

The Monkey unrolled the maps given to him by Herr Myer in Amsterdam and said, 'It's time we went to Tibet, and now we don't have to travel in the back of a lorry.'

Now, he is sending WhatsApp messages to our Mao Shan man, ah, the joys of encryption! With a bit of luck, he will pick them up within a couple of days and we can get a conversation with him and find out what he and his Triad buddies have been up to, and get some coordinates so that we can just walk into Tibet from Slough...

10 January

Still nothing back from the sorcerer, and we don't want to use the sat-phone until he gives us the okay – just in case. The Chinese army is very active in and around Tibet making sure all of those naughty Buddhist monks don't go doing any of their peaceful protests and stuff, and we don't want them picking up messages and spoiling the party before we even get there...

Caroline called in an off the record capacity to give us a heads up that the DNA sample of the clone we handed over at Porton Down has come back. It is a match for the base sample but there are anomalies in it. Anomalies? It would appear that the DNA from the angelic entity summoned into the 'lucky' female recipient of the mad breeding experiment of 1841 has been altered by the snake venom that had been pumped into young Whitaker's face and had become something else entirely. This is now why they believe he may be scarred for life from the bites but is seemingly immortal, at least as far as aging goes. Well fuck! This is almost Biblical...

Aleks and Kris have announced that they aren't going with us to Tibet. They have decided that they will help Caroline and the EID with their attacks on the Illuminati. I get the feeling that there is a hidden agenda there somewhere, even though they say that they just want to make sure that not too many of the EID get killed. Like The Monkey says, they are big girls and can take care of themselves. Still, be odd not having them with us...

*

Tony found some more of his old games in the loft, seems he hit the motherlode when he dug out the Scalextric. We now have a full-scale Battling Tops tournament in progress. The Monkey is finding it all highly exciting and has even stopped rolling joints to watch Kev and Aleks fight it out. The girls do seem extraordinarily good at it, and I might even suspect that they are using a little of their occult abilities to make their tops spin faster and in the exact direction they want them to go. Yes, Aleks has just winked at me as her top has literally blasted Kev's out of the plastic arena. I think we might have to instigate a no magic rule, or we are going to get thrashed!

11 January

More silence from the sorcerer, but we have heard from the EID. They are planning an assault on the Greenland base within the next two weeks and want us to attend a planning meeting in Whitehall. The Monkey made the right noises but was noncommittal, although he did tell them that Aleks and Kris would be involved. Caroline, who was on the call, seemed happy about that and quickly shut down any arguments against. The call ended with us saying we would see them at the EID offices the day after tomorrow and then we all checked our noses to make sure they hadn't grown really long...

*

Kev and JudyZ seem to be back on very good terms. Tony walked in on a scene of internet sex, or on-screen virtual lust, or something. Not entirely sure how you would describe it, but there seems to have been a writhing animated avatar and lots of tissues. I think Tony may be scarred for life and Kev is rather red faced! When they are not involved in a virtual wanking session, Kev and JudyZ are writing a Star Wars parody. The hero is a chonky, perpetually scared Jedi called Panickin Piewalker. It has a working title of *The Rise of Piewalker*, Nerds...

*

The Monkey is back amongst the occult books. We lost most of them when we blew up my house, but Amazon have been busy delivering and the girls have given him access to their arcane collection. He disappears off to the bedroom for long periods of time and there are strange noises and occasionally inexplicable gusts of icy wind will blow through the house even though all the windows and doors are closed. I popped my head around the door when I knew he was having a break for a Jack, and he has drawn quite a few very complex occult symbols on the walls. I asked if Tony was okay with him redecorating and he looked at me as if it had never occurred to him to ask. He shouted downstairs for Tony to come up and then showed him his handiwork with a, 'That's alright isn't it mate?' Tony made vague accepting noises and wandered off back downstairs shaking his head in bewilderment. Poor sod. Mind you, at least it's not his bedroom. It's going to be a bastard trying to nod off if those markings don't stop glowing and moving about...

12 January

At last, a response to the WhatsApp message!

The Mao Shan sorcerer said he had run out of credit and had to get back to Lhasa before he could top-up his phone. I guess it happens to the best of us...

Anyway, he thinks that they have found a passageway to the cavern of the Monkey God, possibly the lost city of Agharti, and he is very pleased that we are going to join him. I say pleased, it's hard to tell in a WhatsApp message. He hardly shows emotion when you are face to face with him, but I think the clapping hands emoji he added to his message was a sign! He needs to get out of the city as he thinks that they are being followed, possibly by Chinese government agents, but he is going to call us tonight on the sat-phone via JudyZ acting as our high-tech telephone operator. Not sure she would appreciate me calling her that...

Me and The Monkey

*

The call has just come in. We were of course drinking and watching bad TV and we had to put our game faces on, and act all grown up. It was going so well until Kev came in from the kitchen with a new bong he and Tony had crafted out of plastic water bottles, bits of pipe, and a battery powered mini fan. There followed a lot of giggling and a slightly exasperated ancient sorcerer trying to give us the low down on what they had found. There was much talk of high mountain passes, and a long narrow pathway through the rock that led to bronze doors set into the face of the mountain. Last time he had talked to The Monkey he had been told about the portable energy portal and so he knew we could get to him without the ridiculous overland trek that we had originally planned. His voice got quite animated when The Monkey suggested that we open the portal somewhere he thought was safe from prying eyes and then he and his henchmen could join us in stepping through it right up to the bronze doors. Great idea, but we might not be able to get that close – he would explain when we got there. Lots of chattering in Mandarin while we tried not to choke to death on the new bong. He and his Triad buddies will get rid of, one way or another, whoever is tailing them, and they will find a secluded place and send us the GPS coordinates so that we can meet them there. He will send the coordinates via WhatsApp once they know everything is safe, he reckons it will be early afternoon our time tomorrow.

Awesome! We are off to Tibet. I have always wanted to go there, and the chance of facing death at high altitude again is always a big plus...

We said goodbye to the Mao Shan man and just as we were signing off he said, 'Oh, it is rather cold. Bring a jumper.'

For fuck's sake...

13 January

Well, at least we didn't waste our money when we bought parkas, and snow goggles, and long johns. We packed our kit, mostly guns to be fair, along with warm clothes and the tube of Tibetan maps and writing, plus the monkey finger. I am also, of course, taking the spear to this little party.

As we stuffed rucksacks full of gear last night, we had quite a heated debate with Kev. We had told him that he had to sit this one out and he wasn't happy. Eventually, with the help of Aleks and Kris, we managed to convince him that he was needed here with Tony to keep an eye on what was happening and to keep us informed of how everyone was getting on. He grudgingly agreed and The Monkey said it would also give him a chance to work on his magnum opus with JudyZ, that is if he didn't cyber wank himself to death before it was finished. Well, it made the rest of us laugh and he saw the funny side in the end after a few tequilas.

*

Had a chat with the girls when we finally got to bed, in between all the farewell shagging that is. We know how capable and dangerous they are, but The Monkey asked them to please be careful as the military arm of the EID seem to be a bit cocksure of themselves. To be fair, the operators are going to be professional, hard-core fuckers, but those giving the orders seem to be a little up themselves and may be prepared to make 'sacrifices' that don't involve them... Kris smiled and replied that, 'No one knows how the cards will fall, but we have more chance than most of beating the odds,' and then returned to some quite possibly illegal, definitely deviant sexual act. Gotta love em!

*

So, our friendly Shaw Bros kung fu movie reject sorcerer has sent us a WhatsApp message with the coordinates. Our bags are ready, there is lots of firepower, the mousetrap man is firmly tapped to the webbing of The Monkey's tactical vest, and we have warm pants. The Monkey has double checked the tube of manuscripts from Herr Myer, and I have the monkey finger safe and sound in its cigar tube, and after all of these centuries it is going home. Some last farewells and be carefuls and The Monkey is going to open the portal...

14 January

It's been a long, cold day and I smell of Yak. I should explain...

The location we had been given turned out to be a Yak herder's abode near Namtso Lake, someway north of Lhasa. Picturesque, run down, and smelly, but free of Chinese military. They had managed to give their tail the slip on the outskirts of Lhasa, and the Triad boys may have permanently dissuaded another couple of watchers that didn't look Chinese who suddenly appeared on the road north. Well, they say that they dealt, in their own unique fashion with 'someone suspicious', from a distance (I am guessing through a sniper scope) just to be on the safe side. They have issues...

We had to stay inside the hut because of the strong possibility of a drone searching for them. The sorcerer apologised that his powers were a little depleted since the rest of the Green and Red Society, including their Mao Shan possie had gone over to the Illuminati and been massacred during our attack on the facility in Wales. Man, that seems like another lifetime!

So, we spread out the map and documents from the tube and stared at them in the hope that the sorcerer would be able to shed some light. He stroked his long white beard enigmatically and then after a few minutes he just shrugged and said, 'I do not have a clue.' Seems that the documents are in an ancient script that even he can't read, and he wouldn't have any idea who could read it outside of a museum of maybe one of the big monasteries. We had talked about maybe getting Prof Brian's team who translated the last Tibetan manuscripts for us to have a crack at it, but in the end we thought we were maybe skating on thin ice with the Prof's good will and mental health, and we had decided that we would wait until we were 'in country' so to speak. After all, how hard could it be to find someone to read a document that was a couple of thousand years old?

The map, on the other hand, he recognised. He turned to one of the Triad dudes who had gathered around and talked in Mandarin to him while pointing one of his long fingernails at the map. Triad dude, who is called Li Wei, and is the Red Pole or enforcer in charge of this bunch, traced a path through the mountains on the map with a finger that is heavily tattooed, as is the rest of the back of his hand, and I suspect the rest of him! After the conversation had gone back and forth for a while Li Wei nodded and the sorcerer turned to us and indicated, amongst the many markings on the map, what looked like a stylised flame sitting on a lotus flower at the end of a dark line. This, he told us, was the location of the bronze door at the end of the narrow path through the mountains. It matched perfectly, in a hand drawn, ancient way, what they had found. They had GPS coordinates for the path entrance, although they hadn't been able to get coordinates for the door itself because there was too much interference, maybe from the rockfaces around them, or maybe because of something else – none of their high-tech gear had functioned properly near the doors. But that wasn't a major problem as the path was only about half a mile long, and although a tight squeeze in places, it was passable.

One of the Triad boys has been keeping lookout, and he has ducked back inside and rattled off something in Cantonese. The others have quickly closed the shutters on the two small windows and made sure the door is tightly closed. Mr Mao Shan pointed upwards and simply said, 'Drone.' It is early evening and pretty dark already so any light would be a beacon to a drone's cameras, so no going out for fresh air...

The Monkey has suggested that we go somewhere else using the energy portal, maybe a monastery to try and get the documents translated. There seemed to be general agreement but also a lot of trepidation about stepping through a hole in space. I think that there is general shaming of manhood's going on and the macho bravado of ruthless killers has finally kicked in. But where to go? We need somewhere out of the way of prying eyes and also somewhere that might have scholars who can read this ancient script. When in doubt ask Tony and Kev!

*

We opened the portal into Tony's living room where they were slumped on the sofa playing a Doom death match. We gave them their mission and they both ran off and came back with their laptops and began the search. After about five minutes of them being stared at through a hole in the air by a Chinese sorcerer and a bunch of Triad heavies Tony looked up and announced that he had found the perfect place. Kev looked crestfallen but as Tony gave us the lowdown he nodded with grudging respect.

*

We are about to step into Lhuentse Dzong monastery in Bhutan. Far enough away that we shouldn't be traceable by the Chinese drones, and an ancient enough monastery with world renowned translators of ancient Tibetan Buddhist texts. I do hope that we don't give any of the monks a heart attack...

15 January

Word to the wise – If you ever step out of mid-air into a Buddhist monastery don't be surprised if the monks don't fall to the ground and start to worship you... They were surprisingly unfreaked out. I guess, given the wide range of demons and deities that populate Tibetan Buddhist cosmology we were relatively normal looking. As usual, The Monkey drew all the attention, it was almost as if he was expected...

We had stepped through the portal into a wide hall lined with prayer wheels and full of drifting clouds of incense. The hall had been deserted except for one novice monk who was sweeping the floor. His jaw hit his chest and the broom hit the floor as he scampered off shouting. Rather than wander about and freak anyone else out The Monkey closed the portal, and we stood in a group and waited for whoever was going to come running to come running.

Excited voices sounded from somewhere beyond the entrance to the hall along with the patter of sandaled feet. And then the entrance was filled with saffron robes and shaved heads. They filed solemnly into the hall and knelt, bowing their foreheads to the polished floor before sitting back up and staring at us, this was not worship, just a mark of respect. There was much pointing at The Monkey and talking amongst themselves, and then a very old looking monk in a tall saffron hat was escorted into the hall by half a dozen slightly younger monks. None of these knelt although they did bow very deeply.

I couldn't help feeling like a proper fraud. I know The Monkey is a god, but other than having a metal arm there is nothing remotely God like about me, I am more like a second-rate video game character. And as for our companions, apart from the sorcerer, they are all criminal gang members, and we were all armed to the teeth. But that didn't seem to matter, by association we were obviously elevated to a more divine status by the presence of The Monkey. Ah, if only they knew...

*

Our Mao Shan comrade is quite a dab hand with languages. He introduced us in Dzonkha (I asked him afterwards and it's the language of Bhutan – just in case you thought I had had a genius upgrade!), and I think did the usual 'We come in peace, take us to your leader,' stuff. The old fella in the hat answered him and after a brief conversation he bowed again, and we were led to another room where we were invited to sit on raised platforms scattered with cushions. The monks had followed on, containing their excitement, and the novice who had first seen us seemed to have gained celebrity status in their ranks as they stood in the doorway. The Monkey asked the sorcerer what was happening and to our surprise the old chap looked up and beamed a gap-toothed grin and exclaimed, 'Ah! You speak English! Excellent, excellent!'

Neten Rinpoche, the Abbot of the monastery, was born in Tibet but went to university at Cambridge in the early 1950s and studied organic chemistry before deciding to become a monk. His English is very, very good and he does enjoy a chance to use it.

The Abbot asked lots of questions, mainly about good old England to be honest. He has very fond memories of his time there and a very rose-tinted view of the UK. We did our best not to shatter his illusions. I asked him why he didn't seem shocked that a monkey god and his heavily armed gang had just appeared in the monastery. The gap-toothed grin again and he sent one of the monks scurrying off to another room to fetch a rolled-up scroll held in an ornate copper and brass case. While he unrolled it, he explained how a monk had a vision that 'An incarnation of the God from the Mountain' would visit the monastery seeking help. That was three hundred and eighty years ago, but they had never stopped believing that one day it would happen. 'And today is the day!' he beamed at us as he held open the brightly painted scroll.

You know when you get that feeling, a bit like going over the drop on a roller coaster? Or maybe it's that one where you fall in a dream and jerk awake? Yeah, that one...

We looked at the beautifully painted figures on the scroll. A group of dark robed oriental looking men, a tall crimson robed figure with long white hair, a western looking man with armour on his left arm holding a glowing spear, and there, in the centre, a large monkey wreathed in blue fire, wearing a pendant with a monkey face, and holding what looked like an ornate egg whisk. And behind them in the air hovered a wheel of fire. The Monkey blinked hard at the painting and started ferreting around in his belt pouch. After thirty seconds of dragging out a mixture of crap that he has collected he held up an ornate egg whisk. He looked at me and I nodded that I remembered he had picked it up from the ashes of the zombie monk in the ruined castle on the side of a Scottish loch. There were excited mutterings around the room and the Abbot nodded, his old but somehow youthful face beaming at us.

'What is this?' asked The Monkey. I noticed the sorcerer edging away from him slightly as he waved it around.

'It is a vajra, a thunderbolt. By the look of it very old. Where did you get it?' The Abbot inclined his head, looking for all the world like a child at a conjuring show. The Monkey gave him a brief synopsis of our little adventure with the U-boat, and the zombie monk and the Abbot nodded, a little frown crossing his face. 'Yes, there were some who were seduced by the dark forces that were unleashed during that war.' He closed his eyes for a moment and when he opened them again, he was more serious than we had so far seen him. 'Keep that close and keep it safe,' he indicated the vajra in The Monkey's paw. 'You will need that I think before the end.'

That all sounded a bit ominous but before I could ask him what he meant by 'before the end', The Monkey said, 'But what does it do?'

The Abbot told The Monkey to hold the centre of the vajra in his fist and using his god energy to bang it on the floor. Fuck! With a blinding flash that left us all blinking hard the vajra extended out into a very useful looking club. We could all hear thunder rumbling above us and for the first time the Abbot looked a little nervous. The sorcerer had suddenly put a good deal of distance between himself and the now crackling thing in The Monkey's paw. It was obvious that he knew exactly what The Monkey was holding. The Monkey gazed at it in the way he always looks at shiny things, and I was hoping he wouldn't stick his tongue on it because, well, just because he could.

'It is a weapon, oh Incarnated God of the Mountain. The marriage of a diamond and a thunderbolt. And I would say that it is the first time it has been awake for millennia.' The Abbot explained that it could be closed again by The Monkey's will, which he did, although with some reluctance.

*

Food has been brought out for us and the monks are all looking on as we eat. It's a bit like being specimens in an exhibition. We have handed over the documents we need translating to the Abbot and he in turn has handed them to another ancient looking monk who has taken them off to another room to examine them. The Monkey was a little concerned at first about letting them out of his sight, but the Abbot reassured him, and he is sitting and eating in a much more relaxed manner. He seems to trust Neten Rinpoche although he does occasionally touch the pocket of his tactical vest were the vajra now resides 'for easy access'.

We have been telling the Abbot of some of our adventures – leaving out as much violence as possible – although he does seem very accepting of that, as if it is an unalterable consequence of The Monkey's nature. I would agree with that! He has been translating for the other monks and there has been lots of oohs and ahs along with laughter, shock, and confused embarrassment among some of the novices. That was mostly when we told them a little about the girls, they have that effect on men even when they aren't there.

*

The ancient monk who took away the documents has returned. He has copied the text from our originals, translating it into everyday Tibetan, and handed it to the Abbot. The Abbot shook his head and indicated that it should be given to The Monkey who took it from the trembling hand of the old monk with a nod of thanks. He looked at the Tibetan characters on the pages and handed it over to the sorcerer. As he did so I watched the ancient monk whisper something into the Abbot's ear. The Abbot raised his eyebrows almost imperceptibly and then returned his steady gaze to us.

'My scribe tells me that there are things of concern in your documents,' he glanced over to the sorcerer as he spoke. 'Warnings of what may occur if the old God of the Mountain awakens and returns to his full power.' The Monkey looked over at the sorcerer who was scanning the text, his eyes moving in time with his long fingernail. But the Abbot held up his hand and continued, 'What will be will be. You have come to us as in the vision,' he indicated the scroll again with our likenesses painted on it, 'What happens next is for you to decide.'

*

We have been given beds in a large dormitory and while we are on our own the sorcerer is going to tell us what the documents contain...

*

Quite a lot of dire warnings about letting sleeping monkey gods lie, possible end of the world as we know it, keep your hands clear of the moving parts, mind the gap, yada yada yada... Getting so used to portents of doom that they almost seem an afterthought, you know, like the warnings that they put on the start of video games about some people being affected by flickering lights etc. You know it's there but you're going to play anyway.

There are however several warnings about an army that might try to stop us – nothing helpful, just more scary words. No mention of traps though. Does that mean we have watched all those Indiana Jones movies for nothing?

Mr Mao Shan dude is still twiddling his beard and muttering about 'armies of the hidden city'. He can't make any sense of it, and it is bugging him:

> From the arrow path to the sleeping valley, there the God of the Mountain sleeps.
>
> Left incomplete by the armies of the hidden city, never to wake until the end of time.
>
> There will come thunder, and the wheel will no longer turn unless the new God awakes.
>
> Frozen in solitude, one bell will sound forever. Break free and make the wheel turn.

I think I have written that down correctly. The sorcerer has been repeating it enough that I should have it. It is obviously talking about the ancient Monkey God that we are going to find, but the rest is, like most of this kind of thing, a bit enigmatic. Ah well, I guess we will soon find out. We will sleep here tonight and early in the morning open the portal to the end of this 'arrow path' that leads to the bronze doors. Exciting!

16 January

We are getting ready to leave. It is about 5am and still dark but the monks seem to have been up for ages. The Monkey asked the Abbot if there was anything he could do to repay him for his help and hospitality. 'Try not to destroy the universe. Oh, and I would really like some custard creams. I haven't had any since I left Cambridge.' Potentially not the answer we expected! The Monkey opened the energy portal to Tony's house and nipped through into the kitchen returning with two double packs of custard creams. The nerds looked confused and waved at the audience of bald heads and yellow robes before they were gone in a flicker of plasma. The Abbot looks very pleased with his biscuits, The Monkey has promised to send more, and we have shaken hands all round. Time to go...

*

We have made it to the bronze doors. That doesn't really do them justice, they are fucking huge and have ornate mouldings all over them like something from the Tibetan Book of the Dead! Across the centre of the doors is the relief image of a flame sitting on a lotus flower. Something with lots of eyes squats in the centre of the flame. But back to that in a minute as we nearly didn't get this far...

We stepped out of the energy portal onto a wide ledge a few hundred feet up the side of a mountain. It was snowing lightly and still quite dark as the sun was only just poking its lazy face over the mountain peaks behind us. In front of us was a rock wall that reached up and up as far as I could see, but it was split by a narrow crack that disappeared off into darkness. The Triad boys produced massively powerful LED flashlights, and in their beams we could see the path into the mountain made by the crack in the rock. The Monkey thought it would be a good idea to see if he could use his SatNav paws to guide us via the portal to the bronze doors. The sorcerer looked on in fascination as The Monkey held up his paws in front of the split in the mountain and the occult patterns on them glowed and shimmered. After a couple of minutes, he frowned and put his gloves back on. 'Nothing,' he grunted, 'It's as if there is nothing down there.' So, he closed the portal and hooked it onto the back of his pack and then, following Li Wei and one of his men, we started into the darkness.

The flashlights did a fair job of keeping us from tripping over each other, but as we could only walk two abreast that wasn't really an issue. Looking upwards I could see a thin strip of light way up above where the gap opened at the top of the rock. As we walked I kept glancing up, possibly as an antidote to the claustrophobia I was starting to feel, and the strip of light gradually brightened as the sun got higher in the sky that was out there somewhere. I mentioned to The Monkey that it seemed to be taking a long time to cover the half mile that the path supposedly ran for. He turned to the sorcerer who was directly behind us and asked him if they had estimated the distance correctly. His reply was that as technology didn't seem to work so well the closer you get to the bronze doors, they had used an old-fashioned pedometer to work out the distance. 'But there is an anomaly with the passage of time. Not only does technology falter, time itself seems to run at a slower pace.'

After plodding on for what seemed to be more than an hour, although the little phosphorescent hands on my watch assured me it had only been twenty minutes, we began to see a warm glow ahead of us in the gradually dimming beams of the flashlights. Ah good, I thought, and then the first bullet snapped off the rockface above our heads. The man with Li Wei in front of us went down, blood splattering back across us and we all hit the deck as the flashlights went out.

It should have been like shooting fish in a barrel but whoever it was, was shooting into pitch darkness, down a slight incline and the narrow rock walls seemed to be putting their aim off. The lucky misses couldn't last long though and there was a command shouted in what sounded like German and the next burst of fire was full auto. There were cries of pain from just behind me as some of the Triad guys bringing up the rear were hit, and I felt a body fall across my legs. The bulletproof vests that most of them were wearing weren't going to help for much longer. I nudged The Monkey and asked, 'Spear?' but he shook his head and said that in such a confined space it would probably kill us all – fair point. So, what to do? 'Fuck it!' he said.

I hadn't seen The Monkey 'power up' since the fight in Bolivia so it took me a little by surprise that he went from nothing to large burning wrathful entity in the blink of an eye! He barrelled down the passageway bouncing off the walls as bullets snapped around him. There was another shouted command, this time higher pitched and panicky, and the hollow wump of a grenade being launched. I had a moment of expecting the grenade to explode in the middle of us and that to be it, but The Monkey almost casually swatted it back as if he was playing tennis. There was an explosion that illuminated the bronze doors momentarily in fire and a fair bit of screaming. There was more screaming when The Monkey made it to the doors. He had his Glock in one hand and K-BAR in the other and he disappeared off to the right. Figures staggered back across the opening of the passageway and Li Wei cut two down with the H&K SP5K that had been slung across his side. Other bodies went flying across our field of view and then The Monkey's burning form stalked after them.

I pulled my legs out from under the body that had fallen across me and followed Li Wei, who had set off at a run towards the doors. I could hear the other Triad dudes following and I checked that there was one in the chamber of my Sig as we approached the end of the passageway. The narrow path terminated in a large open space which I afterwards realised had eight sides with the bronze doors set in the face directly opposite. As we burst out into the area the first rays of sunshine crept in from above and partially lit the scene of carnage. The Monkey was standing with one foot on the neck of a face down figure while he held up another limp body and wiped blood from his knife on the dead man's jacket. Bodies lay in a heap, bits of bodies were strewn across the ground, and it looked like the only one of our assailants still living was the one who struggled feebly under The Monkey's foot. The Monkey looked over at us and for a moment there was no recognition in his eyes, just a crazed savagery that made my blood run cold, possibly from the realisation that I may have looked like that after a few of our previous battles. He took in some deep breaths and gradually began to return to his normal size, the blue flames flickering out.

Li Wei directed his men to check the bodies and to drag our wounded and dead out of the passageway along with our packs and discarded kit. One of them gingerly handed me the spear and it moaned slightly as if it could smell the blood and death. The Monkey squatted by the man he had pinned down and poked him with the tip of his K-BAR until he turned over. The man was sweating profusely despite it resembling a refrigerator in the octagon chamber. I think the trembling figure was only alive because it looked as if he hadn't been holding a weapon when The Monkey had spoiled their little surprise party. The Monkey holstered his Glock and then flipped his Zippo and relit his cigar. Then, after carefully putting the lighter away he examined the glowing tip of the cigar, asking, 'And you are?'

At first it looked like the man was going to be stubborn, but Li Wei said something to one of his men who reached inside his thick jacket and produced what looked suspiciously like a meat cleaver. The man gave a little whimper, and his eyes went wide as he looked from The Monkey to the cleaver and back again. 'I told them this was a bad idea, that they should have sent an advance party to secure the doors, but they said that the Chinese had disappeared around Lhasa and that there was no way they could get back here, to the doors, before we had gained entry. And no one said anything about you...' He raised his hand feebly to indicate The Monkey, although I think we all knew who he meant. Then he sniffed loudly and wiping a lock of floppy blond hair from his face looked around at the dead with a sort of lost resignation. He spoke good English but with a strong German accent that kept cracking up and I thought he might cry. But instead he nodded over at a body slumped against the huge doors, or at least most of a body. The grenade that The Monkey had batted back had made quite a mess. 'He was in charge. Kaskel, is, was ex-Foreign Legion. He disliked me, but how do you say, the feeling was mutual.'

It seems that Elmar Laske, our chatty German, had been recruited by a shady corporate entity called Zukunft der Erde (roughly translated as Earth Future). Although he claims to have no neo-Nazi sympathies himself, he found out after he had started work at their Berlin headquarters that they were well to the right of the political spectrum. Their corporate mission statement is *To help lift the World out of darkness through the use of modern and ancient science* – so, another bunch of mad bastards who think that they know best... Why didn't he leave? Seems that once you are in it is very difficult to extricate yourself, and besides, they gave him some interesting research work that made it easier to look the other way. And what was this research work that had resulted in him being halfway up the Himalayas with a bunch of hired guns? A lost city and possibly the tomb of an ancient Monkey God – well

Me and The Monkey

there's a surprise...

Our Shaw Bros reject wanted to know how the corporation had found this location. Elmar explained how they have archives of documents that were rescued from the vaults of the Third Reich before the Russians got to Berlin in April 1945. Some of these documents had remained hidden in East Berlin after the wall was built and had only come to light after the wall came down again in 1989. With the end of the Cold War, Zukunft der Erde were able to piece together the fragments of intelligence and rumour that had been collected over the years and corroborate them with official Wehrmacht documents. Then they began the task of translating and decoding the often top secret material. Fast forward and Elmar Laske became the latest scientist to be set to work on the project. His speciality lies in cryptography and how it relates to ancient cultures, a bit like Prof Brian and his colleagues, and he had found several mandalas that when overlayed on each other form a map pointing to our current location. He had jumped at the chance to come here and make a real scientific discovery, but there had been intelligence warning of other interested parties who might also have knowledge of this location. The Monkey wanted to know where this intel had come from, but Elmar didn't know other than that it had come from an 'external source'. They had been tracking the sorcerer and his men using drones and knew that they had found the passage to the bronze doors, and when they had gone back to Lhasa the decision had been made to go in themselves. That is why he had suggested that they send an advance party to secure the site just in case as he isn't a big fan of guns and violence.

Li Wei eyed him suspiciously and asked what we should do with him in a way that suggested a permanent solution. I could see The Monkey weighing that option, but the sorcerer held up a long pointy fingernailed hand and said, 'He could be useful to us.' The Monkey shrugged, Li Wei looked disappointed, and Elmar looked as if he might faint.

We turned our attention to the doors. They must weigh a couple of tonnes each and were undoubtedly cast and then moved here which must have been a titanic undertaking! Off to one side there was a grey metal box with leads coming out of it terminating in a sort of stubby gun. I asked Elmar what it was, as it obviously wasn't part of the décor, and he looked all embarrassed and said it was a plasma cutter. The sorcerer shook his head despairingly, but the rest of us, including the Triad guys when it was translated, all thought it was a sensible idea.

The sorcerer removed his heavy coat and stood in front of the doors raising his arms as he did so. His robes floated around him as if he were suddenly under water, and he began to move his arms in what looked like tai chi movements although his feet did not move. As he did this he chanted, his voice hitting overtones that echoed around us and upwards towards the octagonal patch of sky high above. Another note gradually joined his chanting and I realised that it was a vibration coming back from the metal of the doors. I looked over at The Monkey and he was entranced. Slowly he moved forward until he was between the sorcerer and the doors and then he held out his arms and placed his palms on the bronze. Light radiated outwards from his paws and traced the patterns cast into the metal, particularly the flame design in the centre, it reminded me of the way my arm lights up when it holds the spear, and with an almost imperceptible push, The Monkey opened the doors.

*

I for one wasn't sure what to expect on the other side. The map in our possession only really has the straight path and the flame on the lotus symbol. Most of the rest of the imagery beyond that is faded and ours is not the original, it looks like a copy of a copy, and probably of a copy. The reality is a lot more dramatic than a bit of paper…

There is a valley out in front of us, the path continuing unbending through the middle of it, and there, set amongst green lawns and flowering trees, rise columns of white shining stone scattered up the lower slopes. Those slopes join mountainsides that rise to a dizzying height, the tops obscured by cloud. But regardless of the beauty of the rest, the eye is always drawn to the tall jade green pagoda that sits on a base of black stone blocking the way past the valley's centre. And behind that, glowing in the rays of the sun as it came up above the mountains behind us, is what appears to be a chunk of dark amber-coloured glass, larger even than the pagoda. The glass caught the rays of the sun and shimmered, seeming almost to move like fire, and even at this distance we can see a cloudy, distorted shape within it.

Stepping beyond the doors and the rockface they are set into has meant a drastic change of temperature. It shouldn't have done, but it's hard to argue otherwise when everyone is stripping off layers because they are too hot! We have a bit of a walk ahead of us to get to the pagoda which is where the sorcerer says we need to be, so we are leaving nonessentials here, and fortunately our wounded aren't too serious and are mobile so they can come with us. The Monkey is in high spirits and wants to race. Dickhead…

*

Perhaps it's the thinness of the air or the quality of the light but judging distance here is crap! It has taken us all day to walk to the jade pagoda and we are all knackered. Even The Monkey slowed down to an amble.

We have seen no one, at least no sign of human life. Brightly coloured birds, I think they are finches, have been swooping around in rainbow flocks and landing noisily in the trees. We have also been watched by small foxes and cute creatures that look like short eared rabbits. Li Wei says they are pikas and are all over Tibet. Some of the Triad boys were sighting at them through their rifle scopes but the sorcerer told them to stop. I don't think it was through care for the animals, more likely that he doesn't want blood spilled in the valley unless we must. Anyway, we have enough rations for a couple of days so no need to get all Bear Grylls just yet.

We have set ourselves up in the entrance hall of the pagoda. It is huge and even with the flashlights we aren't going to be doing much exploring now that daylight has almost gone. The sun seemed to travel with us along the straight path running through the valley and now it has crossed behind the pagoda and is dipping past the mountain peaks beyond. Night is falling – rapidly. I asked Mr Mao Shan dude why this place wasn't plastered all over Google Earth and his cryptic answer was, 'Some things are not meant for the eyes of the profane.' I did ask if he had actually met The Monkey and he just wandered off to look at some carvings by the inner doorways in the remaining light.

I think The Monkey is a bit pissed that we didn't have time to get through the pagoda and to the giant volcanic glass structure beyond. But impatient as he is he sees the futility of trying to navigate the pagoda in the dark, and as we can't go around it, we will have to wait for the morning. Elmar seems happy as a pig in shit. The decision has been made not to tie him up as he is not really a physical threat, and as long as he doesn't stray out of view, he is welcome to examine his surroundings while Li Wei's men set up a perimeter and tend to the wounded.

The Monkey is interested in looking at the mandalas that Elmar used to create the location map followed by the neo-Nazi nob heads, so when we have heated and eaten our freeze-dried meals, we will compare notes. Ah, The Monkey has just produced a flask of JD from his backpack, things are looking up…

17 January

Fucking terrifying dreams!

Everyone seems to have had the same nightmare – except The Monkey of course who was still spark out and snoring while the rest of us woke up sweating.

In the dream I was standing looking out of one of the top windows of the pagoda. The sun was shining but a shadow passed along the valley coming towards me. As it touched the white columns along the sides of the valley, they began to rotate and descend into the ground. The flocks of birds settled onto the trees and became very still and quiet as the air became colder, and a palpable sense of dread began to fill me. The columns had fully disappeared and suddenly there was movement from the holes they had left behind. Grey shapes began to bubble out of them, tumbling over each other as they spread outwards. At first, I couldn't tell what they were but then they came clearly into focus. Grey, twitching bodies. Dead bodies. Spilling out of the ground and staggering to their feet to begin running towards the pagoda. Thousands of the dead rushing towards me like a wave. The first ones hit the base of the pagoda and looking down I could see them disappearing inside. A groaning filled the air, and I could hear a crashing and meaty thumping sound inside the building, getting closer, and closer. I tried desperately to move but it was as if my whole body had gone numb. Slowly I seemed to rotate on the spot until I was facing the opposite direction, and there, through the windows on the other side of the pagoda I could see a gigantic face looking directly at me and snarling. A hairy distorted many-eyed demon face surrounded by strings of human skulls and fire. And then out of an opening in the centre of the floor flooded the dead, their teeth bared, and fingers clawed, coming for me...

The Monkey woke up when he heard us all talking and after calling us, 'Noisy bastards!' he asked what was up. We explained as he lit up a cigar and for a change he didn't mock. Elmar pointed behind The Monkey and in a trembling voice asked, 'Was ist das?' From the open top of The Monkey's pack was emanating a throbbing amber glow. He reached inside and took out a pouch through which the light was pulsing and tipped the contents into his paw. The monkey pendant, eyes glowing like malevolent suns stared back at us.

*

We didn't sleep much for the rest of the night – surprisingly... We can see the first grey light of dawn outlining the mountains back in the direction of the bronze doors, and after some coffee and whatever passes for breakfast we are going to see what is on the other side of this pagoda.

*

It has taken us the best part of the morning to weave our way, with many wrong turns, through the maze of passages that make up the ground floor of the pagoda. We have followed one of the mandala sets that Elmar has brough with him. Examining it last night we realised how similar it was to the shape of the pagoda, another octagon, with smaller ones nested on top which can only be the upper floors. The overlaid sets of designs form a sort of flattened map and stripping the layers back has given us a map of the path through the lowest level, although it didn't stop us from getting a bit lost. We have marked the route back by spraying arrows on the floor.

So, now we are in front of another bronze door, once again moulded with the flame and lotus relief that was on the double bronze doors. The sorcerer is getting ready to do his chanty arm swingy thing again, and The Monkey is warming up his paws. The Triad boys are unusually subdued and Elmar has commented more than once on the oppressive atmosphere that seems to have settled over everything. I think we are all feeling it, but of course, we are pressing on regardless. Well, what other choice do we have?

18 January

We are back in Tony's living room, well what's left of us anyway. The Monkey is sitting on the floor nursing a nasty bite wound on his shoulder. I know he heals quickly but it is closing up at an even more unnaturally rapid rate. Dave has reminded us of how fast Tony's gunshot wound healed, so maybe that other dimensional demon blood that we drunkenly licked is still doing its thing? The sorcerer and Li Wei are trying to patch up one of the last remaining Triad foot soldiers, and even with the sorcerer's powers it is going to be hard to sort out a sucking chest wound. And as the sorcerer keeps saying, he's not really a healer, although he looks better than he did a couple of hours ago.

So, how did we get to this busted up state of affairs? Here's how...

*

Once again, the sorcerer's overtone chanting made the bronze door resonate at a similar pitch, and then The Monkey stepped in and put his paws on the bronze surface and the moulded patterns outlined in brilliant glowing lines. With a sort of mechanical wheeze, the door slid upwards into the wall above it, and we were left blinking into the reflected sunlight coming from the gigantic volcanic glass lump before us.

Through the distorting layers of the glass, we could see something locked in its depths. A huge figure slumped over as if it had fallen asleep and, like some prehistoric insect, trapped in amber. We couldn't make out its features, the head was bowed over, but we could make out enough of its form to know that this was the Monkey God.

One of its massive paws was pressed against a glass face as if it had attempted to prevent itself being sealed in this glass tomb, and we could see where one of its fingers was missing. We had left most of our gear by the entrance of the pagoda with the two wounded Triad guys, but The Monkey was wearing the pendant and the light coming from its eyes was almost blinding. He walked forward in a daze and stared up at the figure, 'Big bastard, isn't he,' he said as he touched the surface of the glass.

The sorcerer stood next to him and nodded, 'Yes, he is,' was all he said as he too gazed up at the God of the Mountain. 'Is that me?' The Monkey asked, and the sorcerer nodded again and answered, 'A version of you, yes. You have walked this earth many times before, in many different forms, but you always return to your true form eventually. This was the most extreme version of you. The bringer of chaos, the destroyer, the lord of death.'

'Life goals,' The Monkey quipped.

Ignoring him the sorcerer continued, 'This is what the Illuminati want. It is also what they fear. With your power they could have dominion over the Earth without the need for their complex plans and plots. But they fear your power because it is the essence of chaos, the very thing they want to drive from the world. They want order above all else, the sterility of endless inertia, but they are not sure they could control your power, that you can control your power. So, they will bend science to their will and in the coming storm they intend to remake society in their own image.' He turned and looked hard at The Monkey. 'You can stop them, but you must accept who you are and be able to control your power or you will be more terrible than they could ever be.'

'So, what do I do then?' The Monkey pushed his face against the glass, failing to resist the urge to blow his cheeks out as he peered inside.

'I think you need to make the god whole again. I don't know what will happen next, it could be nothing or it could be the end of us all.'

'There is never any grey area with you lot is there? It's always black or white, yin or yang, cute baby ducks or fucking crocodiles.' The Monkey chewed on his cigar as the pendant blazed on his chest.

'You must walk the line between. You must find the balance. In the stillness of the centre can all things be possible without them destroying each other.' As he spoke the sorcerer's hair and robes did that thing again as if they were being blown by their own air current.

'Yeah, whatever. It still sounds like fortune cookie crap.' The Monkey blew a smoke ring as Mr Mao Shan sighed and his hair and robes went back to obeying gravity. The Monkey looked at me and asked for the monkey finger. I took the cigar tube out of my pocket and emptied the tissue wrapped mummified digit onto his outstretched paw. Blue flame started up across the finger and the fur of his paw burning off the tissue paper, and he held the finger up and looked at the giant paw pressed against the inner surface of the glass. 'There's a bit of a size difference,' he observed, and then shrugged and held the finger up to where the finger had been severed from.

As we stood and watched the finger was slowly drawn into the surface of the glass, growing until it met the giant paw and then it was obvious that it was knitting back together. 'Is that right?' I asked, rather alarmed that we might just have done something rather foolish, which of course would be totally unlike us...

The sorcerer looked on enraptured as the giant Monkey God became whole again. The Monkey had his paw pressed against the surface of the glass again. And the rest of us? Well, we just sort of stood there stupidly gawping. As the minutes ticked by and nothing happened, I am ashamed to say that I started to get a bit bored. It just wasn't the great event that I had pictured.

And then the God of the Mountain raised his head and the glass shattered...

There was that fucking face from our nightmares. Too many eyes set in a huge, distorted simian face. Lips curling back over fangs that looked to be the length of my body. Have I mentioned the eyes? Holy fuck! The thing uncurled itself from its crouched position in a slow stretch. I guess after 700 odd years of being stuck in one position we would all need a good stretch. The Monkey had taken several large steps backwards, as had everyone else, and as the titan emerging from its prison settled its many eyes on him, he slipped out of his tactical vest and handed it to me. He stopped for a moment and reached into a pocket and pulled out the vajra, and then he looked at me with a sort of crazed gleam in his eyes and said, 'Get to the doors. Run!'

Me and The Monkey

If there's one thing I have learned to trust, it's The Monkey's instinct for imminent death and destruction. So, grabbing Elmar by the arm I shouted, 'Come on you bastards!' and ran for the doorway into the pagoda. The bronze door had begun to lower, and we only just made it through. We fumbled for the flashlights and following the trail of arrows we quickly made our way back to the entrance hall. Behind us there was an awful lot of roaring and crashing and the pagoda shook violently. The wounded Triad dudes were already up and pointing guns at anything that moved and Li Wei shouted something at them, and they grabbed their packs and headed for the valley. I gave Elmar my pack to carry as he only had a small day pack, and then grabbed The Monkey's pack with the portal strapped to it and ramming his vest inside it, threw it onto my back and followed the others outside.

At the bottom of the steps leading up to the pagoda I stopped and turned to try to catch a glimpse of what was happening. My mum had a saying, 'It's black over Bill's mum's,' I have no idea where that saying originated but it meant, 'Oh, it's gone rather dark and cloudy over there'. Well, looking upwards towards the jade pagoda I could definitely say, It was black over Bill's mum's! The sky seemed to be boiling as the blackest clouds I have ever seen spread out from the top of the jade finger that pointed at them almost accusingly. Angry flashes of light appeared in it, followed instantly by a massive clap of thunder that made us stagger with its violence.

My attention was wrenched back by panicked voices and Elmar grabbed me by the shoulder and shouted above the echoing thunder, 'Look, look! The columns!'

What about the columns? Oh fuck! The columns were corkscrewing into the ground. We began to run, and my first thought was, *We are never going to make it to the doors. It took us half a day to walk here!* I think that had occurred to the others as well and there was an overwhelming sense of dread as we watched the columns slowly descending.

Running in thin air is a killer, quite literally. We had made it no more than about two miles from the pagoda when we had to stop as we gasped for breath. The sorcerer didn't seem as affected as the rest of us and instead of gripping his knees and trying not to be sick he was turning slowly and surveying our surroundings. The columns were just disappearing into the earth and behind us at the pagoda there were titanic crashes and flashes of light. Through my watery gaze I could see blue flashes of lightning and then the pagoda split in two with a sound like a gigantic bell tolling. For a moment the halves seemed to hang in space before toppling out and down. Revealed behind them was a scene from the craziest Buddhist hell painting – or maybe a Ren and Stimpy cartoon...

Two massive figures wrestled in the black cloud that had come right down to touch the ground. Flames blazed and billowed through the rolling cloud, bursting through, and casting freakish shadows up the sides of the valley. I could see the ancient God of the Mountain flailing around with what looked like burning chains, and The Monkey... The Monkey was vast and terrifying, and in his gigantic paws he held the vajra club, diamond and thunderbolt, grown massive, and he was swinging it like a baseball bat.

I heard more overtone chanting and tore my gaze away from the battling gods. The sorcerer was moving his arms in complex patterns again as he chanted, and a swirling wind began to form around us. The air seemed to thicken, and it was as if we were standing in a semi opaque tube that stretched away down the valley. I opened my mouth to ask what the fuck he was doing when suddenly we were all moving at high speed down this tube of air, like being on the London Underground but without the smell and the drunks. It was as if we were being pushed and falling at the same time, and as we were rushed towards the bronze doors, I got a glimpse of the columns or rather the holes they had descended into. My blood ran cold. The dead were coming...

Then the rushing stopped, we were jerked unceremoniously to a halt, falling over each other. And there was the vomiting. Instant travel sickness. I knelt there with the rest, retching pitifully, and groaning as the sorcerer clung to the bronze mouldings of one of the doors and steadied himself. He shook his head and snapped orders in Cantonese then he looked at me and said, 'Quickly, they are coming!'

Emptying out of the ground, the dead were swarming in a mass of moaning frenzied grey bodies. They seemed oblivious to the apocalyptic battle at the valley's centre, they only had milky white eyes for us. Li Wei formed up the Triad boys with their automatics and shotguns in a line in front of the doors, and despite the occasional fit of retching they started shooting the nearest dead. As the bullets hit them great chunks flew off as if they were made of rotten wood. Grenades were fired and they blew groups of the animated corpses to pieces, but they weren't stopping. The bits lying on the ground continued to twitch and convulse with a parody of life, and even partial corpses, if they still had a head, dragged themselves towards us. The sorcerer had slumped down against the door. Whatever he had done to transport us along the valley had taken its toll and he could do nothing but look on as the valley floor filled with heaving grey shapes.

It's at times like this that you really have to kill some shit, so I unlaced the leather hood covering the spear. The voodoo that the girls had worked on it kept it wet inside and prevented the spear from erupting into flame, but now was not the time for health and safety measures. Now was the time to get medieval!

As I gripped the spear shaft in my metal hand the runes lit up along its length and were mirrored on my arm. The tip of the spear began to glow like the sun, and it howled its killing lust. I could feel it moving in my hand like a living thing and with a roar of insane joy I threw it into the valley at the oncoming army of the dead. Yes, it was a roar of joy. I know it sounds a bit pretentious but the more I use the spear the more it produces a demented battle lust. Don't look at me like that, you're not my mum!

Anyway, the spear ploughed through the oncoming dead, splitting them apart and causing them to burst into flames. Those who weren't dismembered continued to stagger forwards, but now they were on fire. Oh, good, burning undead hordes attacking us! But the flames caught hold of the desiccated dead flesh and rapidly ate through it causing them to collapse into piles of charcoal. The spear rushed onwards finding more victims ahead and I quickly realised that we would be overrun before it turned and headed back. A thought hit me (shut up, it's not that unusual) and I held up my left hand and focused on the spear. The runic markings on my metal arm began to pulse and I found that if I turned my hand, I could direct the flight of the spear. That was more like it! I made it do a 180 and head back towards us, nudging it over into a dense mass of heaving grey bodies and it was like watching a truck plough into the back of a crowd.

Li Wei had spotted the effect that the fire was having on the zombie horde and shouted to his men, and they began to lob phosphor grenades. White explosions erupted and more burning dead gradually collapsed into smouldering heaps. Out of the corner of my eye I saw a very pale Elmar hoist up an AA-12 automatic shotgun that must have been amongst the kit brought in by the German mercenaries and left in the octagon chamber beyond the doors. He planted his feet and opened fire only to be knocked back against the door jamb. I shouted for him to brace against the door, and he nodded and fired again, a look of grim determination on his ashen face. AA-12s, as I know from our little adventure into Area 51, do a lot of damage very quickly. It was obvious that Elmar had next to no experience with a gun but to be honest, with a gun like that and so many targets he didn't need to be a marksman. Chunks of grey were flying in all directions, and it was blowing some of them in half, but it was clear that we were going to be overwhelmed by the sheer numbers of the dead and the fact that they just kept on coming.

A decision was made, and we pulled back into the doorway, dragging the heavy bronze doors with us to narrow the field of attack. I swept the spear across the nearest zombies but more took their place almost immediately. As I stared down into the valley at the struggle still raging, it occurred to me that until The Monkey had defeated the God of the Mountain, we couldn't close the bronze doors and escape along the path through the mountain to get to the place where we could use the portal. Unless the sorcerer could close the doors, and he was still a mess from transporting us up the valley, only The Monkey could seal them shut and stop this army of the dead from escaping into the outside world. I had to make a choice, and so I summoned the spear back to me. It snapped into my hand, and I took a deep breath and gathered all my concentration as I hurled it towards the giants battling above the remains of the jade pagoda.

I watched the spear burning through the air like a shooting star and I prayed to whoever would listen that I didn't hit the wrong monkey god. There was a moment, like an indrawn breath, when everything seemed to be silent as the spear entered the black clouds and struck one of the gigantic figures. A roar of pain and anger reverberated from the valley walls, louder even than the thunder and gun fire, and then I saw the immense vajra club swing down and strike the god who the spear had hit. Again and again the club rose and fell pounding away like an angry butcher, lightning lashing as it struck. And then... Only one colossus was standing, and he strode from the boiling clouds and dust. The Monkey.

Me and The Monkey

The dead were piling up at the doorway as they scrambled over each other to get at us. I called the spear back and it came screaming through them but a little too late. We would be overwhelmed because there didn't seem to be an end to the dead who just kept spilling out of the earth. We tried to drag the doors closer together but three of the Triad guys were grabbed and dragged through the opening to be torn to pieces with rotten teeth and clawing fingers. I stood in the centre and used the spear like a scythe, slashing from side to side and creating a mound of burning dead that momentarily kept the others back. But the pile of bodies collapsed and more of the horde took their place. We couldn't run, the narrow path would just mean we were dragged down one by one.

It's funny how time seems to slow when you are at crucial moments. Li Wei was holding up one of his men who had been stabbed in the chest with what looked like an arm bone, with the other hand he fired his H&K SP5K into the twisted faces that loomed between the doors. Elmar had run out of shells for the AA-12 and was using it like a club to hit anything in front of him. The sorcerer had dragged another of Li Wei's men away from the door; he had been slammed against the bronze and struck his head hard. 'So, this is it,' I thought. 'Ripped to bits by what look like animated, past their sell-by date bits of beef jerky.' I think I probably smiled at my own stupidity, I usually do, and as I was probably grinning foolishly as a massive simian head reared up behind the zombies pressing through the gap in the doorway.

I had to blink a couple of times to make sure that it was The Monkey and not the other fucker. The lack of a bazillion eyes convinced me it was the right one and I lowered the spear I had instinctively raised to throw into the snarling mush. A ripple spread through the dead by the door and then they were swept to one side as a diamond-tipped club the size of a bus swatted them away. The Monkey wasn't having it all his own way. The dead were swarming over him like fleas, and he rubbed one hand across his body to get them off. His tail was in constant motion in an attempt to free himself from the bastards, and he stepped in front of the doors and turned to face the hordes in the valley. Thunder roared as he hammered them with the club and lightning flashed out reducing many to ash. It looked as if they were the failsafe because in the end there were that many of them that they may eventually drag down even a God, so big and bad or not, The Monkey needed to get his hairy arse out of there...

It was clear that he couldn't get through the door in his god-engorged state. He would have to shrink, quite a bit, or be trapped in the valley. As he went from King Kong to NBA Basketball player size, we did our best to keep the dead away from him. He kept swinging the club, which reduced in size with him but didn't seem to lose any of its violent charms. The doors are around twenty feet high and so as soon as he had shrunk to less than that he forced his way between the partially closed bronze slabs, and gripping the mouldings began to drag them shut. I used the spear to chop up anything that tried to get through the gap and the fire disintegrated the bodies that lay across the threshold. Slowly the doors closed on the valley and the dead, and we sank down gasping for breath. Elmar was sobbing as he cradled the shotgun. Li Wei looked up and started laughing, it was infectious and after a while we were all laughing – maybe a little hysterically, and even Elmar managed a smile. The Monkey stood there, drooped shoulders moving up and down in time with his slowly relaxing breathing, gradually returning to something more like his normal size. He asked me where his vest was, and I rooted it out of the pack and gave it to him. After putting it on he held the vajra up in front of him and closed his eyes, and it shrank back down to the ornate egg whisk once again. Into the vest pocket it went and out of another came a cigar and Zippo. I noticed as he lit the cigar that his paws were shaking, and he looked up at me as if challenging me to say something. I just smiled and squeezed his shoulder. That had the unexpected result of him dropping to one knee with a loud groan and a, 'Fuck's sake!' There were large bite wounds on his shoulder which I hadn't noticed with all the general gore, blue flame, and Alice in Wonderland size changing. Li Wei tossed over a bag of medical supplies that he had been using to try to stop the bleeding of his man with the chest wound, and I found some Quick Clot gauze and placed it on The Monkey's shoulder and strapped it in place with the webbing of his vest.

The sorcerer had staggered to his feet and was standing in front of the doors, his hands against the bronze. There was a continuous vibration coming from the metal and it took a moment to realise that it was the dead hammering against the other side. 'They must never open these doors,' he whispered, looking back at us.

'No shit, Sherlock,' I heard The Monkey mutter as he tested his shoulder, wincing through a cloud of cigar smoke. Elmar dragged over the plasma cutter that his crew had brought to try to open the doors and I put the hood back on the spear and gave it to The Monkey to hang onto and then went to help him. Did he think it would work? Well, he knew it would melt the surface of the bronze so if we could weld the two halves together it should stop the dead fuckers getting through (my words, not his).

After a few minutes there was a lot of molten metal and a very unsightly weld line from above head height down to the ground. It wasn't pretty but it looked like it would do the job. The sorcerer gave some orders in Mandarin, and Li Wei and his last uninjured man began to set charges around the octagon walls opposite the door, then they disappeared into the narrow path between the rockfaces and set charges there as well. I looked at The Monkey, he was hurting, and he simply said, 'It all has to be sealed.' So, we gathered our stuff, and picked up our wounded, and squeezed our way along the narrow path.

I kept looking behind me half expecting the doors to crash open and a frenzied pack of zombies to pile into the gap behind us and tear us into little pieces, but there was nothing but the sound of them beating on the doors and that got fainter as we got further away.

After about thirty minutes of us dragging our battered arses along we came to the split in the mountain face and then out onto the snow-covered ledge and freezing bastard cold! The Monkey got me to open the portal and then he tuned it in to Tony's house and one by one we stepped or were carried through. Li Wei was the last apart from The Monkey and just before he came through, he handed the detonator to The Monkey. We watched from the safety of Slough as The Monkey triggered the explosions and then jumped through the energy portal dragging it with him. Our last view of the passageway was lit by balls of fire and then it was gone.

*

The wounded Triad guy has stabilised, seems the sorcerer is a bit of a healer after all. And on the subject of him, I have asked him why the fuck he made us walk all that way down the valley to the pagoda when he could have just whizzed us there like he did on the way back. His response was partially in Mandarin, and I think may have been very offensive, but he has delicately explained that he did that in an emergency and almost wiped himself out doing it. Oh, and had I forgotten the vomiting? Okay, fair point...

What to do with Elmar? He was freaked out by the energy portal, it was the last straw after a very heavy day, and I more or less threw him through it. He is in a state of shell shock and Kev has only just managed to pry the AA-12 out of his grip. Kev does like an AA-12, his eyes lit up when he saw it. I think Elmar gets a pass from us all after stepping up at the doors, even though he was working with the enemy. Tony seems to have taken a shine to him and is trying to coax him with nerd stuff. Good for him.

Kev has ordered a delivery of Chinese and pizza, and The Monkey is demanding booze and drugs. The sorcerer wants to talk to him about what happened, but The Monkey isn't having any of it, at least not until he has anesthetised himself and probably the rest of us...

19 January

Slept until around mid-day. I think the Jack, beer, and skunk, as well as the exhaustion of having been in a life-or-death fight helped...

As we breakfasted on cold pizza and prawn balls the sorcerer asked The Monkey what had happened down in the valley. 'There was a massive fight, and I almost got my arse handed to me on a plate,' was the grunted answer. The sorcerer gave a long sigh and tried again. What exactly had happened? The Monkey poured himself a Jack to go with his coffee and sat back in the chair. For a moment I didn't think that he was going to answer, he just shovelled forkfuls of Singapore fried rice into his mouth between sips of Old No 7, then he put down his fork and rubbed at the almost healed wound on his shoulder.

'When the finger merged back with that googly-eyed dickhead, I saw a dark shadow descend from the sky and settle inside the glass. Then that fucking thing raised its head and looked straight at me. I knew right then that we were one and the same thing but that only one version of us could leave the valley, and my friend, it was damn well not going to be him! That's when I told you to go. I knew it was going to get messy and I didn't want to have to watch where I was standing in case I crushed you lot.' He stopped and chewed on a prawn ball, dipping it in sweet and sour sauce from the little polystyrene pot. 'I could also feel something stirring underground, and after all of your bad dreams I had a feeling that something bad was on the way up. Anyway, me and the big bastard started on each other. I smacked the vajra on the ground and it turned into that wicked club while that ancient fucked up version of me had these burning chains with hooks on them. We seemed to be fighting forever in this flashing black mist. Then the bastard sunk his teeth into my shoulder and dragged me down. That was when there was an explosion, like the sun had appeared and gone supernova. Something tore through him like a comet, and he let me go. I realised that this knobber,' indicating me of course, 'had chucked the spear.' He smiled, a savage smile. 'It gave me a chance to get back up, and I knew that if he got hold of me again, I wasn't coming home. So, I battered his ugly bug-eyed fucking head in with the club and didn't stop until it was mush.' He popped another prawn ball into his mouth and then grabbed a slice of pizza, 'Man, I am hungry!' Then he looked at the sorcerer, all humour leaving his eyes. 'That dark shadow – it left the God of the Mountain and I felt it enter me, like it was sucked through the pores of my skin.' He paused, you could have heard a pin drop, and then he belched loudly and said, 'Ah well,' and crammed a triangle of meat feast pizza into his face.

I wanted to know where all those zombie things had come from. Mao Shan man had said that we might find the lost city of Agharti, and now he believes that it is the hidden city mentioned in the Tibetan texts we had translated, and that the dead came from there. So, it was underground then? Yes, he believes that beneath the valley, in the heart of the mountain is a city of the dead, a necropolis that is thousands of years old. The dead were waiting in the darkness to be released and the waking of the ancient Monkey God was their cue. Perhaps it was some end of the world scenario or maybe they were there to stop the Monkey God from escaping his prison. Who knows? But they nearly did for us and if he hadn't managed to get out of the valley they may well have done for The Monkey. Like soldier ants, eventually sheer numbers would have won out over brute strength.

*

The wounded Triad dude is stable but needs proper medical assistance, so The Monkey is going to open the portal to their base in China and get them home. Li Wei is a good guy to have on your side in a fight, and I think it's not the last we will see of him. The sorcerer has said he will be in touch again soon and has cautioned The Monkey against going God Mode if he can help it. He seems to think that it could be 'too unpredictable'. Like that's not The Monkey's middle name...

*

Our Chinese friends are back at their base now, and we seem to have won a German!

Elmar and Tony have hit it off big style, I would even say that a bromance is in the offing. Nice to see Tony smiling, and you never know, Elmar might just stop shaking at some point...

Kev filled us in on the news from the girls. The attack on the Greenland base has been moved up due to some intel gained by the EID. So, Aleks and Kris are at some staging area with Caroline, the EID techs, and the British Army's finest stormtroopers. That's as much as they could let him know apparently.

It's a shame the girls missed out on Tibet; they would have enjoyed the floor show. Although the 'all you can eat' buffet might have been too much for even them! Pity we didn't think – could have brought them back a doggy bag...

20 January

Today we are mostly indulging in some R&R. Not R&B, that would be a whole different story...

The Monkey's shoulder wound has just about closed. Mad healing skills to go on the long list of mad things associated with him! I asked him what it was like to be that massive and godish, and he just puffed on his cigar and said, 'Was alright.' Fuck off with your 'alright'! 'Nah, it was epic,' he admitted with a broad grin. 'The power was mental. I literally felt as if I could lift up a planet. It was like my entire body had a hard on.' I said that I had wondered what that other little bit had been in the shadows cast by the lightning. He just laughed and called me a pervert for looking. We are now playing a drinking game involving tequila, I'm not sure if there are any rules so I guess it's last man standing...

*

We ran out of tequila. We are having to drink beer as the shopping delivery hasn't arrived yet with new supplies of JD. Kev has a stupid look on his face. He has spent most of the morning in his room talking to JudyZ, I fear he may go blind. As for Tony, well he seems quite smitten with Elmar, and it appears to be reciprocated, who would have thought? I asked Elmar if he had any family or anyone he should be contacting, and did he want The Monkey to drop him off anywhere via the energy portal. But he seems quite happy to stay here, and his tequila-slurred back story seems to involve a freak bobsleigh accident leaving him as an orphan. How very continental!

Ah, the doorbell! Groceries, by that I mostly mean booze, delivered straight to your door. What a time to be alive!

21 January

Just had a quick chat with Aleks. They are about to use the EID energy portals to assault the Greenland base. The Monkey wanted to know if they needed us to tag along (sweet, you see he does care) but she says they will be fine although they aren't guaranteeing the safety of anyone else other than Caroline. Fair enough. They both sent kisses and said they would see us soon. They have questions about Tibet; seems that they had some interesting dreams while we were there… The Monkey signed off by saying that if they needed help, they should let JudyZ know and we would come running.

*

Got a chance to have a proper chat with Elmar and ask about Zukunft der Erde and their intentions. He said that he was kept out of most of the corporate goings on as he was just employed as a scientific researcher. He began to suspect that their sympathies were a bit right wing when his induction involved rather a lot of excuses as to why Hitler wasn't such a bad guy – more misunderstood. And then there was some stuff which Elmar says was getting into the realms of Holocaust denial. He had made noises about leaving, other job offers etc etc, but the HR department had made it very plain that accidents seem to happen to those who just up and leave the company.

The Monkey stopped mid drink, very unusual, and with narrowed eyes asked if Zukunft der Erde were responsible for the death of Herr Myer. Elmar looked uneasy and said that he had heard jokes being made about a 'death' in Amsterdam where the victim was left to look like it was a self-abuse sex act gone wrong. He didn't know anything else about it but from the description and particularly the knowledge that Herr Myer had shared he thought it was highly likely to be the same incident.

The Monkey disappeared and came back with the energy portal. He fired it up and said he would be, 'Back in a min.' He stepped through and shortly was handing me Claymore mines through the portal. I poked my head through and could see that he was in what looked like an MOD weapons store. After he had borrowed a dozen Claymores he came back through and stood there with a thinking look on his face. An evil smile spread across said face and he refocused the portal and dragged me through with him. We were in a basement which I soon realised was in a hospital, and in front of us were large oxygen cylinders. Between us we wrestled three of them through the portal and then he closed it again. Elmar looked at me and I shook my head.

Twenty minutes later and The Monkey had gaffa-taped four Claymores to each cylinder. Okay, nasty big bombs. What now?

Well, now The Monkey asked Elmar for the headquarters address of Zukunft der Erde, and after getting Tony to do an internet search he got the GPS coordinates. Ah, okay…

Kev walked in just as The Monkey was opening the energy portal to the Berlin HQ coordinates. The, 'What the fuck?' he silently mouthed was ignored by The Monkey who recruited the four of us to heave the, what can only be described as massive pipe bombs, through the portal. He looked at us with the sort of look that Lieutenant Colonel William Kilgore gives his men in *Apocalypse Now* as he calls in the napalm, and as he closed the portal, he pressed the remote trigger for the Claymores. There was a fireball just before the portal span into black nothingness and he beamed at us and went to get a bottle of Jack.

*

News reports of a colossal explosion in Berlin that has destroyed the headquarters building of a secretive research company. Quite a few lives lost, and fire crews are trying to contain the blaze. Footage on Sky News of a high-rise building, or what is left of it, and the adjacent lower-level buildings on fire.

The Monkey has raised a toast, 'For Herr Myer, may you be drinking in Valhalla. Payback is a bitch, mutha fucker!'

22 January

Last night I dreamt that Kris got into bed with me. I asked her when they had got back, and why everything smelled of cordite and burning flesh. She just smiled and said, 'In the morning,' and went to sleep…

Woke up this morning to find Kris wrapped around me and Aleks asleep in bed with The Monkey. There is still a strong smell of cordite, but the burning flesh smell is much fainter. So, not a dream then… I slipped out of the tangle of limbs and woke The Monkey. The girls were dead to the world, so we were going to sneak out of the room, but on the way out The Monkey picked up some of their clothes that were dropped on the floor. They fell to bits in his fingers, and we took the remains out onto the landing to investigate. They were charred as if they had been on fire. Fuck! We went back into the bedroom and turned on the light. Both girls are burned pretty badly. I had a minor panic with thoughts of fetching tubes of Savlon or something vaguely medical running through my head. Aleks partially opened her eyes, one side of her face is scorched, and whispered, 'It's okay. Let us sleep.' We turned out the light and came downstairs.

*

In the kitchen there is an energy portal, not ours, propped against the sink. There is also a pile of thawing out food on the floor by the freezer. I opened the lid and there is a badly charred and now frozen clone, another one, jammed down amongst the ice pops and frozen peas that never made it out. There are some quite significant chunks missing from fleshy areas of the body, no points for guessing who has had those!

There is a note stuck on the energy portal – MAY HAVE A TRACKER. GET KEV AND TONY TO CHECK XX. Ah, bollocks! The Monkey has legged it upstairs to wake the nerds…

*

Kev and Tony immediately put the portal into their security net thingy and have now blocked and removed the tracker and are super intrigued by the portal control chips. It is one of the Brightstorm ones, not an EID knock off, so we must hope that whatever went down at the Greenland base does not result in Illuminati stormtroopers materialising in Tony's living room. We have already had to blow my house up when they followed us through the black hole into Cornwall, it would be a shame to have to do it again…

We are going to take it in turns to stand guard just in case. By stand guard I mean sit and watch TV while holding the AA-12 until it is time to pass it on to the next on the list. Elmar is a bit bemused, but after explaining the situation to him he has agreed to join in. Tony can't stop smiling, ah, love…

*

The Monkey nipped out to get some supplies. He needed cigars and took a stroll to the all-night garage, and while he was out, he paid a visit to the wannabe roadman he gets his mad skunk from and procured a bag. As he was leaving, he saw a car with blacked out windows turn up, so he waited in the shadows and watched. Turned out to be some serious gangster and his heavies who was delivering a load of gear to skunk boy. We now have quite a bit of coke, and a couple of bags of pills. Gangster and heavies will be in hospital for a while, and skunk boy is so scared of The Monkey that he won't be telling tales, even if he knew where to find him.

Well, at least we shouldn't have any trouble staying awake now. It's not exactly *Scarface*, but there is more than enough to go round, the only problem we might have is avoiding shooting each other in a fit of over exuberance…

23 January

We didn't take it in turns to stand watch. No point really as we were all buzzing that much we couldn't sleep. So we played a really intense game of Monopoly which was on the verge of turning violent until Kev fetched the electro bong that he and Tony had invented, and we smoked quite a bit of skunk which took the edge off. We called the game a draw and put the TV on. I found the season 3 box set of *Sons of Anarchy* and we settled down to watch. Kev loves the AA-12 so we let him cuddle that – just in case. And we had chocolate Hobnobs…

*

The girls have woken up and come downstairs. They don't look like BBQ meat anymore, just a bit scorched. They laughed at us because we all look so battered from a sleepless night of overindulgence, and then they went to the freezer for a snack. They have promised to tell us what happened in Greenland when they have had some sustenance. I can hear the electric carving knife going, and the microwave, and there is a very odd smell…

*

The girls came back into the living room and squeezed onto the sofa between me and The Monkey. They look considerably better after eating, if a little dishevelled. We passed them large glasses of Jack. I looked over at Elmar, I had forgotten he was new to all of this. His eyes were very wide while he kept having to close his mouth. He said something in German and the girls both fixed on him as if it was the first time they had realised he was in the room. He sank back a bit and Tony hugged him protectively. How cute. I introduced Elmar to the girls and explained how we had met at which point it seemed like the right thing to tell them of our adventure. So, between us we gave them the whole crazy tale.

They were duly impressed and, as we suspected they would be, fascinated by the thought of that many dead. Although they said that from the description they would be 'a bit tough', quite a long way past their best by date...

They gave Elmar the once over and seemed to immediately take a liking to him. Kris said something to him in German and he blushed. Tony looked at him and he whispered into his ear and then Tony really blushed! Kris and Aleks laughed at their embarrassment and held out their glasses for more booze. The rest of us just sat there none the wiser and waited for the 'meet the new housemate' session to finish so that we could find out what had happened to them.

Right, their turn...

At the EID staging post on the outskirts of London two platoons of troops, a couple of dozen weaponised techies, and an unspecified number of spec ops warriors had been gathered. Aleks and Kris were going in with Caroline, one group of technicians, and two spec ops units, while the rest were dropped into and around the base to deal with the armed opposition that was expected.

Caroline had expressed concerns at the briefing the day before about the possibility of there being some of the Illuminati super soldiers at the base. The military, who had decided that they were in charge, had made lots of, 'Well, if there are then we will just deal with them, won't we', noises. Aleks and Kris had tried to explain that they had seen these souped-up clones in action and that they weren't to be taken lightly, but they were ignored by macho dickheads who didn't see why the girls where there in the first place.

The EID energy portals were set up and tuned in, and then opened simultaneously. Through they went, although the girls used their voodoo skills to make sure their party was as invisible as possible, something they couldn't do for all the other units.

Their portal was set to open in the area of the cells that Caroline had been held in, although the coordinates had been tweaked to put them into the corridor rather than a locked room. So, they stepped out into an empty corridor that ran the length of the holding cells. Aleks and Kris did their thing, made the security cameras go haywire, and at the same time did that cloaking thing they are so good at, and then their party set off in search of the base labs. There were fourteen of them in total: Caroline, Aleks and Kris, three EID boffins, and two, four-man SAS teams that Commander Greyling had assigned to them, although one of the SAS teams would be peeling off to help suppress resistance at the main doors. Other members of EID were dispersed amongst the other attack units so that they could advise on anything 'unusual' that was discovered and loot any shiny Illuminati/Brightstorm bling that was worth having.

Caroline's unit made it out of the cell area and into a large vehicle repair bay without any contact. They could hear over their comms that the other units had hit the ground running and the sound of small arms fire began to intensify. What looked like a service corridor led off from the repair bay in the direction of the main doors and with a nod the designated SAS team headed off at speed in that direction.

Then there was a huge explosion some way off in the base and comms chatter confirmed that they had blown the main doors to the bunker. That would mean the units who had stepped through the portals on the base's perimeter could get inside and join the party. Well, that was the theory anyway, but as some Prussian General once said, 'No battle plan ever survives contact with the enemy'...

There was suddenly a lot of screaming over the comms and the firefight stepped up a notch. One of the SAS boys told Caroline that they could hear M134 gatling guns, so resistance was far from light.

As they exited the repair bay, they came to a metal staircase leading up to the next level. A couple of guards appeared at the top of the stairs but were quickly dispatched with silenced handguns, and then they were up into a long corridor with technical workshops and labs on either side.

As they worked their way along the row, the Illuminati scientists either surrendered or made a hasty exit through other doors. Some of them had quite obviously been in the process of destroying computer hard drives when they had guns shoved into their faces. They were gradually rounded up and locked in a storeroom except for the most senior one (identified by his lanyard – they are suckers for hierarchy), who was then frogmarched from room to room as the EID techs went about collecting anything of interest.

The gunfight going on in and around the rest of the base had quieted down somewhat and our side seemed to be getting the upper hand. There were reports over comms that the exterior of the base was secure and so was the main entrance. Units were working deeper into the complex and had managed to take out the M134s.

The team entered a large lab where there were rows and rows of portable energy portals, a new version, and the EID techs immediately had a bit of an orgasm over the new computer control chips that were on display in a couple of open service panels. They began collecting them up, sending them back through their own portal to the UK staging area. That was when someone turned on a massive fan and threw a tonne of shite at it...

Comms went wild with shouted warnings and requests for back-up. There was another almighty explosion which caused the lights to go out and the emergency lighting to kick in. Aleks and Kris immediately got very bad vibes, and moments later a clone soldier stepped through an energy portal at the far end of the lab. It took out two of the SAS team in short order and everyone else took cover and opened fire on it. Aleks recognised the same sort of body armour that the one in Bolivia had been wearing and knew they were in trouble. She and Kris did that thing they do that makes the air go thick so it was as if the clone was moving underwater. It only bought them moments, but they were able to get back out to the corridor before it came crashing through their magic like an angry bull. Their captive scientist ran like fuck through a side door, and they saw him bounce off a door frame and then disappear into the complex, shouting frantically. The scientists who had escaped when they had first breached the labs had obviously been able to alert the guards fighting in the main complex and through the open door bundled a crowd of armed men and women. They started firing and Kris and Aleks dragged the others into cover in another lab. The two remaining SAS boys lobbed grenades and laid down covering fire.

And then the guards ceased fire as the clone came charging through the lab doorway Caroline's team had just deserted and into their line of fire. The automatic weapon it was using ripped up the partition walls and blew out the lab windows. As it killed the SAS troopers Caroline made the call that they should escape through the energy portal. One of her techs opened it to the staging area and they jumped through, but it seems they haven't practised with the portals and didn't immediately close it. We know how quick the clones are so what came next wasn't too much of a surprise.

Super soldier clone came straight through the portal after them. Big time fuck up! It killed two of the techs before they could even react and once again Aleks and Kris pushed Caroline and the remaining tech into cover behind a stack of crates. The reserve units at the staging area took a few seconds to register what was going on and then they opened up on the clone and absolute fucking chaos ensued as more energy portals opened up and more of the souped-up bastards came through. Bloodbath is a standard newspaper cliché but when the girls use it you know it must have been bad.

They quickly realised that the super clones were only after one thing, and it wasn't casual sex. They wanted the energy portals that had been appropriated from the lab and were now heaped in the centre of the staging area. While some kept up the remorseless massacre the others carried the portals back to wherever the clones had come from.

Aleks spotted a box of phosphor grenades and lobbed several into the midst of the clones. These had much more of an effect. The super soldiers kept firing but now they were on fire, and it was only a matter of time before they were too severely compromised to continue fighting at full capacity. As they dropped, the one that had followed

Caroline's unit headed straight for them stripping burning body armour off as it came. It crashed into the crates and managed to ignite them as it sought to batter its way through. Caroline's last remaining tech was still holding an energy portal taken from the Greenland base and Kris grabbed it and ran to the end of the stack of crates. Aleks grabbed the shocked Caroline and shouted at her to use the EID energy portal and get out of there, and then she went to help her sister.

I have seen the girls fight up close and personal and they do not take prisoners. The clone followed Kris and the energy portal. It had run out of ammo but that makes little difference to these killing machines and it closed in with a big old combat blade. Aleks jumped onto its back and Kris hit it from the front, it was still on fire and within moments they all were. It had obviously been weakened by the fire and the girls used their knives to take out its tendons and bring it down to the ground. Then Aleks knelt on its back and emptied the clip of her Desert Eagle into its skull. She said that even then they were amazed at how, as they watched, its tissues were trying to regenerate, and so they cut off its head.

A quick look around showed them that Caroline and tech were just disappearing and that the reserve units had managed to contain the last few clones who were jumping back through their own windows in space. So the girls did some quick and dirty voodoo to confuse whatever tracking devices were on the portal they had acquired and then they opened it up to Tony's living room, and came home, dragging the clone corpse with them.

*

That explains their scorched state. But why bring back the clone? Well, it seems that they had a little taste of the last one we inadvertently brought back (I knew I had seen bite marks), and the flesh of these super soldier clones has some rather special properties which the girls would like to partake of. How could we possibly object? As for the new energy portal, or rather the control chips, well that is apparently something else. Our resident nerds are champing at the bit to have a close look and now that we have heard the background story, they feel free to run off and do science things.

We have all warned them not to reactivate the tracker accidentally. The girls voodoo kept us safe when they first got back but we don't want super troopers materialising in the kitchen because Kev gets a bit, 'I wonder what this does?' They have given us their best, 'You know nothing, John Snow,' looks and have departed to their makeshift laboratory with the portal and a rather bemused Elmar.

We shall administer healing JD, chocolate cake, bad TV, and hugs, to speed up the healing of our femme fatales...

24 January

Very interesting… I say that even though I don't have a clue what they are getting excited about because, well, it does sound interesting!

The nerds worked through the night on the Illuminati energy portal control chips. I think they may have been aided by the last of the Columbian marching powder, I know that they were definitely aided by JudyZ, who seems if anything even more excited than Kev and Tony. Elmar is helping, but as computers aren't really his field of expertise, he isn't as ecstatic as the others.

It would appear that Brightstorm (we are guessing it is them) have created a new type of computer chip that had previously only been a theoretical possibility. In fact, JudyZ has just told us that she wrote a thesis at uni on the possibly implications of such a chip and the theory behind producing one. Tony's statement that, 'This defies physics', made even us technologically challenged sorts prick our ears up. There was talk of something called 'Time Crystals', and at that point we were asked to leave the room as The Monkey started making sci-fi noises and I must admit I couldn't help joining in.

*

Well, we have left them to it and are awaiting an update at some point when they have stopped shouting techno babble at each other.

The girls, who are looking much better after another frozen clone snack, are keen for us to contact Caroline and check that she is okay. So, The Monkey has dug out the sat-phone and we are waiting for her to answer…

*

Seems that they, meaning the military lot, are calling the Greenland attack a success. There are obviously some odd metrics being used! They seem to be measuring success by the fact that not all their men died, and they managed to take control of the base. Caroline thought this was very funny, particularly as someone had managed to set off some sort of self-destruct protocol and most of the base blew up in their faces. Still, the top brass declared it a victory so it must be true.

Caroline and her last team member had managed to use their portal to escape to EID's Whitehall headquarters, and some of the other EID techs who were with the other units found their way there as well. One of them had even carried back a handful of unusual computer chips that he had found just before one of the super soldiers appeared and started killing everyone. He had chosen survival over valour and had opened an energy portal to the research floor at EID, stepped through and closed it after him.

None of us said anything about the chips other than to make interested noises, we like Caroline but it's hard to show all your cards when secretive cabals keep trying to fuck you up! Aleks did tell her to make sure that they weren't fitted with trackers, and Caroline said that they have some sort of interference loop set up around the research floor which prevents unauthorised signals getting in or out.

Caroline was pleased that the girls were okay. The last time she had seen them they were on fire, and I think she was amazed that they sounded so chipper. They just laughed it off and said that it had looked worse than it was. Caroline thanked them for their help saying that it would have gone badly for her team without their assistance, and then she said that she would be in touch as Commander Greyling and the suit from MI6 wanted to have a meeting regarding 'next steps'. We could almost hear her rolling her eyes.

*

The Monkey wants to go out. He is pissed off that we haven't been to a club in ages and thinks it would be good for us. I wasn't sure Aleks and Kris would be up for it but they never fail to amaze and disappeared to get some barely legal clubbing gear on. The Monkey told the nerds that they needed a break and no arguments, so we are waiting for a couple of Ubers to take us somewhere dark and noisy...

25 January

We had a great night making total dickheads of ourselves as usual, and it was even quite conflict free for a change except when some knuckle draggers decided to give Tony and Elmar grief. It was funny watching Kris bitch slap them, one of them actually cried – bless. It was some club in Reading that had the pleasure of our business, no idea what it was called or where it was. We ended the night sitting on the edge of a fountain in some gardens and eating doner kebabs. It was when we finally climbed into the Ubers we had booked to take us back to Tony's that we heard the news reports on the radio about the terrorist attack on Whitehall. Our driver said that it had happened a couple of hours before and that a large part of London was closed off. I checked the news feed on my phone and there were videos of burning buildings and explosions which looked like they had been shot on mobile phones. And then another news flash appeared – there had been a massive underground explosion at Denver International Airport. Reports said that something had gone wrong with a train running on the tracks bellow the airport and a massive detonation had occurred causing a huge crater to appear amongst the runways. The Monkey looked at me, a lot more sober than he had been a few minutes before, and said, 'No such thing as coincidence'...

*

Back at Tony's we tried to contact Caroline but there was no answer. JudyZ got us some close-up satellite images of both London and Denver airport. Being night in London those images were just a lot of orange fire, black smoke, and not much else. The Denver images showed a sizeable hole in the tarmac but not a lot else. There were no gaping caverns full of subterranean city structures, or indeed any hint that there was anything below the underground rail line.

JudyZ said that she had some news regarding the chips, we explained that we were a bit worse for wear and even with the sobering news reports we needed some sleep before we could manage anything remotely technical. Surprisingly even the nerds agreed and JudyZ conceded to wait until the morning as it was, 'Too amazing to waste on drunks.' Harsh but fair...

*

Managed to get some sleep after watching about an hour of pretty much the same reports repeating on Sky News and BBC News 24. The sat-phone woke us up, it was Caroline. The Monkey put her on speaker phone, and we listened blearily as she told us as much information as she could, or would...

Her technicians had been working late in the Whitehall laboratories. There was a lot of pressure from senior levels to discover what was so special about the computer chips they had managed to recover. She had gone home to get some rest; she had also taken a couple of minor wounds so was in need of some down time. There had been a call from the lab to say that external computer systems engineers had been brought in by another agency (she thinks MI6) and they had ignored warnings regarding the possibility of tracking devices. They demanded the power to the floor be cut so that they could use their own portable, clean power source to run their kit, which disabled the EID interference loop, and were busy plugging the chips into testing boards and activating them. It was then that she heard gun fire and she told her techs, who had been excused from the lab by other officials, to get to safety.

She had been called again by her senior tech who said that they were all safe outside the building but that there were explosions. He believed that at least one of the super clones had used a portal to home in on the activated signals from the chips and that they were running amok.

Caroline had been in emergency meetings since the attack which was why we couldn't reach her. The government have decided to classify it as a terrorist attack which gives them opportunity to clamp down on right wing and Islamist terrorist groups who are on their radar, and it avoids them having to mention to Joe Public that the capital actually was under attack by an international secret organisation who have an army and a selection of shock troop super soldiers at their disposal! After all, the Illuminati don't officially exist other than as lunatic conspiracy theory or as some quaint gentlemen's club with secret handshakes – you get the picture. As Caroline said, this was an act of war perpetrated by an enemy that doesn't technically exist, although as The Monkey pointed out, sending troops to attack their Greenland base that doesn't technically exist was also an act of war – probably...

She will let us know what she can when she can, but she says that it is all a shit show and that the interdepartmental blame game has already started.

*

JudyZ couldn't contain herself anymore and kept pinging email and any other app she could until Kev dragged himself out of his hangover fog and screenshared her feed onto the TV in the living room. After the obligatory cyber smooches, we were allowed in and all sat around feeling a bit wounded, drinking coffee, and eating Wagon Wheels which the supermarket had for some reason substituted for tomatoes in the grocery delivery – result!

Our extra-terrestrial computer whiz kid launched almost immediately into a hugely complex, and very excitable dissertation on her results with the chips. Kev and Tony both said, 'No fucking way!' almost simultaneously. Elmar looked lost, but in an intelligent way. Me and The Monkey looked lost, but like some cavemen who have just seen the moon and are throwing rocks at it. Aleks and Kris had gone back to bed, they are still mending, and so mercifully missed the science lecture.

There was a great deal of stuff talked about that made my head hurt even more than the drink-related thundering of chariots racing around my cerebellum. Graphs and charts appeared on screen and a whole bunch of equations that might have been cuneiform for all the sense they made to me, and actually made me feel sick to look at. I amused myself watching The Monkey push entire Wagon Wheels into his mouth and then try to eat them without hurting himself – I'm sure they aren't as big as they used to be... And then I became aware that the others were all looking at us with that, 'Well, what do you think about that then?' look on their little nerdy faces. Even Elmar joined in, fuck him! So, while The Monkey tried to wash down oversize biscuit remnants with gulps of hot coffee, I did the only decent thing and said, 'What the fuck are you lot talking about?'

Between them JudyZ, Kev, and Tony tried to break it down, and this is what I got: The chips contain something that they insist on calling time crystals. It seems that a time crystal is both stable and constantly in flux, with these defined states repeating at intervals which can be predicted without it ever dissolving into total randomness. Are you keeping up? Me neither. But there's more...

They tried to explain it by saying that it would be like having a chess board set up with all of the black and white pieces in their start positions and then tapping the board and causing all of the pieces to switch sides but without expending any energy. The time crystals don't seem to give a shit that they are breaking the second law of thermodynamics and doing something impossible, they are just doing it.

So, what is the consequence of this? Well, there seems to be a nerdy consensus that these time crystals could be used to create almost instantaneous processing, and to create computer memory that verges on the infinite. They defy entropy (no wonder the Illuminati have them) and could be the technology needed to create a virtual universe of their own.

But so what, we can use the energy portal to go to different universes using the power of the black holes? Why are these time crystals such a big deal?

JudyZ summed it up. 'With these the Illuminati could build a world in their own image, and if they could get humanity to give up their physical form and enter this world then they would have won. They could rule an Earth devoid of humans except those they wanted or needed to be still physical, and at the same time they would be lords of their virtual utopia.'

The Monkey had finally cleared the biscuit backlog and he had that, 'What would I do if I wanted to create a scare big enough to make everyone want to live in a computer?' look. Alright, that's a bit specific for a look, but it was his scheming look. 'If they create a big enough catastrophe then they could manipulate you dumb humans into doing pretty much anything. They don't need all the hi-tech weapons to rule the world they just need a biblical flood and to have the only ark.'

They have attacked London and seemingly blown up their own underground city. What are the sneaky bastards up to?

26 January

Caroline called again. The GCHQ code breakers had been hard at work on the images that I took of the Post-It Note collage from the Denver base. It took a series of pure flukes involving an ex-member of an occult group, a part-time games programmer, and a chance encounter with an old chap on the London Underground to make some sense of the notes. The ex-occultist had spotted some resemblance to pathways on the Kabbalistic tree of life; the games programmer saw a nested series of levels, like you would find in a role-playing game; and the old chap on the train? Well, that was the odd one. He had glanced over the shoulder of one of the code breakers who was sitting on the train next to him on her way home for the weekend. She had her notebook open and was looking at the arcane characters she had copied down from a couple of the Post-It Notes. No one had been able to decipher them or even find an alphabet that might be similar, but this old fella had gripped her by the arm, and staring at the notebook he had whispered. 'They are rebuilding Eden, and it will be terrifying!' He had got up to get off at Hampstead Heath and she had asked him how he knew, just humouring him because she thought he might be a bit senile, and he replied, 'It is the new language of the angels,' and then he had left the train and disappeared into the crowd of commuters...

Back at GCHQ on Monday morning she had explained what had happened thinking that it would just be an amusing story and the ex-occultist had gone into a frenzy. He had rushed off and come back with printouts of an esoteric alphabet called Enochian and a bunch of background information. Enochian (The Monkey, Aleks, and Kris had all pricked their ears up at mention of this) is a language supposedly transmitted to Dr Dee, the Elizabethan magus and seeming ancestor of Arno Whitaker, during his rituals with con man Edward Kelly. But the characters from the Post-It Notes don't look like Dee's Enochian, well, not entirely. They realised that they had been merged with some form of computer machine code to form a new version of the alphabet and had started to piece together some of the details. It had something to do with the computer chips...

She couldn't tell us any more because she had been sworn to secrecy, and also because they don't know a whole lot more. She said that Commander Greyling had allowed her to keep us in the loop, but that was possibly on the off chance that we had some information that might help. Well, we did, but once again we had decided that it was probably best to keep it to ourselves for the moment.

Oh, and one other thing. The background printouts about the Enochian alphabet had included an image of a painting of Dr Dee. The code breaker from the train had been a little confused when she saw it, because she swore that the old man on the train, barring the robes and ruff, was the spitting image of the figure in the painting...

*

Aleks and Kris, who, by the way, are almost back to their pale perfection, are unusually excited by the code breaker's assertion that the man on the train looked like Dee. They say that there were stories about the good doctor dying a pauper's death in Mortlake, but the parish registers and Dee's gravestone went missing. And then there were tales that he had been seen in Rotterdam the following year, and then again in Copenhagen about twenty years after that. They were only rumours and there had never been any corroboration, but the girls have a nose for these things, and if they were Peter Parker their spider sense would be tingling.

*

Arno Whitaker's company Brightstorm, even with his links to the Illuminati, is still operating as if it's business as usual. They have no UK presence anymore since we blew up their plant in Wales and the EID took the opportunity to ransack what was left under cover of helping at an industrial accident. And because they are outwardly a US based tech company with US government and military contracts, they are pretty much untouchable. Plus, we know Whitaker is an evil, quasi-immortal dickhead but there is no evidence that we or anyone else can officially show that would make him public enemy number one. But JudyZ has just informed us that she has found a connection between Brightstorm and a manufacturer of cheap smart phones based in India. It would appear that Brightstorm have been secretly pumping funds into the company and backing development of a new generation of 'People's Mobiles', with the express goal of getting one to every person on the planet. We have seen these phones making an appearance in supermarkets and garages at bargain prices. I'm sure Arno Whitaker has no intention of just giving people roll over minutes or more opportunities to show their tits or knobs on social media so there must be something else behind this. We all think that it could be part of the plan to gain control – but how? Spying on people through their phones – maybe… But if Kev and Tony are to be believed then that is nothing new. No, there must be bigger game afoot than just grabbing people's food/cat/baby pics and their sexts…

27 January

More news reports from Denver. They are now putting the explosion down to an earthquake as a massive sink hole has opened up. So, unexpected tectonic plate activity – that was convenient, well if you want to get rid of a dirty great underground facility it is. There are no reports of strange buildings being found in the crater, so we are guessing that one of those jumbo black holes like the one we saw in Bolivia had been used to basically suck all the evidence down the cosmic plughole!

While we have been sitting here and watching the on-the-spot reporters spouting clichés and the in-the-studio experts arguing with each other as usual, there have been more reports flashing up on the screen of further earthquakes around the globe. Pakistan, Turkey, Hungary, Siberia, Canada, Mexico, and Bolivia. With the one in Denver that makes eight, eight earthquakes in less than 72 hours. The scrolling text at the bottom of the screen keeps saying '…a sequence of seismic events occurring over a short period…,' and '…there have been tens of thousands of tremors, the strongest with a magnitude of nearly four…' Either the world is going to end, or it is just a coincidence, and as we know, coincidence is just another way of saying that although you were sunbathing on the tracks you never expected the train that ran you over. Well, something like that…

JudyZ has confirmed that the Bolivia quake is in the same location as the base on the outskirts of La Pas. We don't know about the other locations, but Aleks is willing to take big money bets that they all have an epicentre that is located on an Illuminati underground base. But why, what the fuck are they up to? And then it hits you, or to be more precise, The Monkey, Kris, and Aleks look at each other at the same time and say, 'They are cleaning house!'

I caught up quick. The consensus is that the Illuminati are freaked out that three of their bases: La Pas, Denver, and Greenland have been compromised, and rather than wait to find out that the rest are on the hit list they have decided to take matters into their own hands and press the self-destruct button. That would have given them chance to move any goodies they didn't want either us or the EID pillaging, and the opportunity to hide their bases from the world's media by burying them forever. After all, it's no good being a secret organisation operating on the fringes if Aunty Beeb and company come stomping into your house with the cameras rolling, is it? This can't be them giving up though, this must be part of their game plan, even if that game plan has had to alter because we have strutted around knocking over the pieces and shitting on the board – metaphorically… Kev thinks that this has something to do with the chips and that just maybe what they are sacrificing is no longer important. As Elmar has just said, 'Like a magician. How do you say? Making you look the wrong way while they do their trick... Yes! A distraction!'

'Making you look the wrong way while they do their trick' – well, this is a bit of a step up from an alcoholic kid's party entertainer pulling bunches of flowers out of his clown pocket...

28 January

Okay, a couple of weird things have happened. Yes, I know we live in weird central, but stay with me.

First, the girls decided to get out the tarot cards again. They did a few different spreads and then Kris got up and went to the bedroom and came back with a square wooden box, about eight inches across and two deep. Opening the box, she took out something wrapped in black velvet cloth, and after carefully undressing it, we could see that it was some sort of thick circular black mirror. Aleks and Kris sat side by side, holding the mirror between them, and then they began to whisper in a language that I couldn't understand. The Monkey watched fascinated as they stared into the mirror until suddenly their eyes rolled back so that all you could see was the whites. Shit, it looked creepy and Tony, who had just walked into the room, walked straight back out again. This white-eyed staring went on for about thirty minutes and then their eyes snapped back to normal and Aleks exclaimed, 'He still lives! We have found you now, we have found you!' The Monkey asked them who lives, who they had found? and Kris smiled a really eerie smile and turned the mirror towards us. There was an image frozen in the black, like someone had hit the pause button on a video, and the image was of an old man with thin collar length hair and a long white beard. His long narrow nose and pronounced cheekbones gave him a vulture-like aspect, and he was captured carrying a tray with a teapot, cup and saucer along the hallway of an old-fashioned looking house. And he was looking straight out of the mirror as if he knew he was being watched. The Monkey gave her a puzzled look and Aleks answered, 'It's Dr Dee.' Well, fuck me!

Second weird thing, Kev came clattering down the stairs to tell us that JudyZ had picked up a message – for The Monkey. It had come in on the same sub aquatic hidden signal frequency that she had picked up before. It was very short and straight to the point. Arno Whitaker wants a chat with The Monkey, not face to face, probably for the safety of all concerned, but over an encrypted internet connection – sort of an evil Zoom call. He says that if The Monkey is agreeable (that would be a first) he should respond on the same frequency and then Whitaker will set up the virtual meet... How the hell does Whitaker know we can pick up those messages let alone respond?

JudyZ thinks it is possible that there is some sort of reverse tracking of the messages, sort of like an echo that pings back to the sender when they are accessed. That set Kev and Tony arguing about algorithms and shit like that, JudyZ says it's okay because she is in orbit, and they aren't going to be looking there...

The Monkey has drafted a response, two actually. The first one went along the lines of, 'You bat shit crazy clown, I am going to find you, rip your head off and shit down your neck!' It might not be quite as polite as that. We had a rethink over a couple of Jacks, and he compromised with, 'Yes, when?' Ah, the master rhetorician...

*

So, now we need to wait for Whitaker to set a date and time. I had wondered if it was a trap to try and locate us and then drop loads of super soldiers on us, but Kev thinks it would be impossible for them to get a bead on us because of the way the message is transmitted and passed through JudyZ. She agrees and says that conversely it would be impossible for her to pinpoint Whitaker's location. Looks like it will just be a pleasant conversation, probably with a lot of threatening vibes, and maybe some offers of an invite to the party. I will make sure we have plenty of popcorn as this could be entertaining.

In the meantime, the girls are trying to narrow down the location of Dr Dee. They seem very keen on finding him, perhaps they want to chat about the good old days? I have to say though, he hasn't aged anywhere near as well. Although, to be fair, he was born in 1527 so he's not doing too bad.

*

Well, the girls are busy with their scrying, Kev has locked himself in the bedroom with JudyZ avatar, Tony and Elmar are canoodling somewhere, so what shall we do? The Monkey has suggested Deadpool, nachos, Mexican dip, JD, and Kev's electro bong. Who am I to argue against such sound logical reasoning...?

29 January

The girls want to go on a Dr Dee hunt, so we are in the Lancia, singing along to Type O Negative, and trying to navigate around the congestion. Central London is still a shit show after the explosions at Whitehall and there are areas that have been closed off for 'security reasons'. So, round the M25 north and then down the M1 seems to be the plan.

Why are they so keen on finding Dr Dee? Aleks says that as the original source of all the 'prophets' kept locked away serving the crown he may be able to provide some useful insight into his descendant Arno Whitaker. Plus, given his longevity, they suspect he may have stumbled on some serious occult knowledge which they would like to share in. And, if he can decipher the text used by the Illuminati in their planning then he can tell us what is written on the Post-It Notes from the Denver base. Got to love 'em! Always thinking ahead, which is I guess one of the reasons they have managed to survive for so long in a world not friendly to them. If it was left up to me and

The Monkey, we would just crash from one situation to the next. He thrives on the unpredictability of the next moment, and I seem to get swept along in his wake…

*

Aleks and Kris have narrowed it down to Willow Road on the edge of Hampstead Heath, but they couldn't be more specific as, 'He has been covering his tracks.' Therefore, I had to drive slowly along Willow Road while the girls were tranced out in the back. It took three runs but in the end their eyes snapped open simultaneously and they said, 'Here.' I slowed down and we got horns blaring and cheerful Cockney banter bellowed at us, but we now knew that the three storey, red brick house with the unkempt front garden was our goal.

*

It took a while for the door to be answered, and when it was the old fella just opened it and walked back into the gloomy hallway, his tartan-slippered feet making no noise on the tiled floor. We followed him inside and I shut the door onto the twenty-first century.

The house was Victorian, the decor was 1930s, but the ornaments and paintings belonged to other centuries. Napoleonic cavalry helmets sat next to Renaissance brass scientific instruments. Late medieval paintings hung alongside framed 1950s 'Duck and Cover' Civil Defence posters. The house has the feeling of a small museum, like the ones that always seemed to be at the end of the pier in dying seaside towns when I was a kid. On the top of a corner cabinet a large stuffed eagle owl gave me the evils from its glass eyes and The Monkey glared suspiciously at a stuffed hooded cobra that was permanently rearing up from a side table.

'I have been waiting for you,' the old man's voice was weak but got stronger as he spoke. He obviously didn't do a lot of talking and was out of practice. 'I knew I would be found eventually. I suppose it was talking to the young lady on the train about her notebook. But you are not really what I expected!' He spoke as he fussed with cups and saucers and pouring water into a large china teapot. When he had finished, he placed the tea tray on the low table in front of us and perched on the edge of a large wingback chair, his eyes alive in the dim light. He leaned forward and put his bony hands on the hands of Aleks and Kris and said, 'I remember you. Such a long time ago…' The girls smiled and I looked at The Monkey and mouthed, 'What the…?'

Then without any prompting he told us how he had faked his own death in 1608 and how a recently deceased geriatric had stood in for him at his burial at St Mary the Virgin in Mortlake. He had then slipped away to the continent where he had spent the next hundred or so years until he was sure everyone who might know him would have died, apparently the plague had helped, and returned to England, eventually ending up back in London, and in fact living in the very same house in Mortlake that he had occupied at the time of his supposed death. Over the centuries he had been forced to move many times and assume new identities so as not to draw attention to his unnatural longevity, but oddly, as the modern age arrived, he found himself less noticed, almost as if people didn't pay attention to anything but the tiny screens in front of them.

Kris wanted to know how he had managed to cheat death and he had to admit that he was at a loss as to the exact reason. 'I believe, although I cannot prove it to be true, that the angelic rituals I performed somehow conferred upon me a form of immortality. At least the wretched form of immortality that you see before you,' he spread his hands wide and in the yellow light of the table lamp his paper-like skin was almost translucent. There was a deep sadness in his voice, a terrible longing when he next spoke. 'You have no idea what it is like to watch the world die around you, to see those you cherish grow old and pass away while you remain – a withered husk unable to either regain youth or to end this existence.' He looked at the girls and said, 'At least you have each other.' Then he turned to me and staring straight into my eyes he asked, 'Have you noticed that the world is not the same? Yes, I believe you have. You woke up one morning and everything was different, there was nothing left of your old life.' Then he turned to The Monkey and his bony hand trembled as he brushed stray white hair from his forehead. 'And you. I do not know what you are, but you could be the end...' He reached into the pocket of his cardigan and pulled out a tarot card which he handed to The Monkey face down. 'I had a dream several decades ago and found myself holding that card. I have carried it in my pocket ever since and now I know that it is meant for you.' The Monkey turned it over and there, being struck by lightning was what looked like the castle from a chess board with flames coming out of its windows and a human figure falling from its battlements. The Tower. I had to ask, The Monkey just said, 'Destruction and chaos.'

*

We are now on the way back to Slough. Aleks is driving, I am shotgun, and Kris, Dr Dee, and The Monkey are in the back. We have changed the music for the doctor's benefit, he seems okay with Dead Can Dance, and even a bit of Nightwish. He has asked if we have any Glen Miller or maybe some jazz but there are some things even we won't do...

He is very agreeable about coming with us, he had his coat on even before we had finished suggesting it. There was an old crumpled leather bag in the hall, and he grabbed that, a wide brimmed felt hat, and a walking stick with a lead-coloured skull handle. I asked him if he wanted to get anything else as he might be away for a couple of days and he just said, 'No, I packed everything I may need yesterday,' and he patted his leather bug-out bag. As we got to the front door, he let us out and then turned and muttered a few unintelligible words that I could barely hear. There was a sound like heavy footfalls from the room above and then he stepped out and closed the door. I asked if he was going to lock it and he gave me a cryptic smile and said, 'No need for that,' then he turned and taking Kris's arm walked up the path to the front gate. I brought up the rear carrying his bag and as I reached the gate I glanced back and could swear I saw a large, hunched silhouette through the second storey windows. The hair on the back of my neck stood to attention and I was glad to close the garden gate and follow the others to where we had parked the car.

We have explained to Dr Dee about Arno Whitaker. He is saddened but not entirely surprised that the ritual to produce a seer for the Crown continues and thought it only a matter of time before one of the progenies escaped into the wild, in fact he was surprised it had taken so long. After telling him Whitaker's back story he is fascinated by the idea of a juxtaposition of angelic seed and the 'Serpent of Eden', as he called the face bitey rattlers who had a go at young Arno. Even though he has survived all these centuries he is still a product of the Elizabethan religious beliefs and sees everything through a distorting mirror of Dante's Inferno style imagery. To be honest, after all the shit we have seen I'm not ruling anything out!

Kev has just called. Whitaker wants to do this conference call thing at 6pm tomorrow. The Monkey is good with that. This is going to be even more interesting than anticipated...

*

Kev has moved his stuff up into the loft so that Dr Dee can have a room to crash in, and we have given him the tour. He was very interested in the spear but wisely wouldn't go anywhere near it, but when he saw my arm, he gave that a long inspection. He was also fascinated by the energy portal and The Monkey opened it up to some other random dimension in which giant whale-like creatures glided through magenta clouds and green lightning flashed around them as they basked in an endless sky. The doctor seemed to take all of that in his stride and made the comment, 'That would have been so much simpler than constructing an altar and spending a fortune on candles!' I asked him if he had seen such worlds before and he casually said, 'Oh, yes,' his face glowing in the magenta and emerald light emanating from the portal.

I decided to ask him what he had meant by, 'Have you noticed that the world is not the same? Yes, I believe you have. You woke up one morning and everything was different, there was nothing left of your old life.' It has been bugging me ever since he said it – that itch in your mind that you can't scratch. So, I sat him down, and with The Monkey peering narrow eyed through his smokescreen in the background, I asked Dr John Dee what had happened to make him think that about me? And the answer was even stranger than I could have imagined...

It was 1907, and while attending an art exhibition at the Bruton Gallery in London's West End he struck up a conversation with a young man who turned out to be the artist being exhibited, one Austin Osman Spare. Spare had a deep interest in occultism and was developing the use of sigils which he believed could, in conjunction with the will, be used to create a physical effect in the real world (Dee tapped my metal arm and told me that the markings on it were very similar to Spare's sigils). They kept in close contact although Dee never gave away his true identity or his great unnatural longevity.

And then Spare introduced him to Aleister Crowley. During a party at a hotel in Surrey, where Crowley had been performing rituals and smoking a shit tonne of hash, Dr Dee was introduced to a very different type of occultism. At some point during the bacchanal Crowley had given him a pipe that he said contained the powdered carapaces of beetles mixed in an aromatic resin to make a glittery metallic looking paste. By this point the doctor was a little worse for wear and so took the pipe outside into the grounds of the hotel and smoked it. He said that the last thing he remembered was Crowley, standing nearby, watching him and smiling. Boom! He was somewhere else, in a rushing vortex of dark clouds and vivid electric flashes. It was like his angelic rituals but far more intense, and the angels led him through other worlds and into the deepest hells where he saw what he described as the 'Great Dragon'. This beast was so large that he couldn't see all of it, but he did see the massive claws that it unfurled to reveal a book containing the past and future of the World. Then he woke up on a bench in Regent's Park and got moved on by the police…

I called a halt for a bit and made him a cuppa whilst getting JD for myself, The Monkey, and the girls who had come to join us, and while he sipped his tea, I did a bit of Google searching. It seems that the shiny metallic blues and greens of beetle shells contain DMT and the gods only know what the other stuff in the pipe was, but it does explain the visions and the eerie feeling that the DMT is some sort of link between us. Maybe even the key...

Anyway, from that day he knew there was something different, dare I say wrong, with the reality he found himself in. He tried to find Crowley, but Crowley had headed for the US of A so Dr Dee didn't get chance to question him, and then World War 1 happened – obviously not quite like that, but you know what I mean. There were very strange happenings on the Western Front. Sightings of giant angels striding across the battlefields and creatures from another world descending to take part in the conflict. Dee used his occult knowledge to ask some questions of, well, some form of metaphysical Google search, and was told emphatically that the conflict was a cover up by the major powers of Europe and America who were hiding the invasion of 'alien beings' by blowing each other up. Right...

The war ended and at the same time the world was struck down with Spanish Flu which Dee claims, and is strangely reminiscent of War of the Worlds, was used as the last resort to defeat the alien beings (this is alarming stuff when you know that it was the fledgling version of Whitaker's Brightstorm company that was involved in poison gas manufacture and in producing treatments for the flu pandemic. Was it them who created and weaponised the flu strain in the first place?). It apparently worked but took around 50 million humans with it on top of the death toll from the trenches. Although classified reports leaked out into the press and for a short while there was public outcry there then seems to have been what the doctor describes as 'collective amnesia'. It looked like the world needed a bad guy to point the finger at and make the thought of aliens go away, so, because Germany had, early on in the conflict, attempted to arrange peace talks with the alien invaders they drew the short straw, and the rest is – well, some version of history.

I asked the girls if they remembered any of that and their response of, 'That definitely sounds familiar from a couple of timelines,' does nothing to reassure me...

Then Crowley resurfaced and Dr Dee tracked him down to Sicily and his Abbey of Thelema, where, amongst all the sex magick he managed to get Crowley to admit that he had slipped him a mickey. Good old Uncle Aleister was quite open about it, in fact he felt that it would open up the doctor's chakras and help him reach new heights with his occult explorations, and apparently there was no going back from the reality switching effects of the drug. What a dick!

It seems that both me and The Monkey have at least that in common with Dr Dee. The experiments done to The Monkey with DMT in Thailand when he was a nipper, and my experiments with DMT in Amsterdam just before I met The Monkey have seemingly flipped us into a shared somewhere else that is both familiar, and at times, totally alien.

*

Dr Dee is getting used to all of this at the moment so we haven't given him the stuff from the Denver city to look at yet, we thought it would be better to let him acclimatize this evening and then have a go at decrypting the Post-It Notes in the photos after breakfast tomorrow.

*

Dr Dee likes a drop of wine, so we have sent Tony and Elmar out to get a dozen decent bottles of red. The doctor is aware of television but doesn't own one, or any form of computer. Now, rightly or wrongly we have him sat in front of *The Lord of the Rings*, and I don't think he has blinked for over an hour...

30 January

I got Kev to make a bunch of printouts of my Denver wipe board photos and with the aid of lots of Sellotape we have stuck them all together in the correct order – I think!

Dr Dee is a bit groggy this morning from all the wine and hours of watching Frodo and co. He swears he didn't, but I am not sure that The Monkey didn't spike the red wine with something psychedelic, it's like playing Russian roulette when he is in that sort of mood – you never know if you are going to wake up on a traffic island in a giraffe onesie. Anyway, that's a different story... The good doctor is eating toast and drinking tea while staring transfixed at the taped together printouts. We have given him a big pad of paper and The Monkey's contribution, a rainbow pack of glitter gel pens, and are going to leave him to it.

*

It's all go today! Caroline called and we spent a tense twenty minutes on speaker phone with her, Commander Greyling, and the MI6 suit. They have managed to salvage some stuff from the EID Whitehall offices and are now slumming it in the MI6 building over the river. They have come to the same conclusion as us regarding the earthquakes. Although they can't be certain if there were Illuminati bases in all the locations, they think it's safe to say that there was some sort of presence there. But they don't agree with us about it being distraction. MI6 feel that the Illuminati have cut their losses and rather than face more troops dropping in unannounced they have destroyed the bases and moved somewhere else. We suggested that they might be using it as an excuse to change direction under the guise of running scared but there is a definite lack of willingness to take on board what we suggest. On top of that we also get the impression that the military top brass, despite their earlier victorious posturing, are rather glad that they don't have to commit any more troops after the Greenland debacle, or as Greyling called it, 'That Greenland cluster-fuck!' Despite our warnings they were taken by surprise by the level of resistance and totally blindsided by the clone super soldiers.

The UK Government has, of course, sent rescue teams to the quake hit areas, and by 'rescue teams' I do mean EID crews and MI6 spooks. Oddly reminiscent of the 'aid team' who had got hold of the second monkey pendant that had led to us being co-opted to go looking for the Monkey Temple in Peru… I guess they are hoping to find something of interest while poking about in the wreckage – good luck with that! We didn't get a chance to talk with Caroline separately, but I hope that she can see the wood for the trees, so to speak…

*

Back in the living room Dr Dee is a bit concerned. He has translated a good deal of the writing from the Post-Its and it is now spread across the coffee table on sheets from the notebook in technicolour twinkly ink. What he has written still doesn't make total sense to us, but this is his synopsis of it: They are building an Arcadia that he insists on calling a 'New Eden'. They are using what he has translated as the 'power of the void' as the energy source (by that we think they mean the black holes). There is a lot of stuff that he doesn't understand but when Kev and Tony looked at it, they both agreed that it has something to do with the time crystal computer chips, and an equation for creating a series of tunnels through quantum space, most one-way but a significant one that is two-way. The Monkey looked perplexed, fractionally beating me to it, and Tony explained that it was like the way data flows through your smart phone. It didn't help. Elmar, even though he is not a computer nerd chipped in with the observation that it looked very much like the mandalas that he had been working on for his employers Zukunft der Erde; not the writing but the layout of the letters and the way certain lines overlapped. Dr Dee is fluent in German, and they had a brief, excited exchange, and then he picked up a green glitter pen and joined groups of the characters together like doing a large, abstract dot-to-dot picture. It wasn't a bunny. As Tony pointed out it had a remarkable similarity to the 3D computer map that Prof Brian had sent over, the map of the runes on my arm and the spear shaft.

There was something else that Dr Dee kept repeating. He had found lots of references to someone called Adam. We thought that maybe it was to do with his obsession with this New Eden idea of his, but he shook his head and told us that we had misunderstood, it wasn't a person, it was a thing called Adam. Tony reminded us that JudyZ had picked up the name 'Adam' from the hidden messages she had intercepted, so maybe not just a Biblical fetish…

*

6pm and time to talk with the man who is the continual turd in our swimming pool…

*

Well, that went well – HA, HA, HA!

Me and The Monkey

The Zoom type video link took ages to open and when it did there were issues with the audio breaking up and then the video freezing. Whitaker sat in his executive villain black leather chair and drummed his fingers on the desktop as several members of what could only be his IT support team pressed stuff and adjusted things. Kev and Tony kept tutting and laughing derisively about the lack of technological competence. It seems that even evil cabals intent on world domination have IT nerds!

After five minutes of fucking about we were ready to go, but to be honest it had just become something of a farce. Whitaker opened by thanking us for agreeing to talk but then ruined it by saying that we really didn't have any choice. The Monkey grunted and got up to walk out until Whitaker backtracked and blamed all the technical issues on his impoliteness. So, The Monkey sat down again. I got the feeling that IT support heads would roll after this was over, and not in a metaphorical sense. Now the picture was clearer we could see that there was a row of others sitting someway behind him, just out of focus.

'Despite the problems you have caused us we are willing to welcome you into the ranks of the Illuminated Ones. We,' he waved his hand to indicate those behind him, 'have been forced to dispose of some of our assets sooner than we had planned, but that has just precipitated the deadline for the completion of our great work, and in many ways, we have you to thank for that.' The crazed grin slashed across the blur of a face seemed to get wider until it looked like his head would fall in half. 'We have come to realise that the masses will not submit, even using righteous force, to the will of order. Not while there is the seed of entropy growing in their midst. But you can join with us and become part of the solution, part of the glorious whole!' He spread his hands in a grand gesture, but they went out of camera shot and it just looked weird.

There was a signal from somewhere off to the side of him and he beamed at the camera and said, 'Please, excuse me for a moment.' The screen went black and then came back on again and this time with the image perfectly clear, and Whitaker was framed as if he was in a TV studio. 'Sorry about that, you know how technology can be.' I was suddenly very conscious of the fact that we were crammed onto Tony's sofa, and that there were beer cans, bottles, and bags of nachos liberally scattered around the coffee table and floor along with copies of *Guns and Ammo Magazine*. Ah well, I guess it was always going to be his show.

'Now, where was I?'

'You were just telling us about your glory hole...' Ah, The Monkey doesn't miss an opportunity does he!

Whitaker ignored the crude humour and continued. 'Our plan for the people of Earth has begun. The attempts that we made to create supermen using the US Armies experimental drugs, something which I believe you are intimately acquainted with,' this was a reference to the testing that was done on The Monkey in Thailand, 'proved to be a dead end. Not least because you blew up our Nevada facility.' His voice was unemotional but his eyes, staring from that messed up face told a different story. 'But you have met some of our new improved super men I believe? We have you to thank for that as well.' Again, the grin nearly split his head. 'If it hadn't been for your attempts to kill me, we would never have discovered the DNA splicing techniques that have allowed our scientists to create the ultimate humans. Those who will act as guardians and shepherds for this planet in the millennia to come.' He put his palms together and bowed his head slightly, it was difficult to tell if he was mocking or genuine.

'We are going to take away the necessity for humanity to struggle. We are going to set them free and all they need to do is submit!' All evangelical, the Baptist snake charmer was back.

This seemed to be the moment The Monkey was expected to go, 'Oh, ah, brilliant... Where do I sign up?' but instead he leaned forward intently and asked, 'What do you have in mind then if you aren't going to bully them into submission? We all know how stupid and pig-headed humans are. Even if you crush them and take away all their hope, they still somehow manage to surprise with their determination to fuck up whatever party they get dragged into – invited or not.' Grudging respect for humans from The Monkey even if it was a backhanded compliment?

Whitaker leaned forward just as The Monkey had, conspiratorial, and said, 'The ways in which humans can be manipulated seems unexpectedly to have increased in this new century in which we find ourselves. There was perhaps too much emphasis on the 'medieval' in our previous thinking and because of a change in circumstances we have realised that the subtle blade is much more effective than the crushing axe.'

'Not going to share then?' The Monkey sneered.

'When you have fully committed to us then you will be allowed to see the vision of the glorious world to come which you can share...'

The Monkey took the cigar from his mouth and gazed at its glowing tip. 'I am going to kill you, you ugly dickhead.'

Once again, the even more insane grin as Whitaker sat back in his chair. 'I told them that you would never join us, but they did insist that I try.' There was vague out of focus movement behind him from the row of seated figures. 'I am glad that you have rejected the offer. There can be no room in the coming world for the personification of disorder.'

The Monkey pointed the cigar at the image of Whitaker and growled, 'You are going to find your plans, your super men, your utopia, and any of your totalitarian buddies I find along the way, fucked up.'

'Are you threatening us, Monkey?' this was said with pretend shock.

'I don't threaten. Listen freak. You know what chaos theory is right? Well, I am the fucking butterfly and I'm gonna do more than just flap my pretty wings.'

It was at this point that The Monkey reached forward and moved the laptop camera to face the chair off to our left, the chair in which an old, white bearded man sat engrossed in the exchange.

'Have you met Dr Dee? No, of course you haven't. He's your great, great,' he stopped, counted on his fingers, and gave up, 'Lots of great's granddaddy. He's the man who knows how you were created. Fuck, he wrote the book and made the original!' Dr Dee stared at Whitaker with something like wonder and gave a little, slightly self-conscious wave. I think that was the first time I have ever seen the corners of that evil clown grin droop.

'What? What?' Yep, that struck a nerve.

Whitaker began to say something else, a look almost of panic crossing his face, and The Monkey reached out and clicked the button marked End Call. 'Well, that went well,' he said, and wandered off to the kitchen for a new bottle of Jack.

*

JudyZ came on after Whitaker had been cut off. Her avatar, not the one that siren calls Kev to the bedroom I hasten to add, had a bit of a frowny face. Aleks asked her what was wrong, and she took a moment to answer, and when she did, she asked Kev and Tony if they agreed with her. 'You know I have been looking at the new pictures of the information you took from the Denver city? Well, based upon the translations of Dr Dee and the hypothesis that we came up with regarding the time crystals and the tunnels through quantum space, I think, no, I know what they have built. It is a computer, a supercomputer that is powered by the energy of the black holes and uses the chips containing the time crystals to create a virtual reality. The diagram that you drew from the Post-It Notes is a worm hole into this virtual reality and there are lanes, like a motorway, some only go in and some go both ways.' She stopped for a moment and her avatar gave a little expectant head bob. Kev and Tony both gabbled over each other agreeing with her. They were obviously very impressed with the way she had stitched the pieces together.

'So, it's a really powerful computer. So what?' Asked The Monkey as he swallowed alcohol.

JudyZ's avatar smiled patiently and set about explaining. 'It will be big enough and powerful enough to contain all of humanity, everyone. They will be able to take the consciousness of every living human on the planet and transfer them into the computer. Humans will no longer have a physical form; they will exist only as sentient code within the machine.'

It was my turn to pipe up. 'I read a couple of years ago about the possibility of people giving up their physical life and transferring themselves into an artificial intelligence, living happily forever in some virtual world. It was being proposed as the natural conclusion to human evolution, at least as physical beings, and the only alternative to capitalism. Is this what you think they are doing?'

'Sort of, yes. But I think it may be more like living forever in some totalitarian vision of heaven. Let's face it, it would be very difficult to rebel if the Illuminati controlled the off switch. They could identify and cull, or reprogram, any dissenting voices because they would control the virtual world, the operating system in which all of this happened. As I predicted, these time crystals seem to defy entropy, and so the Illuminated Ones could have their perfect order – forever.'

Dr Dee cleared his throat and leaned forward to talk to JudyZ's image on the screen. 'I keep telling them, they are creating a new Eden. Not metaphorically, really. I don't understand the technology or terms of reference you use but I can see what they are planning. To go back to the garden, the utopia that existed before the Fall, they would have to make everyone as new. They would possess their souls and in a very real sense could banish them from the garden if they disobeyed. But this time there would be no original sin, because, if I have understood correctly, the sinners would just cease to be.'

JudyZ nodded, at least her avatar did. 'And the references to Adam? It's the name of the computer. Not a biblical reference to Adam and Eve, but I think, a mark of respect to the founder of the modern Illuminati, Adam Weishaupt, who created the coalition of the ancient secret societies that has become the Illuminated Ones.'

'What about all of the bodies once the consciousness has left them?' I noted a little professional interest in Kris's question, and couldn't help a smile for which I got a dig in the ribs.

'These "lanes" running into the virtual reality. Could people go back and forth between here and the virtual world?' The Monkey was on his second large glass.

'Yes, it would depend on which of the lanes you were allowed to take, but theoretically that could be possible.' Tony is a bit of a genius with the whole quantum physics thing, so we all bowed down before his judgment while Elmar gazed at him with adoring pride.

Kris looked at The Monkey and he said, 'That's what will happen to the bodies. Not everyone will get a one-way ticket to this New Eden. I guess that the ruling elite of the Illuminati, their families, their henchmen, and their super soldiers will remain here to run the planet as they see fit, and to stomp out any pockets of resistance. I would imagine that the dedicated faithful will be put to work disposing of the remains, probably chucking them through a black hole – that's what I would do. Then the new lords of Earth will be able to nip back and forth between this world and the virtual Eden like gods. And when they get old or ill, they can move permanently into the virtual world and carry on as before.' We all stared at The Monkey, it's a horrible thought but he was right, it was spring cleaning on a global scale. I think we also stared at him because his throw away, 'That's what I would do,' line seems to indicate that he has given the idea some previous thought!

'Is it going to be like the *Matrix*?' it was the most I could contribute at that moment.

'Nah, more like *Tron* but without the cool bikes,' replied The Monkey, while the JudyZ avatar rolled her eyes.

I tried again, 'Okay, smart arse, but what is going to make the entire population of Earth want to give up all of the shit they have bought from Amazon, and their new cars, and their chance to fuck the hot girl/guy who just started at the office?'

'Do you remember when I said that they needed the only ark? Well, when it starts to rain everybody is going to want to get on board. And those that don't? Well fuck 'em. They will either drown or get cleansed later, there won't be any witnesses'...

31 January

Nice weather today, frosty but sunny, so we have decided to take Dr Dee out for a drive and have a break from all the impending doom shite. We are quite close to Avebury, so we are going to go there and wander about in the stones like new age hippies – or something!

*

We went for lunch in The Red Lion just by the stones. There was a mixed bag of crop circle T-shirt wearers and some more goth looking sorts who I would put in the Wiccan fraternity. At a large table in a far corner a group of randoms was playing a game of Magic: The Gathering, and excitedly chattering away as they threw cards on the table and consumed craft beer and crisps. We sat as far away as possible...

While we waited for our food I asked Dr Dee about Aleister Crowley, what he was like and if he was 'all that'. He smiled and replied, 'He was, I believe you would say – a bit of a dick.' That made The Monkey chuckle, I think we are having a bad influence on the doctor. He continued, 'He was very charismatic, he knew how to get and hold attention. But in the final reckoning he was far too narcissistic and unable to let go of his ego in order to attain the greatness and knowledge he was so close to. He destroyed a lot of naive souls along the way, burned out on his altar of self-aggrandisement. I would be doing him a wrong to say that he had no skill in the arcane arts, but he was by far and away a more successful manipulator of people and showman than he was a magician.' He sipped his red wine, looking at the glass appreciatively. 'He didn't try to have sex with me fortunately, I think I was a little too old for his tastes...' That made us laugh out loud which drew some looks from the fantasy card players across the room.

The Monkey asked Kris if she and Aleks had known Crowley, 'Yes, we spent some time in his company when he was in New Orleans, and then again years later in London during the Blitz. He was back on the heroin then and had lost much of his edge.'

Aleks laughed and added, 'He was very naughty! But I think we would have to agree – he was a bit of a dick.'

*

After a long lunch and quite a bit more booze we sat outside in the last of the winter sun at the long wooden tables with our drinks, and The Monkey sparked up a cigar and handed one to Dr Dee. It was an unusual moment of peace, the girls in their sunglasses drinking tequila, and me in the middle with an arm around each. As we sat there a faint mist began to rise from the still frosty grass and the stones took on an even more ethereal look. Shapes seemed to form, sort of darker patches in the mist and I realised the doctor was looking at me. 'The spirits here are strong, I think because so many people still come here and share their energy with them. All of those young people in the pub are looking for something mystical but they don't have the eyes to see yet – maybe they never will. We have been changed; the world will never be the same for us. We get to see the beauty and the horror, and there is nothing between that for us, no filter. We are not catching glances of other realities as reflections in the mirror anymore, they are staring us straight in the eyes.'

As he had been talking the shapes in the mist had become figures that marched down the avenue of stones and then disappeared into the rays of the low winter sun…

*

Back at Tony's, and he and Kev are very excited by the prospect of one of their favourite comic book artists doing a signing at a comic shop in Reading. So tomorrow they are getting the train and going to nerd out taking the bemused Elmar with them. But this evening we are going to show the doctor the *Matrix* movies in an attempt to sort of explain what the Illuminati might be up to. Not the best analogy possibly but the nearest we can get, and they are very entertaining – even *Revolutions* will be forgiven this evening.

Once again pizza delivery is on the way and snacks and drinks are piling up on the coffee table. Aleks and Kris have surreptitiously had a snack on the super clone in the freezer. They don't need to eat much of it to be satiated and they haven't been out grave robbing since they brought it back. We did have to get another freezer for Tony though as none of the rest of us fancied our frozen food nestling up to a corpse.

Ah, I can also see Kev's electro bong so this could be a big evening – yet again. I hope we have enough chocolate Hobnobs…

Me and The Monkey

1 February

The Mao Shan sorcerer contacted us today. He has been watching with interest the attacks in London and the earthquakes around the globe. When The Monkey told him about our chat with Arno Whitaker, he didn't seem surprised, he thought it was long overdue that Whitaker should try to bargain with him. After all, he had tried before, and it would make perfect sense for the Illuminati to recruit The Monkey. To have a god on their side would give them an air of legitimacy, and more fire power than any opponent. We told him about what we think they are now up to, the supercomputer, the virtual Eden, what we suspect is their end game. That did surprise him, and also possibly fitted in with the real reason he had called us.

A virulent disease has started up in Mongolia. It is thought to be a version of pneumonic plague but spread through human-to-human contact rather than by rodents. Even though it is contained it has got the Chinese authorities worried. The region where it began is home to a medical research facility owned by a subsidiary of Brightstorm. 'Ah, balls!' was The Monkey's only comment...

One more thing. The sorcerer's friendly contacts in the Chinese military advised him of some unusual satellite signal traffic coming from an unknown source and being received and returned by a satellite they could not trace but which was pinging the ID code of a supposedly decommissioned Chinese spy satellite. There had been a hell of a lot of signal traffic which had defeated their best efforts to decode, and as he knows about our orbiting friend, he thought we ought to be aware that the Chinese authorities have authorised a major search for the phantom in space.

We thanked him for the heads up, both lots, and then The Monkey looked at me with a frown and said what I was thinking, 'JudyZ hasn't told us about all of this activity. Is she doing a bit of extracurricular activity which she hasn't mentioned?' Not that she isn't entitled to her own thing, it's just that it's a bit unusual. I guess we will have to ask Kev if he knows anything when he gets back from his expedition to the comic shop with Tony and Elmar...'

*

Something else has happened as well...

An obscure Polish industrial band have released a track that uses some of the black box recording from the Ecuador plane crash. How they got it they are not saying and between being bad taste and car wreck entertainment they have managed to become quite famous. There have been over 500K plays on their YouTube channel. So, of course, I had a listen. The track begins with one of the band members explaining how, when they slowed down part of the noise that ran over the end of the recording, and then put it through some filters, it sounded like words. So, the track thrashed out of the speakers and then I went all goosebumpy as the black box sample kicked in and the distorted electronic words that have become the title of the song hissed out at me – 'Die, American bitch!'

The Monkey came in as I was listening and read the track description over my shoulder. He looked at me with a frown. It sounds like JudyZ, there is no getting away from it. She swore that she had nothing to do with the crash, but this would seem to indicate otherwise.

That can't be good...

Andy Darby would-be Viking, and lover of the bizarre. Mission – infest the world with his strange creations. He is the author of *Me and The Monkey*.

Son of a WW2 Commando, growing up in 1970s Birmingham, as a teenager Andy became a fan of heavy metal, fronting several metal bands over the years. His passion for martial arts also began in the 70s and has continued to the present. Competing as a bodybuilder and playing American Football for the Birmingham Bulls took up much of his 20s.

Following a mixed career involving working in a jewellery factory, spraying cars, and office work, he finally managed to follow his other passion, art, and began a career as a designer. A marketing department honed his skills, and he became aware of the world of designing for live events, joining a small production company, and eventually becoming creative director of their larger parent company. Moving to Cornwall he decided it was time to go freelance, setting up his own business focusing on motion graphic design.

In the late 1990s he began to get the urge to write and his laptop drive is littered with the unformed creations that have popped into his head. Volume 2 of the Chronicles of the Monkey God is obviously the third release in the series but what else would you expect?

Andy lives on the north coast of Cornwall with his artist wife, teenage daughter, cat, two ponies, and constantly growing library. He still secretly thinks he could be a big wave surfer regardless of what reality tells him.

...the lovechild of Hunter S Thompson and Terry Pratchett... this is an alcohol and cigar fuelled thrill ride. Booze, ghouls, guns, magic, black holes, and the Illuminati – need I say more? – The Ritual Blog

Not mainstream? Proudly so? Monkey speaks to you – Geeknative.com

Completely bonkers and one of the most enjoyable reads I have had in ages

Me and The Monkey: Chronicles of the Monkey God Volume 1

Available at www.amazon.co.uk and all good bookshops

The Paddington Incident, a prequel to The Monkey's story...

Come on Chapman! Stop punching that anarchist bastard. We are missing valuable drinking time, and I need a brandy to take the edge off the opium...

Available at www.amazon.co.uk

Wear The Monkey on your back... go to www.meandthemonkey.co.uk/merch

BAD PRESS iNK,

publishers of niche, alternative and cult fiction

Visit

www.BADPRESS.iNK

for details of all our books, and sign up to
be notified of future releases and offers

www.ingramcontent.com/pod-product-compliance
Lightning Source LLC
Chambersburg PA
CBHW082104280426
43661CB00089B/847